John Miller

**Questions Awakened by the Bible**

Second Edition

John Miller

**Questions Awakened by the Bible**

*Second Edition*

ISBN/EAN: 9783337100025

Printed in Europe, USA, Canada, Australia, Japan

Cover: Foto ©Lupo / pixelio.de

More available books at **www.hansebooks.com**

# QUESTIONS

# AWAKENED BY THE BIBLE.

### I.
### ARE SOULS IMMORTAL?

### II.
### WAS CHRIST IN ADAM?

### III.
### IS GOD A TRINITY?

BY

REV. JOHN MILLER,

Princeton, N. J.

SECOND EDITION.

PHILADELPHIA:
J. B. LIPPINCOTT & CO.,
1877.

# CONTENTS.

## I.
### ARE SOULS IMMORTAL?

## II.
### WAS CHRIST IN ADAM?

## III.
### IS GOD A TRINITY?

# I.

# ARE SOULS IMMORTAL?

# PREFACE.

THE sole object of this book is to show that the immortality of the soul is not taught in God's holy word. The impulse to conceive of such a book was not given by science, but was bred of texts of Scripture. The author was not studying Materialism; and indeed denies that philosophy can determine whether the soul is or is not immortal. That will appear. The surprise that such changed views awakened, came upon him, not in the Porch, but in the Temple, and in his wrestlings against them he had to contend, not with science, but with the word of God. To illustrate his helplessness in these respects take this sentence, " So man lieth down, and riseth not: till the heavens be no more, they shall not awake, nor be raised out of their sleep " (Job xiv: 12): or this, " In that very day his thoughts perish " (Ps. cxlvi: 5); or Paul's very unobserved passage,—" These all, having been attested by faith, received not the promise, God, out of reference to us, having looked to the future for the something better, that they without us should not be made perfect " (Heb. xi : 39, 40).

The manner of a book, however, needs a preface, as well as the matter. The naked denial of the immortality of the soul, without the gentleness of a careful definition, would needlessly shock people: and to mark upon our gate, " The Soul not Immortal," when we wish to admit the guest, and lay before his candor something entirely different from what he would at first sight suppose, would be anything but skilful.

There are two questions: Will the soul be immortal? and, Is the soul immortal now? To say " The Soul not Immortal," would needlessly jar upon the former. The immortality of the soul is one of our sweetest confidences. All the ecstasies of faith are wrapped up in the very expression. It has grown hallowed. And though " The Soul not Immortal " is really the correct title for the belief that it dies between death and judgment, yet we must really not turn faith too suddenly even out of a heathen temple. Our doctrine is, that man dies at death : that the body is mortal, and that the soul is mortal : that the body will live again, and that the soul will live again : that the body will live forever, and that the soul will live forever : and therefore, keeping them together, that the whole man will die, sleep, rise, live again, and be immortal. This doctrine is taught in Scripture, and does not touch a fibre of the tree of grace. It touches fatally the errors of the Papacy. It is this literalness of the soul's not being immortal, to which we ask the attention of the church; and we beg her to perceive, that this is all that we attempt to teach, and that if she considers this a wreck, we have fallen on it over our charts and compass, and not by peering to the land for the decoy lights of a false Materialism.

JOHN MILLER.

PRINCETON, Aug. 6th, 1876.

# CONTENTS.

## I.
THE SOUL NOT IMMORTAL.......................... 13

### CHAPTER I.
THE DOCTRINE STATED............................ 13

### CHAPTER II.
THE DOCTRINE ABHORRENT TO THE VIEWS OF CHRISTENDOM. 17

### CHAPTER III.
THE DOCTRINE ABHORRENT TO CERTAIN CORRUPT FORMS OF FAITH............................................ 21

### CHAPTER IV.
THE DOCTRINE ABHORRENT TO CERTAIN PREVALENT SUPERSTITIONS........................................ 23

### CHAPTER V.
THE DOCTRINE, IF TRUE, IMPORTANT ................ 24

### CHAPTER VI.
THE DOCTRINE, IF UNTRUE, UNIMPORTANT............. 26

## CHAPTER VII.

ORDER OF DISCUSSION ................................... 27

## II.

THE IMMORTALITY OF THE SOUL NOT IN REASON ............................................... 29

### CHAPTER I.

CAN REASON BE UNMISTAKABLE? ......................... 29

### CHAPTER II.

REASONS IN FAVOR OF THE IMMORTALITY OF THE SOUL .... 34

### CHAPTER III.

REASONS AGAINST THE IMMORTALITY OF THE SOUL ......... 47

### CHAPTER IV.

A PROVIDENCE IN THIS DISCUSSION ...................... 57

## III.

THE IMMORTALITY OF THE SOUL NOT IN SCRIPTURE ............................................. 64

### CHAPTER I.

CAN SCRIPTURE BE UNMISTAKABLE? ...................... 64

## CHAPTER II.
The Fourteenth Chapter of Job............ 69

## CHAPTER III.
The Fifteenth Chapter of First Corinthians.......... 73

## CHAPTER IV.
The Two Adverse Passages.................... 78

## CHAPTER V.
The Spirits in Prison.................... 93

## CHAPTER VI.
What might we Expect of Scripture?.............. 98

## CHAPTER VII.
The Whole Man, Body.................. 105

## CHAPTER VIII.
The Whole Man Dead .................. 109

## CHAPTER IX.
The Whole Man Buried...................... 113

## CHAPTER X.
The Whole Man Raised from the Dead ............ 128

## CHAPTER XI.

The Whole of Man, Soul ........................... 136

## CHAPTER XII.

Spirit ........................................ 158

---

# IV.

## THE IMMORTALITY OF THE SOUL A RELIC OF PAGANISM ................................. 167

# I.

# THE SOUL NOT IMMORTAL.

## CHAPTER I.

### THE DOCTRINE STATED.

HE who wishes to propound a doctrine, and has in view any conscientious object, will discover it to be discreet not to define as far as he is able, but only so far as his conscientious object obliges him to do.

It is like ship-building. The packet has to meet the billows. The wily draughtsman will curve its lines as crank as he dare. If he satisfies the great need of carrying the freight, he will make the resistance of the sea the slightest possible.

We have our own theory of the soul, and that theory will incontinently appear as we complete our book. But that theory is not necessary to our purpose. We think it is hinted at in the word of God; but it is not vital. And as we wish the greatest number of adherents, it is obviously discreet to define as little as will barely meet our end.

We may mention for example three hypotheses:

First, the hypothesis of those who think that thought is an attribute of matter. They think that Abraham is nothing but carbon and phosphorus and other elements, and that Abraham's faith will physically follow when these are felicitously combined. We scout anything so rude as this; but still, let us not exclude its advocates. We find in the word of God that the soul dies. These men think so. Let us not haggle at the specific form, since *qua essentia* we agree,—that Abraham passes from life when his body is struck with dissolution.

Again, there is another school. They would treat matter like the orders of Masonry. They would speak of different endowments. First there are the brute molecules. Then a different endowment makes them grow, and we have the bean stalk; or a different endowment makes them feel, and we have the calf or the elephant. Incident to this feeling is thought, and it is the direct gift of the Most High. Then we have another endowment that is necessary to man. The question whether these endowments are simply matter would be answered by asking, What do you call matter? It would soon be found that these men think matter itself an endowment; that is, that it moves and acts; that it is forceful, and is all in motion; and therefore that matter is not life, because life is an additional gift of motion; and that life is not thought, because thought is another dose, so to speak, from the same Efficiency; and that, therefore, thought is not life, yet added, and inseparable from it; and life is not matter—the doctrine of this school

## The Doctrine Stated.

being, that the first dust of earth is a divine efficiency, and then life another, and then thought another, and then conscience more; all bred of God, and yet dependant back the one upon the other; dust having this supremacy, that it appears to abide, the conscience and the thought and the life following the fortunes of the dust, so that when that is disorganized, its endowments fail, and the bean-growth and the calf-life and Abraham's faith perish and become extinct together. This is another theory. We might subdivide with lesser shades, but we will deal generically.

We will give now another. It is that of the Soul-Sleepers whom Calvin attacked. They had not reached modern notions of the restlessness of matter. Boscovitch had not lived. They were ready to admit substantial spirit. They therefore thought matter one thing, and soul another—I mean *in esse*. And reasoning just as we do, I mean from Scripture, they argued out a common history ; that is, admitting that the soul had essence, and the body also, and that they existed permanently, they affirmed a participated lot, and that the soul sank into unconsciousness the moment it was driven forth from the refuge of the body.

Now we will enforce neither of these theories. We believe the second ; with the added proviso, however, of appeal to the unknowable. There is more than can be possibly conceived in both soul and body. When we speak of efficiency therefore, we are merely giving our last idea, and when we say that thought is but an added efficiency, it is rather giving an apology for a truth. We only mean that the mind, as a separate substance, has not a thing to show for itself in the world's analogies.

Behold, therefore, our doctrine. It is not to be encompassed by any one of these theories. We believe that Scripture inclines to one of them ; and we may be often tempted to use its language. But if we do, we are earnest to warn our readers that it is illustrative rather than enjoined. The whole doctrine that we plead for is, that the soul dies at death.

If Abraham lie in the grave, Abraham will think and act again no sooner than I. It was so with Christ. These simple inferences will shed light over all our purposes of teaching. When our Saviour died, He was out of being, *qua homo*, till the day He rose again. There is abundant sense in His descending into hell (*hades*). Adam is still extinct ; and if the judgment should be after millions of years, you and I will wait for it. My brother who dies to-night, sinks into his original nothingness, with nothing to show for it that he be raised again, except his dust that is sleeping in the grave, and his spirit, if you choose to think so, existing in its dreamless essence.

We take in all the consequences. But we consider it honoring our Master to believe that our life is hid with Christ in God ; that our souls, if they rest, rest as in John's vision (Rev. vi : 9) under the altar of our blessed Redeemer ; that we have a life in court ; that justice will call up the lost (Jo. v : 29) ; that the thousands of years that intervene shall be to us as they are to the Lord but as one day (2 Pet. iii : 8) ; and "that He which raised up the

Lord Jesus shall raise up us also by Jesus and shall present us with you"(2 Cor. iv: 14).

CHAPTER II.

THE DOCTRINE ABHORRENT TO THE VIEWS OF CHRISTENDOM.

THE view of the immortality of the soul in which we have been brought up is, that the soul is independent of the body. I mean by that that it lives with it on earth, but that it will soar away from it when the body arrives at dissolution. This pictures two essences, the one divisible and organized into life; the other one ; and this one essence incapable of death, and held back from sleep by the necessities of its being.

Now arrayed about this queen-cell, as though it were the centre of the hive, will be all the faith of nearly all believers. I cannot attack it without injury. It is not a vital doctrine. In fact it is a very incredible doctrine, if we think of it as a new thing as it would first strike us when we heard it for the first time promulgated,—that there is a floating spirit that is nested in us like a bird, and which a bullet crushing our brain would set flying at once as we scare an eaglet from his rock! But I may impair half the catechism, suspect the covenant of grace, doubt the atonement, deny the imputation of Adam's sin, and advance a creed that will shake all the doctrines of the Gospel, and it will not meet so sharp a recoil as a denial of existence between death and judgment.

Now why is this?

1. Partly perhaps from the innocence of the doctrine. Men's hearts have fiercely grappled with the doctrines of grace, and the church has been obliged to become aware of subsisting differences. But death—whether it be a sleep or a change,—or indeed which is to be preferred, whether a sleep till we are judged, or a state in which we cannot be tormented in the body,—these are vague questions; and therefore sinners have not thrown themselves upon them with opposing force. At any rate, the doctrine being rarely called into doubt, has giant hold. The immortality of the soul has so thoroughly pervaded thought that the man who challenges it throws the glove into nearly all the camps of believers.

2. Again, it has scenic force. The heavier doctrines, like the sumpter wagons of a pilgrimage, travel slowly. Immortality is every where. It fills all our visions. If we threaten, we call this up. If we soothe, we use this. And marvellous as is the thought itself that when I die I live still, it is not so marvellous as the feeling of certainty with which I administer to the dying so wonderful a consolation. It is so detailed. 'You are not dying: you are going on to live. Your body is sinking in decay: but your soul will free itself. You will be in the higher world to-night.' There is something startling in the scenic vividness with which these things are offered; as though there had been historic search, and as though men had come back as from Spain or Palestine and reported the things that are to be witnessed. Death, a weird spectre in itself, is made

more startling; for we tell men without a moment's hesitation that dear friends whom they have lost will be in their embrace the next moment. We shrink not from sending messages to them. And we let the brother launch out into the dark with as strong a conviction as we can make that he is going among friends, and that a message to Christ Himself would reach Him the next hour, warm from the lips of those who stand round the bed.

Of course such scenic certainties are not to be displaced like colder thinkings.

3. And then the rhetoric of such thoughts. They have pervaded language. What chance for different reasonings when each man in the tongue in which he was born finds immortal life imbedded? This is the unfair difficulty. The flight to heaven, the parting with the vesture of the body, the advent among the blest, are beautiful words with which we comfort children; and we mix into their very souls the tender conviction that lost relatives are waiting for them beyond the tomb.

And the people's literature! What hope is there that we can bend the current of universal thought? and what comfort can there be, through one lifetime at least, for any school who shall so thwart common speech as that Shakspeare shall have to be emended on every page, or allowed for, at least, in beautiful but obsolete conceits, where he permits himself to travel in the customary path in speaking of immortality?

4. Warning, too,—what must become of that? How can we afford to relax anything, and to give

up the idea that the sinner will go down quick into hell?

5. It is precisely here that the fifth difficulty will appear most pressing. 'How can you imagine that you are right when the whole world is so continually against you? Almost anything can be thrown in doubt; but when man, with singular harmony, has almost every where adopted this doctrine of the disembodied state, why do you disturb the preaching to the impenitent?'

6. Particularly, as men will say, 'If this doctrine be not true, how can we be sure of anything? If a teaching can lie quiet a thousand years, and then the Bible itself be suddenly found to undo it—then what next?' This is indeed our sad circumstance. We find the Bible squarely denying immortality. Almost the whole of our race squarely assert it. Quixote and his wind-mills will in spite of ourselves heave into view—nay Hobbes, and his bad skepticism. What are we to do? We have kept these Scriptures long enough for motives of prudence. May we repress them altogether? We think deliberately not. Though the church is in one sense infallible; that is, has never been deserted by the doctrines of the truth,—yet in single ones it has; in Christ's time, as to His temporal reign; in Paul's time, as to salvation being for the Jews; in Calvin's time, as to the use of the sword; and in Cranmer's time, as to the right of kings; and though it seems baseless to say so, yet we believe that scores of errors are sleeping unwatched under the cloak of Christendom.

Let each man light his farthing candle. If it be a folly, it will go out. If it be a shame, it will be his. If it be a mischief, it will not be to the Church; for all things will work together for her good. If it have a particle of truth, it will help even the light of the sun. And if it be fetid error, it will help the triumph of truth; for truth, like a horse's hoof upon the pavement, is kept only healthy by being beaten to the earth, and made ceaselessly to put in practice its wonderful defences.

CHAPTER III.

THE DOCTRINE ABHORRENT TO CERTAIN CORRUPT FORMS OF FAITH.

THE doctrine that souls live in a disembodied state has been made the vehicle of the chief curses of the Papacy.

1. The Papacy, like many another creed, exposes us to the unwarranted dream that all men may finally be saved. The theatre of uneasiness, certainly, is moved back just beyond the grave. The great doctrine of Purgatory becomes a paramount one with the saint, and a means of influence in extorting from the people.

This doctrine builds itself upon the fact of immortality. If we were mortal like the body, Purgatory would be a phantom like the spirit. Rome takes the passage, "Went and preached unto the spirits in prison" (1 Pet. iii: 19), a passage that we shall explain hereafter; or she takes the passage, "For for this cause was the gospel preached also to them that are dead" (1 Pet. iv: 6); or the passage, "Else what shall they do which are baptized for the dead, if the dead rise not"? (1 Cor. xv: 29), and building equally upon the general belief that we are immortal, they erect the great fabric of purgatorial devotion.

2. There comes in logically Prayer to the Saints.

3. There comes in with equal consistency of course, Prayers for the Saints:

4. Then Masses for the dead:

5. Then direct gifts to pray the departed out of Purgatory:

6. Then Indulgences:

7. Of course Canonization of Saints:

8. And then, lastly, Mariolatry, with all its accursed rites, preferring a sinner to the Almighty.

Of course Papists would abhor our work more poisonously than the tenderest believer. Protestants are not affected by what we advocate. The doctrines of grace, like the works of a scratched watch, are not entered. But Romanism would be struck with death. Grant the infallibility of the Popes, and the scores of them who have pronounced for Purgatory become testifiers against the system.

The pence that built St. Peter's were for a mistake. Indulgence had a theatre the whole dream of which was a fable. Purgatory aimed at that which was the dust of sepulchres. Mary was sleeping in her grave. And masses for the dead, and intoned prayers, and millions of consecrated gold, were lavished upon that which is as senseless as a clod, or

# Abhorrent to Certain Superstitions. 23

upon saints whose tutelar watch was about as precious as of the vanes above their resting place.

CHAPTER IV.

THE DOCTRINE ABHORRENT TO CERTAIN PREVALENT SUPERSTITIONS.

NOR would what we are convinced of be less fatal to certain prevalent superstitions.

1. This ghastly Spiritualism which has been stalking out of its grave ever since the Witch of Endor,* if men would quit reading in their Bible reports of spirits, would appear in its naked foolishness. Clairvoyance and mesmeric utterances and supernatural feats and inspirations would come down to their natural Christian measure, either as, in excessively rare instances, by demon spirits, or as legitimate plagues to the church for having mistaken the teaching of the Bible, and taught men about these disembodied sprites in derogation to the doctrine of a blessed resurrection.

2. Of course all ghost stories would become child's reading at once.

3. And, thirdly, all Schleiermacherism and Swedenborgian conceit, and spiritual-body dogma which seems to be coming up again with renewed vigor in our day—a doctrine that would give Dives an actual

* We do not doubt that the witch summoned Samuel ; and we do not deny that among the endless juggles of necromancy, the devil may have been allowed to work occasional miracle : but if our doctrine be proved, of course ghosts as ghosts must disappear from the imaginations of men.

"tongue" (Lu. xvi : 24) the day he was buried,—all this would have to be disowned at once; and we must teach the doctrine, not that a finer frame sails off from this at the moment of dissolution, but that all life extinguishes itself in dying, and that the gracious gospel truth is, "that all that are in the graves shall hear his voice, and shall come forth, they that have done good unto the resurrection of life; and they that have done evil, unto the resurrection of damnation" (Jo. v : 28, 29).

## CHAPTER V.

### THE DOCTRINE, IF TRUE, IMPORTANT.

So that the doctrine, if true, is important.

We wish we could present it as it lies in our mind. We wish we could present it better than it ties in our mind. For the doctrine is of so radical a nature, that so full a book as the Bible ought to determine whether we have a separate soul or not. We wish we could exhaust the evidence, and like some fine judge in the Supreme Court, lay the testimony on both sides so deftly that the case could be determined,—

1. For how grand if this could be found to be the Providential method for cleansing the Augean stable of the Papacy.

I do not know that the polarity of the magnet raises bread or cooks victuals. I do not know. It may operate in these things: but I cannot see it.

I do not see that the immortality of the soul does much for our Saviour's doctrine.

But I do see that its *not* being immortal corrects a host of errors.

I do not see that my soul's perishing at death obscures redemption, or affects in the least degree inability, the soul's depravity, the saints' perseverance, imputation, expiation, or any of the decrees of grace.

But I do see that if you will "hide me in the grave" (Job xiv: 13), I sleep over the time, that the Papist has polluted with his myths. And as I see nothing but resurrection in the Bible, I am determined to strike at immortality; and who knows that this seton in the neck of the Church, viz., a disembodied spirit, may not be the thread that has gathered through the ages much of the corruption of the church, and, poor figment as it is, that it may not be the will of the Master that it may finally be pulled away, with all the foulness that it has gathered through the ages of its history?

2. But not only would Spiritualism and Popery and Swedenborgian conceits perish if the spirit did, but we foresee another triumph, with a miserable Scientism.

The studious are periling the doctrine that man can think without a body. We deny that they can settle it; but they can throw probabilities forward that can beguile many an unstable soul. The scalpel has certainly moved nearer to the facts; and consumption of material cells has actually been seen in every pulse of thinking.

What a strange Providence it would be if men should taunt the Christian and say, Look now at your doctrine of immortality, and as in the instance of Galileo's globe, should rear amazing probabilities against our thinking,—if, as in late geologic revelations they could so fortify their analogies as to make it well nigh certain that a man cannot think without a brain,—how marvellous, just as the last battering ram boomed, and the enemy were shouting our discomfiture, if the Bible should appear, as in the instance of the Mosaic attack, nestled in another camp, divine Providence having shed fresh light upon the word of truth, and men having arisen who found in the Book itself that priceless proof—I mean unknown agreements with the facts in nature!

## CHAPTER VI.

### THE DOCTRINE, IF UNTRUE, UNIMPORTANT.

ON the other hand the doctrine, if untrue, could work but little mischief. The most serious evil that could possibly arise from it is that which has been already alluded to in the unsettling of Scripture. Men would say, How can we be sure of anything doctrinal? But bating this, which I confess should be an occasion of misgiving, the promulger would be as innocent as a child. For let us trace consequences. Where would the belief impugn orthodoxy? Suppose a soul, sinking into death, supposes that it will wake again only for the judgment. Does that affect the Gospel? Suppose the whole world goes to sleep thus universally convinced. Suppose they fare differently, and the whole turns out to be a mistake ; where will it affect salvation ? When a soul is garnered in the grave, atonement and pardon, justification and all the forensic doctrines both of grace and penalty, are safe no matter when we rise. The feat of living disembodied could not help any of the promises. The times and the seasons God might safely keep in His own power. And that a soul cannot sleep at death would be as vain a principle of ethics as that a man could not sleep over night for that it would destroy his responsible identity to break the thread of his thought as between night and morning.

We work, therefore, with a less troubled conscience. If we mistake, the gospel is untouched. If we do not, we pull down, as far as men accept our reasoning, shameless conceits, which have grown venerable in age; and which have so dazed the Church ; and which have made our Protestant tribe but a slender part of it.

CHAPTER VII.

ORDER OF DISCUSSION.

To keep paramount the fact that Scripture suggested all that we are writing, we intended to put Scripture first, and indeed all our book was to be chiefly under this head,—"THE IMMORTALITY OF THE SOUL NOT IN SCRIPTURE." But as a mere mechanical device we changed this for the convenience of the reader. It being altogether unnatural to complete a work like this, and say not one word about the philosophical question, we devised a short space for that: but observing that there it would be that by the necessities of the case we would be driven to the closest definition, we saw the advantage of arranging that first. Will the reader, therefore, understand our policy? Scripture is our whole appeal. Our resort to reason is chiefly to show that reason never could resolve the difficulty. That will be our very thesis. But in bringing that out we will have to define our being immortal very accurately. To avoid doing that twice, we find it mechanically better to fix an order of discussion that shall place reason first. Let it be under a sort of protest. This is a book entirely bred of texts of Scripture. And that we cannot put them first and all the time, is a grief to us; and is only submitted to, to avoid that hateful thing in any writing, a striking twice unnecessarily upon the same descriptions.

A clear idea, therefore, of all that we mean to teach will be reached best in the outset under the heading,—THE IMMORTALITY OF THE SOUL NOT IN REASON. Then will follow the main body of the work,—THE IMMORTALITY OF THE SOUL NOT IN SCRIPTURE. And then, to anticipate the retort, How did the world come so universally to believe the opposite, we shall consider as our last head,—THE IMMORTALITY OF THE SOUL A RELIC OF PAGANISM.

# II.

## THE IMMORTALITY OF THE SOUL NOT IN REASON.

### CHAPTER I.

#### Can Reason be Unmistakable?

1. IF common sal ammoniac be put in a glass shade under certain circumstances of heat and moisture, it will effloresce into the most exquisite growths, shooting up over the surface of the glass into the most plant-like shapes of leaves and branches. Is it alive? Nobody dreams it. Is it dual? No. So that I can heat the glass more, and melt all back into a mass, and no body dreams that there was more than matter.

2. Next I plant a bean in the glass. Presently I get an efflorescence not a whit more beautiful. What have I now? The bean has wonderful dignities. It can climb. It can observe wholesome laws. It mounts with the precision of an animal changelessly from East to North. Put it in the ground, and without eyes it will know the way upward. Put a bone near it; and if it be like the grape, it will burrow a whole yard towards it, and though in the lap of the dark earth, go pilgrim to it with many

roots, and web its spongelets over it, and peer in into all its pores, that it may eat up all its substance. Does matter do this? Certainly. Or rather (for we prefer always to speak of the efficiency of Jehovah), God blesses it with life. And yet no mortal thinks that there are two things in the bean, first, matter, and second, life, in any such sense that if we could kill it shut up in the vase, a something would be shut in with it other than its material molecules.

3. Now take a dog. What have we in him? Suppose I shoot him, and tumble him into the earth. Is there a spirit that floats away? And yet remember, that grey cur was very intelligent. He had thought, and arrangement, and memory, and fine judgment, some said, more than his master. He had discriminating affection, and conscience, and remorse, —at least it seemed so. What had he not that served to ally him with what is purely human? We tumble him into his grave, and what remains? Not one man in a thousand but believes that that is all of him. We cover him with the earth that we have dug out, and the analogies perfectly smother us if we dream of his surviving afterward.

I say, analogies; for if the dog lives, then the chalk cliff lives, and there has been a survival from the whole coast of England. If the dog lives, then the coral lives, or at least the coral worm; and whole continents must account for their immortal builders. If the dog lives, then lime mountains and whole Saharas of calcareous plain, and ribs of provinces that have dropped some day shell by shell under pressure of the sea, are the charnel houses of existing spirits. And the grasshoppers with their drumming hordes, the horsemen of the prophet, outweighing in tremendous mass the mammals of half a province, and preying on each other as plant devours plant, are nevertheless, all distinguishably in life, and continuously kept; for the analogy that would spare the dog, would crowd us with immortals in a way that would make the Hindoo doctrine of Transmigration a delightful relief from the nightmare of an impossible arithmetic.

4. But deny the dog, and where is your analogy for the man?

Now we drop at once to the right level when we say, that the immortality of man must depend solely upon Scripture.

The salt effloresces, and melts. The bean grows, and withers into dust. The dog dies, and that is all of him. Now if a man survives, it must be by a special gift; for it is surely out of analogy with the whole creation.

Let us show what the Bible will have to do, by proceeding in order:—

1. In the first place it will have to overcome a distinct analogy. Ten million vertebrated species give up their life, and are buried hopelessly in their grave. One species claims to be immortal.

2. And yet the analogy in all outward respects is singularly perfect. All die. All carry to the grave the same heart and lungs, the same brain and life. They have originated in the same birth, and are nourished by the same food, and possess the same

senses, and the same fear of death, and the same zest for life, and jealousies and affections, as each other. Moreover they have a like intelligence. Now I do not dream of settling the question where they differ. I only say, that they agree: and that there would be a violent presumption, save on a religious ground, against believing that the dog unconsciously sleeps, and that the man eternally wakes; when the dog falls into his grave with an intelligence so like the man's, and with a heart and a life so physically similar in all that was previous in his being.

3. Add to this that the scalpel of the student increases this analogy; and the torch of the chemist —in fact the search of the metaphysician. The leaning of modern thought advances sensation. The body is asserting a wider scope. And when we find that its tissues actually exhaust themselves in thought, and that its brain-substance and nerves actually telegraph thought we cannot tell how, but with appreciable physical results,—the analogy between the dog and the man is actually growing greater all the time, so long as we confine ourselves to facts other than those which we gather from the pages of the Bible.

4. Besides, analogy is the whole of argument. Why is this not more insisted on? Butler's Analogy is in fact Butler's attempt at every possible reasoning. There is an immediate consciousness; but this is no field for reasoning whatever. Accepting immediate consciousness, all that we build upon it is its analogies; and as few people will be so hardy as to say that we are conscious of immortality, we

will ignore those who do,\* and then the analogy as to the soul is the one determinate test of all that we are to believe.

5. But Scripture! What are we to do with Scripture? Let us recapitulate. 1. We have shown that the analogy is against our being immortal. 2. We have shown that that analogy is very strong. 3. We have shown that it is growing stronger under modern light. 4. And we have shown that analogy is our only expedient of reasoning. We would seem therefore to have settled the whole question at a blow.

But then, fortunately for man, there are higher analogies. We have higher consciousnesses. And on those consciousnesses are built higher foundations of reasoning. There are analogies of testimony; and when those analogies carry me to the receipt of the Bible, I weigh it with other analogies still, namely, with my conscious moral light, and with my chief experimental impressions. The scalpel may deceive me. So may the Bible. They are both by analogy. But my poor reason is so much more helped in the region of revelation; that is, to express it critically, so much more able to use the stepping-stones of my more certain forms of consciousness,—that my whole appeal is to the Bible. I think it in the very highest degree unlikely that the soul is immortal: but show me that it is, out of the Bible, and the unlikelihoods

---

\* We have no choice. It is impossible to reason about consciousness. If a man says, I am conscious I am immortal, what can we say? We can only remind him that he is declaring that he is conscious to-day of his existence to-morrow!

are all the other way. Let me be thoroughly understood here. All the analogies of earth are in favor of my being mortal. This we shall attempt to prove. Analogy, moreover, must decide the fact. Analogy, however, is not infallible. And as there are higher analogies for man which furnish the base for a revelation, these are the ones that must end the appeal. We will bring out the others; but it will be like race-horses which we expect to be outstripped. It is only the fact that the Bible has taught me that I am mortal, that emboldens me to premise the proof, that reason is of the same idea.


CHAPTER II.

REASONS IN FAVOR OF THE IMMORTALITY OF THE SOUL.

To give reasons against immortality in their clearest shape, it will be wise to exhibit first those that appear to be in its favor.

To do this, it will take too much time to exhibit all the forms of immortality, and to fit the proof to the specific nature of the doctrine as each man may choose to hold it.

Some are supernaturalists. They hold that the body now-a-days is necessary to thought, but that when we die, the soul is supernaturally lifted and set off upon an independent being.

Some are naturalists, and believe with the great herd that the body and soul are distinct existences.

Some are materialists, and get their immortality

like the arrangement of a Chinese box, one body inside of another.

And some are transmigrationists.

It is not necessary that we should go over all the list. Some arguments suit one form better than another. But it will suffice if we exhibit all in gross. The doctrine is, that consciousness survives death. Before we oppose it, it will become us to make the very fairest exhibition of the arguments that have been thought to make it good.

1. And in the first place it has been said that thought is so different from extension—or, to talk more comprehensively, that color and shape and motion and all the more usual attributes of body are so different from consciousness, that we cannot conceive of one of them as the attribute of the same substance as the other. This, in fact, is the old triumphant demonstration. Matter has gross particles and brute traits; mind has the attribute of intelligence. The perishing of one, therefore, is nothing, satisfactory at least, as to any decay of the other; nay, Butler would hold, leaves room under the light of analogy for a higher spiritual being.

Now what is this reasoning exactly?

If it be, that thought is different from motion, and that therefore the thinking thing and the moving thing must be different substances, that proves too much, for color and sound are different, and yet the one harp breeds both of them.

If it means that they are *so* different, and in fact so very and essentially different, that will not answer; for so are other attributes. Light, for example, is entirely different from hardness; and so are polarity and attractive force. What is the exact gist of the argumentation? It will not do to say, Where attributes differ substances differ; for attraction through millions of miles, and extension through an inch or through a yard, are unimaginable as to their accord; and yet who would deny them as attributes of the same materiality?

II. Let us, therefore, change that argument a little. It is not that they are stark different traits, but that we cannot produce both by laying molecules together. We grant that color is different from force, but we can arrange for both of them. All the subtler attributes of body, and even those that *impress* sense, as for example light and fragrance, we can produce by laying molecules together; but we cannot produce thought. We cannot conceive of thought as born in a solution, or produced out of a mass, however subtle the ingredients that we dispose together.

Now what is the exact logic?

*Conceiving* things we throw out of the scale at once. We do not suppose it was intended. We cannot conceive of gravity. We cannot conceive of smell. We do not suppose that any one will shut out as an attribute of matter anything because of what we can or what we cannot conceive.*

On the other hand, our antagonist would not care

---

* Unless the want of conception is at such an extreme that the language employed is positively without idea. In that case of course faith in anything would be, in terms, perfectly absurd.

for the debate if he caught sight of it as a mere question of language. The Nottoway, when it joins the Meherrin River, drops the name of Nottoway, and is called the Chowan. Who would not resent it with disgust if he were entangled a whole day in a debate whether the Meherrin poured its waters into Albemarle Sound? This is a very important remark. If, as it is reasonable to think, matter is called matter in its earlier and grosser exhibitions, to say that matter does not think is simply to say that thought is not a phenomenon that conferred its name. Give it other efficiencies, or let it take in other affluents as the Chowan does, and then it becomes soul, the only question being whether this is an impossible condition of the case; and now the argument that would assert that it is, is nakedly this,—that we can put together molecules and produce color, and that we can put together molecules and produce sound and smell, and so of all those things that we are accustomed to call material attributes, but we cannot put together molecules and produce thought. This is the fairest statement for our adversary that we can possibly achieve.

And it amounts to nothing.

The argument sternly given is that something cannot produce thought. We should be fools if we did not insist that the argument should be positive. But now something cannot produce life. We are insane or else that answer is articulately complete.

I put molecules into a glass vase, and cannot arrange them into intelligence. But I put molecules into a glass vase, and cannot arrange them into a bean-stalk. The man who says that the bean-stalk is not simply matter is making a vegetable spirit. The man who says that a man is not simply matter is making a human spirit; and thereby he is either changing a name like the Meherrin river, or he is building upon Scripture. This argument from what we can *make* is no better for the soul of man than for Igdrasil or a spectre of the cedars.

Remember, we are dealing with but a single argument. There are a whole list yet. We are simply saying that thought as the prerogative of men is no more demonstrative of a separate essence, than the cunning of a bean, of some separate sprite that floats away when it withers upon the ground.

III. But now we bring on more.

Our opponent demonstrates, and with apparent aspect of being exact, that spirit cannot perish with the body, because spirit is conscious of being one, whereas body is seen to be atomic, and its separate parts can die by being separated from each other.

We might contest the premise. We might utterly deny that the soul was conscious of being one. We might say that consciousness to-day is separate from my consciousness yesterday. We might show that their weaving into one was a beautiful provision of the Creator; and peremptorily challenge the far-fetched statement that the soul is imperishable because it is one, and that the fact that it is one is boldly deducible from unitary consciousness.

Let all that pass however.

The argument is, that the soul is imperishable because it is indissoluble; and that it is indissoluble because it is one; and that it is seen to be one by the fact of a single consciousness.

But now I ask, Has not a worm a single consciousness? What shall we venture to say about it? When we prick it, has it as many pains as it has rings in its length? or does it wince under a unitary consciousness much as we do? But I cut it in two, and each part lives! Now how is this? I leave it in the sand, and to-morrow there are two perfect worms. How about the argument for an immortal spirit? Nay, going to higher life: I take a zebra, or an ox; and by the prick of a spear do I inflict one consciousness or two? and if I effect but one consciousness, then has he not one soul, and when his atoms separate, does not some unity float away, from this imperishable fact of his being but one existence?

IV. Fourthly, the soul is independent.

We treat each reason in the list with absolute precision.

Abraham, it is said, was born an infant. Twenty years afterward he had twenty times as much weight, and his body had not a single particle of the substance that it possessed at the beginning. Then he lost an arm, let us suppose. His mind, which has been conscious from the first, is absolutely identical under all this history. Let us suppose him to be dying. The change may mount up, and may reach even to his forehead, and yet he is talking calmly to his friends, and his mind imperturbably waits for the falling to pieces of a tabernacle.

The argument then is this :—Mind demonstrates itself to be different, because it continues the same when every atom has been changed that was in the body; when part of the body has been cut off by the knife; and when the mists of death are gathering upon its more sensuous vision.

But honestly, is not the argument, made strictly emphatic, most positively the other way? The growth from infancy to age,—is not that in the bean and in the conscious ox? and is not the life of the bean and the consciousness of the ox kept unitary under this entire change? If I cut off a limb does not analogy explain everything that happens? Is it not known that we have vital parts? Suppose we cut off the head! We are unwilling that arguments should be used that would prejudice a cause in court; and never have understood why men admit such reasonings in their gravest interests. If I hammer my head, does my thought go right on as before? and if I cut off my leg, is not that known in its very nature as to the result, and never expected, from its analogy with brutes, to interfere with my more conscious living?

I die: and what happens? Why exactly that dying of thought which if the brain could be revealed would lie patent under the eye of the physician. Why will men venture such reasonings? I sit up and talk to my friends; but does not my body sit up? and is not my brain at work just in proportion to my consciousness? I confess that thought is driven to its citadel; but if my limbs are all cold, and a feathery pulse scarce lingers below my forehead, what of that? Is it not rigidly the case that thought is no more strong in me than my brain, and that there is a rallying there just in proportion to my remaining vision?

We complain of such things. The facts are obviously on our side. And yet Bishop Butler himself argues, that because a man is sensible just up to the margin of the sepulchre, he is, beyond it ; when Butler himself would admit that there is a stir in his brain precisely in proportion to the amount that remains of thinking.

Why not give up this argument avowedly and at once? The soul is *not* independent of the body. On the contrary, whatever else may be said, its dependence is complete. A blow renders it insensible. Infancy exhibits it as feeble. Age makes it that way again. Sickness deadens it. Death fades it, up to the very portals of dissolution. And what makes this Butlerian argument singularly insincere is, that all these circumstances are known to enfeeble the brain-action just in proportion to the decay of consciousness.

V. A fifth argument is, that the soul longs for immortality.

Now again let us be exact.

The argument means that what the soul longs for it must have. And the basis of this persuasion is not that we are conscious that such must be the fact, but that, reasoning from analogy, such must be the arrangement of the Most High. But then unfortunately this does not seem to be the case. Lost men desire happiness.

And if it be said, We are speaking of a normal condition: man in his natural state has that which he is born to long after,—we discover a difficulty here. Man in his innocent state may have that which he is born to desire, but surely we are not to infer how long and how much. It would seem unlikely that there should be no air for a bird; but it does not follow because a bird desires endlessly to live, that therefore it is to be gratified. The bug desires endlessly to destroy my vines. Now it seems natural that it should get some vines to destroy; but that it should be pleased endlessly has no warrant of analogous fact.

VI. The argument grows stronger if it moves on to the sixth place, and builds itself upon an expectation founded on considerations of justice. Here indeed have been the strongest argumentations.

Nor will we pause to weaken them by still interjecting the brute.

The brute has conscience. The brute has some appearance at least of a moral part. Is there to be no retribution for the brute? Why should the bad brute steal away to death? And why should the good brute have nothing different? Why should the deformed brute do naught but suffer? And why should the drunkard's brute be beaten and tortured into dissolution? We have our theory of these things; and it reconciles their total disappearance from life. And it does not impair justice. The argument from justice we consider quite unanswerable. Let us define what it is.

B. F. has gone to his grave with a physique so perfect that he has had a perpetual holiday. There are no bands in his death, but his strength is firm.

He is not in trouble as other men, neither is he plagued like other men. Therefore pride compasseth him about as a chain ; violence covereth him as a garment. His eyes stand out with fatness ; he has more than heart can wish. Now this man dies, and is buried ; and there is another man who is just the opposite. All day long has he been plagued, and chastened every moment. Suppose this latter to be scrupulously honest ; nay tenderly benevolent, and scrupulously kind and upright, and pestered with the regret of not having done his full duty to men. Now the argument is this ;—that this good man with the black and mephitic temperament, and this bad man, all joyous and full of life, if they die so, must have an immortality : else there is no justice on the part of our Creator.

The argument is a sound one.

But now look at the folly. It undertakes to show that to be immortal we must survive the sepulchre. That is ; a glorious judgment is not enough, and a resurrection at the last day. It is not enough that there should be an absolute account, and that B. F. shall confront it in the day of God. It is not enough that there should be an absolute forensic quest, and, after that, an eternal retribution ; but justice must be satisfied in their exact thought, viz., a continuance of our being when we close our history.

I say, Here is no particle of proof. Justice is justice. Justice may be done at last, just as well as in the beginning. Justice *has* waited long periods of years. And though justice is a capital proof that the soul will be immortal, it is no proof that it is immortal now ; or that it must begin its recompenses as a floating spirit.

VII. Yes, says our unconvinced antagonist ; for now, as our seventh consideration, justice is not justice unless there *is* a continuance of being. If life actually goes out, and the man has lapsed for thousands of years, where is the equity of bringing up another man? The judgment-day creation is actually fresh. There is no soul ; in fact there is no body ; but a few particles resting in the grave. Indeed it is doubtful whether the Great Builder will go back even for them. The man who lived and acted has passed out of existence, and there is no pretence of his being, except in the Rolls of Court and the accounts of the final judgment. If the man does not exist, then the judgment-man will be a new existence ; and where is the justice of seizing *him* under the judgment of the Great Day?

I ask, Where is the justice of punishing me after the unconscious sleep of yesternight ? One day is with the Lord as a thousand years ; and an utter unconsciousness is as bad in *foro judiciæ* as a break in being. Where is the virtue of my brute particles that they should keep me responsible over night, and deliver me with required identity to the judgment of the morning? These are puerile difficulties. Moreover there are much heavier ones. If lapse of time make against justice, what of the infant of to-day responsible for the sin in Eden? If the Creationist account is to be respected, that each infant soul is newly brought into being, where is the justice of that soul being guilty for federated guilt,—and I not for my own, because dead for some thousands of years?

I live by the Almighty. If He relaxes when I come to my burial, and " takes to Himself His spirit and His breath" (Job xxxiv: 14, 15), what difference does it make, if He breathes on again at the sound of the Trumpet, and wakes the same life after buried years?

VIII. But, says the opponent, it will lessen the terror of death. On the contrary!—A lady, walking in her house, is struck by a part of a cornice, and is carried stunned to her bed. She was just giving an order to a servant to bring her some sugar. Her skull is dented in upon her brain, and she lies unconscious for two weeks. At the end of that time the difficulty is discovered, and she is suddenly restored to life. The sight of the girl seems to continue her unbroken consciousness, and she repeats her order, " Mary, bring me the sugar!"

Now this settles the preaching difficulty. Once let it become sure, that the soul does not survive the body; and let it become familiarly the belief that the whole man reappears at judgment,—and the interval between will give no difficulty. . Between death and judgment there is positively no consciousness. The stride may be a millennium of centuries: to me it will be nothing. What use for a disembodied state, if I lie down to-night upon my bed, and in an instant, *seemingly*, ascend to judgment?

IX. But it may be urged, atheists will take heart. Say what we will of a resurrection at last, infidels will have their foot upon us. Once dismiss sinners wholly out of life, and men will take the risk of being brought into it again.

And this really, it will be urged, is the dangerous aspect of the innovation. When reason wrote over a necropolis, "Death is an eternal sleep," she used essentially the same arguments that we have set up. And men will shudder. They will say, Is there to be no rest? If immortality is unseated, then Scripture! then Jesus! nay, a resurrection at all! What may not be unsettled? And if a man entirely dies, and his existence is ashes of the tomb, then skeptics who have carried their notions thus far, will easily trample the last remaining legend.

Now I grant all this: and I shiver myself lest perchance I am doing mischief. But the like was menaced when Galileo upset the universe. Is it not true that the actual ought to conquer? If it be so, that immortality is a dream of Pagans, and that it is the revelation of the word of God that we die and are raised again, is not the offence the fault of the original heretic? I confess that scandal is created. And if any one asks eagerly, What uprooting will be next? I am unable to answer. But if it be a just uprooting, who dares say, It is a mistake? Heavenly truth is not to be kept in countenance by mouldy error. And if it is a false uprooting, men deserve it. In every age truth has suffered when hoary errors have come thundering to the ground. But who will say, Keep the errors that we may save the truth? Count over the follies of the past; the right to persecute; the divinity that hedges the throne of kings; the astronomic blunders of the church; or the geologic errors with which this century began; and who will say, Better keep all these than disturb religion? or who would hesitate himself to overthow such things as these, even though he knew it would be followed by disorder in more genuine believing?

These are the arguments therefore, that are to be given for the immortality of the soul. There is no charm in them. There is no ghostly privilege that is to hem them about as though they were a particle more venerable than the mind concedes. They are to be tried as one lawyer tries another when he appears in court. And as they are in a very heavy case, they are to be better arguments than the most (a thing which seems to be forgotten), and are to have just that attribute of precision and force of which all these seem to be strangely destitute.

CHAPTER III.

REASONS AGAINST THE IMMORTALITY OF THE SOUL.

I. THE first reason against the immortality of the soul is, that immortality, properly so called, it cannot possibly have. Immortality properly so called is deathlessness, and it belongs solely to the Almighty (1 Tim. vi: 16). Immortality properly so called would make a man so imperishably one, and so defiantly self-sustained, that he would live on forever without the Almighty.

Now the most determined advocates of our being immortal do not pretend to say that we are not dependent upon the Most High. There may be infidel naturalists that may make us eternal ; or Spinozists that may trace us back to the everlasting ; but square religionists there are none who do not say that we live in the Almighty (Acts xvii : 28); and who do not hold that, along with an immortal hope, we must have a concurring Power, else we would vanish any moment under entire annihilation. Then we are not properly immortal in any manner. Then it is a question of Will.. The most pious maintainer of the immortality of the soul will confess that we are not immortal in ourselves, but that it is a mere inquiry as to the will of the Almighty.

It is true there is an immortality second to the very highest, and the idea may be urged that this is all that is necessary in the instance of our race. There is an imperishableness of matter, for example. It is not absolute, and it does not exempt matter from being dependent on the Most High. It does not forbid the thought that if He were to withdraw his hand it would be annihilated. And yet practically it does not forbid the thought that it is imperishable. There is the same sum of matter now, say the learned, that there was in the beginning, and by the conservation of forces all will continue to exist through the myriad of years.

It may or may not be the case; but grant it; whether it may or not, it only may by the will of the Almighty.

And turn the question as we may, we come back at last to Scripture. If we resort to reason, it is as to the analogy of God's will. If we continue to think after death, it must be because God wills it. And if He wills it, it must be for some final cause. Now I can see the final cause for matter. Derange it, and you derange the cosmos. Diminish its volume, and you leave me nothing on which I can rely. But I can see no such cause as to mind. Continue that, and you bewilder me with difficulty. The snail and the stork and the elephant must all keep continuously on, and in the increment of life must submerge rather than uphold the cosmos.

The sole question however is, as to the will of the Almighty.

II. And our second argument shall be as to the analogy of that will.

Rehearsing what we have long ago declared, life when it goes out of the animal and the plant, goes out altogether. There is no soul of the cabbage or of the oak. If there be a soul of the lion, men ought to be willing to declare it. But if it be the prevalent opinion of believers that souls are the appanage of man, then the analogy of brutes should be confessed, and it should be admitted as a region of difficulty in respect to the whole opinion.

Men should deal fairly too in respect to our own analogies. The whole courses of our lives proclaim our dependence on the body. We are weak in infancy. Our thoughts are feeble and small when our bodies are. All through life we have just as much thought as we have action in our brain. If a blow stun us, we sleep. If sickness steal our faculty, it slackens and grows dim. If age deaden, we are embruted that much. Death puts a crown to the analogy. And unless thought actually flashes up by some bold manœuvre of the blood by which it rallies in its citadel, it is diminished as life is; and makes a sort of chicane of helplessness, if it springs into strength at the acme of most apparent impotence.

Analogy, therefore, most distinctly teaches that it is the will of our Maker that our mind should perish with the body.

But mark a difficulty. What might seem to be an overwhelming triumph is lessened, we are willing to admit, by a peculiar appeal. Analogy it might be frankly confessed would be almost perfect; but then how much remains of it when we have admitted one grand and wonderful exception? Plants die, and brutes die, and so we might seem to leap to the conclusion man dies. But then it seems that in every important way man does not die. What is there worth in the analogy if it is admitted that man is an exception after all? It is proclaimed that justly we must live again. It is confessed that we shall live immortal after a final day. What is left of the analogy, therefore? In other words, if man is a great exception to the brutes, why plead the instance of the brutes as any check to his being an entire immortal?

Now this would do grandly if there were any proof that he was, drawn from God's holy word. The fact of a resurrection would shed a great light on man that would justify a faith in any cognate wonder. But surely it could not originate it. The failure of an analogy in one respect would be a queer proof *ab origine* that it must fail in another. The doctrine that man must rise might be an argument that brutes must rise, or that plants might live again in the garden of the blest; but we do protest against an analogy that would declare that because man must rise by miracle under the archangel's trump—that therefore he must never have gone into the grave, or that his spirit at least has lived immortal.

III. Therefore we advance boldly to a third point. While we admit that man is a great exception, and that his being raised to immortality at the last puts a great gulf of dissimilarity between him and the brute creation; while his grafting into Christ and his entitlement as to the Holy Ghost makes it almost profane to think of him as dying like the ox and ass,—yet in the rush of such grand conceptions, it is not necessary that there should follow all manner of possible conceits. It is quietly said that we shall rise again. Unless it is also said that there shall be nothing to rise but the dust of the sepulchre, it spoils things to mix the exaltation at the last with the imagined idea that we are to be continuously immortal.

But it will be said, anything else makes necessary a miracle.

Let us notice where we stand.

Our third argument is that the mortality of the soul makes the simplest eschatology.

We have admitted that resurrection makes a vast exception for our race, but we have argued that that does not involve an original immortality. We are now reaching the argument that it is most natural it should not, but that the simplest eschatology would follow unconsciousness at death.

But says the present difficulty, then there must be miracle. Now no believer in the Bible disowns miracle; but the real gist of the challenge is that it must be constant miracle. The whole dependence of a man for life must be that he shall be raised up in the end totally, body and soul, as when originally created. If a man can live along; if he can have some identity of existence and continuousness of life; if nature can be pleaded as originally designing him and unchangeably continuing him in conscious being, then he reappears more naturally. But to lay the total weight of our immortality upon a supernatural re-creation at the last, shocks belief; and is out of the province of miracle; for miracle does no such permanent feats, but is only invoked for rare interferences in nature.

Now two things have gotten mixed. The warning is (1) that the whole thing is too incredible, or else the warning is (2) that there can be no permanent miracle.

Consider both.

(1) Ideas have moved around till we who teach a mortality like brutes are considered fatally credulous because we teach a total resurrection. That seems strange. We might challenge the reasoning that is built simply on the incredible.

But let that pass.

We simply sketch the circumstances.

One theory is that there is a total resurrection at the last. We hold that a great miracle. The other theory is that there is a partial resurrection at the last. Is that much less? But then in addition to this the arguer for the soul's immortality preaches another wonder. He believes in disembodied existence. That is,—I believe that I die just as I am born, totally and like a brute (Eccl. iii: 19); and that the one great promise is that I shall rise again. He believes most that is wonderful in my being raised, and believes also in a floating life different and in exile from the body. Which believes the most? And which, if both doctrines were stated now for the first, would he fight against with the most doubt, and get his mind to grasp and cover with the higher conviction of helplessness?

We believe most baldly that if we are to live again, as we confidently believe we are, we can get our eschatological conceit most easily through a restoration at the last, rather than through two strange wanderings, the wandering of thought altogether away from its base, and the wandering of it back to reclaim and vivify what is mortal.

(2) Then as to miracle. The difficulty pretended is, that it would be permanent miracle. But pray what was our creation at the beginning? The difficulty is that it is making miracle not casual but by law. A whole race are to come back to life, both wicked and just, under the supernatural. But men forget! How did we all come to life? And where is there anything more permanently supernatural in the resurrection of the whole, than in the creation of the whole originally? And then further; how is the resurrection of the body a whit less chronically miracle than the resurrection of the whole man, body and soul, at the judgment of the last day?

IV. Besides; the analogy of the universe!—we are greatly assisted by that. The wandering of disembodied mind, and that the dead should go on to think!—that is out of the line of the universal cosmos. But that, like the sowing of the dragon's teeth, there should spring up a whole harvest of inhabitants,— that has the prestige of the past. I mean by that, earth bears marks of having been peopled again and again. If she is to be again destroyed; if the heavens being on fire are to be dissolved, and the elements to melt with fervent heat, and then we, according to His promise, are to look for new heavens and a new earth (2 Pet. iii: 13), it is in the analogy of the past that the earth should people itself at a stroke: * and that it should people itself with man, I mean call up the millions of the past, is all that is special in the thing to be supposed. Earth, having been peopled often before, I mean with animals, is now repeopled with man; man having been formed on it as one pair by the miracle of the past, and now *re-*formed; all his buried millions lifted back into existence; a beautiful planet re-covered with homes; not now as in the common instance of creatures for the first time created, but of the just preceding race; a people degenerate by sin, but some re-generate; all of them to be brought back again to life, and some of them to be made gloriously perfect, body and spirit, in a Divine Redeemer.

I know not how it affects other minds, but when I read of the spectroscope,—soda and carbon and fer-

---

* I know this is denied; but I am willing to take with me what still remains as the great body of earnest thinkers.

ruginous vapors and hydrogen and other terrestrial matters seem messengers to me from other stars. They speak of universal body, just as loudly to my ear as anything ever spoke of universal mind. It may be fancy; but they beckon to me as from other seats. I see a universe; of some spirits perhaps, as of angels and principalities of a ministering race; but of great worlds of men, with phosphorus in their brains, like Newton and like Locke; and, like Newton when he rises from his grave, men with weight upon their feet, and with light upon their eyes, and food upon every bough to repair the exhaustion of their living; men who have never seen corruption (Acts xiii: 37; Rom. viii: 21) like us, but who have escaped it by holy living; yet who are nevertheless models of embodied life; rather than of that floating immortality which we are looking for after our dissolution. At least, this much we teach;—that the analogies of our own planet lead us to think that its whole repeopling (the wicked having been sent somewhere else) will be by sinners newly raised, their whole life brought up at once from the sepulchre, the race as a race created as much as if it were a new race, like any new fauna for a resurrected province; and that the only difference from the past is, that in this instance it is not a new race, but one kept reckoned for in the rolls of court; with a life hid with Christ in God (Col. iii: 3); brought back to conscious memory of their acts; and brought up as actually the same as if they had been sleeping but two minutes in their sepulchre.

Our fourth reason therefore, is, that a total planting of a race, I mean of body and soul at once, and that probably as the history of other planets, is the analogy of the cosmos ; with the exception that in this instance of man, there is the metempsychosis across the centuries of a lost but remembered being.

V. Now the last reason! We rejoice that the soul is mortal because it is the more solemn way to preach salvation to the perishing.

By the old plan I told men that they would be disembodied. How long was that to last? Why possibly for ages. Well, what are we to suffer there? Remorse. Well what is remorse? For my part I do not believe that the ungodly man can be brought to tremble before psychical suffering. Then whereto serves immortality? For our part we boldly declare that it breaks the fall that the impenitent is inclined to hazard. But tell a man that he is dust. Tell him that he will rise again. Tell him that it may be to-morrow. Convince him, as you easily may, that though it be after millenniums, yet *to him* it will be at once; and you bring upon his soul all the weight of an immediate torment. Tell him that he will die; tell him that he will be buried; tell him that his soul will live; tell him it will float in some dark Gehenna; tell him according to this doctrine that it will be without the body, and without corporeal pain,—and he will increase his ventures. The longer you count the period, the better he will be pleased with this idea of disembodied perdition.

It is true it may be an evil to unseat this doctrine of immortality ; just as it is an evil to unseat any doctrine that has reigned supreme, and that has struck its roots far into the thinking of mankind. Moreover it may have answered an end, just as one error balances another, as will be seen in the next chapter. But this end it is for God to aim at, not man. We have no right to play at bowls with the errors of the church. The times of ignorance God winks at (Acts xvii : 30) ; or, to correct a very wicked translation, God overlooks or oversees. God watches error to observe its exigent times. And we verily believe the knell has tolled for immortality. This grave mistake can no longer prevent a graver. And to teach men now that they entirely die, and that when they rise from the dead they entirely rise ; and that if millions of ages pass it will be to them unconscious,—bids fair to be the higher method of alarm ; for millions of ages disembodied they might be inclined to risk, but immediate torment they shrink from as inflicted in the body.

## CHAPTER IV.

### A Providence in this Discussion.

WE do not pretend to imagine that God could create error. "He is the Father of lights" (Jas. i : 17), "and in him is no darkness at all" (1 Jo. i : 5). It is dangerous to talk in any way different from this. "Let no man say, when he is tempted, I am tempted of God ; for God cannot be tempted of evil, neither tempteth He any man" (Jas. i : 13).

Yet, though God could not engender the idea of immortality if it were not true,—yet He could permit it to continue, if thereby he could rein in other follies more dangerous to man. God did not create the folly that salvation was of the Jews; I mean, ritualistically, and by the blood of Abraham. Christ did not create the folly of a temporal reign. We see how by both these mistakes the Jews and Christ's earliest disciples could be rallied and kept together. God did not teach the divinity of kings. Christ did not order religious persecution. And so the power of the Pope, and absolution by the priests, and infallibility of the church (like the union of Church and State, and like State education in our day), have been made in dark ages, like a hard bridle upon a horse, to stifle with forged claims more brutal and more dangerous heresies.

But the time comes for a release.

Now I can see, in respect to the doctrine of immortality,—men were brutish. It might suit half civilized children to imagine ghosts; for men might "err, not knowing the Scripture and the power of God." But let the whole world awaken; let the true relation of God to the cosmos be distinctly understood; let the light that modern science sheds upon the text "In him we live and move and have our being" (Acts xvii: 28), enter and prevail. and we can see that ghosts are not necessary to transmit our identity before the Law; that we can die to-night and rise ages afterward, and yet continue responsibly one; that one day with the Lord is as a thousand years; and that an hour's sleep is just as fatal to our continuing the same, as unnumbered centuries before our resurrection.

## A Providence in the Discussion.

The man, therefore, in this period of the world, who, at the suggestion of Scripture, and in fidelity to its claims, can overthrow the doctrine of immortality, may be doing a most timely service under the Providence of Heaven.

1. In the first place, he may be making better *teachers*. Continuing allegiance to the Bible all the same, the man who can bring our dying into analogy with all dying, so that the heart and lungs of beasts can be seen to stop as ours do, and all their animal existence, with the same arrest of conscious being (Ec. iii: 18-21), and who can build our hopes of immortality upon a life brought to light in the Gospel, is making the whole economy of salvation more practically simple, and is building, as bridge-builders do, with far less timber than in the old spans, and with a relief of faith unspeakably great to those who observe the analogies of nature.

2. In the second place, he will make better *polemics*.

Pharaoh and his chariots were so cheaply destroyed, because they had been led by Providence so featly into the trough of the sea. God by wonderful Providences has assembled the corruptions of Christendom within the same sea-walls. Those wretched abominations for the dead, purgatory and the worship of the saints, masses and the multiplication of prayers for our departed friends, indulgences, and all the horrid wickedness as to Mary the Mother of God,—all sink at once with this doctrine of immortality. It is a glorious overthrow. And if Miriam is to dance upon the rocks, we see no nobler chance for it than after this very history of ours, where God has borne with Antichrist, and hardened the Popish heart, and gathered its main conceits into this narrow bottom beyond the grave, and then buried all at a blow by filling up the bed itself under the gulfing waters.

There is no life in Hades in which Mary can appear. And then masses for the unreturning lost, and alms gifts, and invocations, have all been wasted upon myths; and, what is now very timely, the infallibility which has been just decreed, cuts off the retreat of Rome, and gives its assembled multitude an entire overthrow.

3. And so of the heathen field. A recanting of our ideas of immortality makes men not only better *teachers*, and better *polemics*, but it makes them, let me say also in the third place, better *missionaries*.

Immortality, we verily believe, is a Pagan myth. The systems we oppose are therefore all full of wandering spirits. Legends of the past crowd on us pictures of continual Transmigration. We are to cut up such systems. How can we do it better than by one clear message of a blessed resurrection? Paul accentuates this. And not only does he exaggerate our rising, beyond what we could conceive as natural if it were the mere resurrection of the body, but he is eternally harping upon "*that day.*" Every thing is to happen on "that day." And, in a way that would be utterly unnatural if it were the mere date of the rising of the body, he makes it the great day of redemption itself, and seals the spirit for it as though that were the day of universal restoration. We can make the best *missionaries* therefore, on this plea that we are mortal.

## A Providence in the Discussion. 61

4. And lastly, the best *philosophers*.

Savants are undoubtedly worsting this pretence of spirits. They are very wicked: and many of them are ghastly atheists; at least they are attempting to believe that there is no personal account, and no personal judge to hold those terrible Assizes beyond the grave. We know that we are in wretched company, till Christians join us, so long as we teach the doctrine that the soul is not immortal.

And yet, as all reasoning from nature is built on a system of what is *like*, it is not *likely*—and philosophers are making this incontestably to appear—that there is a soul, separate from the body, that can go on, in analogy with facts, to thought and reason after we are laid in the sepulchre.

We have taken pains to say, This is not certitude; but it fixes an analogy: and this analogy is ever growing. It is burrowing nearer the seat of life. In ways that are vital in other search, the phosphorus is tracing itself right up to thought; and the cellular decay to exertion in its mental part; till we can only say this:—You have proved your position subject to appeal. You have settled the cosmical proof, viz., the analogy of fact. We can overrule you by the Bible. You are decidedly the best philosophers, and I who follow you am the best theologian thereby, unless we are overthrown by Scripture. There are higher analogies, that leave with Scripture the final appeal But if Scripture itself suggests our being mortal, then the game is up. He is the best philosopher for Christ who catches the indications of the times, and brings the dicta of the Word into the earliest consistence with God's Providence in the discoveries of science.

Our next step, therefore, is into the citadel. But one word now!

Men will say, We object. The whole thing is a chicane. The Bible is a nose of wax. Free thought has had great triumphs, and has fairly upset the positions of the word of God ; and priests have patched up the break. This is what you are now bent to do. We unsettled Job and Isaiah, and Galileo showed the monks that the earth moved round the sun. The gravest exegetes silenced us by the Holy Word. And yet when we broke our path, and the opposition of the Popes was carried down by the inevitablenesses of Science, presto, there was a shuffle of the text. The oracle now told no such thing! And it has been repeated as to the age of the planet. The Bible now is at one with the geologists. Give the Doctors time, infidels declare, and Lyell and Darwin and Huxley and the very demonstrations of sight may break down the old wall of Scripture ; and a new wall is there behind it. Therefore it is of no use. The ghostly hierarchy maintains its place as by a new revelation. One word now before we proceed, and our enemies themselves shall judge.

I beg to know whether this is a fair view *scientifically considered.* I beg to know whether the Bible ever did teach that the sun rose and set. I beg to know whether it did not hint the contrary (Job xxvi : 7) before moderns found it out. I beg to know whether the way we searched our Bibles was not as these men searched nature, stupidly and ill; and whether the fault was not with Science that they did not post the world quicker, and through it the Popes, with the true way to read and understand the blessed revelation. I beg to know it: and also more,—whether the Bible ever did teach the newness of our planet ; whether when Doctors said so, they were not mistaken ; whether the very first text of Moses does not throw creation back unmeasurable depths; whether the Chaos of the second verse has any scriptural date ; whether the texts that follow have found any geology so agreed on and explained as would carry a case against them of any judicial strength ; and whether the whole fight with Science has not given Scripture some of its very finest proofs, and could at all be spared from the very first chamber of exoteric evidences.

If this be so, come on with us again. We are going again into one of these escapades of Revelation. She can afford to have them. The church has stoutly asserted immortality. Free thought has chased it, as it thinks, by glass and scalpel out of the range of possible subsistence. It thunders away at the wall of Scripture. And we are beginning to believe that there will happen again the old experience,—that just as the rams' horns (less blessed than those of Joshua) have blown their last blast, and the shout has gone up, and the wall of the beleaguered city has fallen to the ground, another, better wall will be seen behind it, and the Bible be found disowning the first, and showing its unaltered page to prove that it never built it.

## III.

## THE IMMORTALITY OF THE SOUL NOT IN SCRIPTURE.

### CHAPTER I.

#### Can Scripture be Unmistakable?

IF Scripture afford us a direct text in favor of a doctrine, we cannot trust it. This arises from the infirmities of language. If it says, "This is my body," it is in favor of transubstantiation: if it says, " Except ye eat the flesh of the Son of Man," it adds proof further: but such are the liberties of speech, that we cannot take such texts out of the category of an engaging rhetoric, until we find them braced up and warrantably supported by all the analogy of the words of Scripture.

When, therefore, the Bible says, "Baptism doth now save us;" or when it says, "Ye ought also to wash one another's feet;" or when it says, "Salute one another with a holy kiss;" "Rise and wash away thy sins;" "Lest I myself become a cast away;" "Whosesoever sins ye remit they are remitted;" or "whatsoever ye bind on earth shall be bound in heaven,"—we are not to run off at once and pronounce gravely what each of these texts seem to teach, but wait till we have compared. I cannot take the text, "In that very day his thoughts perish," and deny the doctrine of immortality on the faith of that single passage.

But what dare I do?

Here is an Indian box. It is built of bark. I wish to fit on the cover. It is built of striped bark ; and if I take the lid and fit it on in a certain fashion, I can know that I am doing right if all the stripes beautifully and simply and in a perfect way agree. That is what I would call fitting it *unmistakably.* But if I take it off, and put it on differently, and some of the stripes refuse to match, I turn it back at once. The fact that some of them tally does not satisfy me the least. The agreement of all of them if I fix it on the other way, carries conviction at a blow ; and I can perfectly understand why a few of the stripes match by a happy accident, or by any cause you choose to state, when I set it differently.

Moreover if a tool has been at work to *make* the lid match the box when it is set on wrong, it only makes it disgust me the more, and only makes me more comfortably convinced when I see it fixed the other way and matched in every direction.

Now this is what I call making Scripture *unmistakable.* Scripture may not be absolutely unmistakable even then. But it may be practically so—if I take a doctrine like immortality and it practically won't fit. You may quote me a text or two, and it shall be like the imagined fitting of the box. If I turn it round the other way and all the texts fit, and there is an easy fitting each one in its place, the effect ought to be decisive. There is an easy falling into place that carries with it unmistakable evidence that all has gone well.

Now as to the tool *making* it fit, we see that in immortality. The world has been steeped in that thought hundreds of years. It tampers with the word of God without knowing what it is setting wrong. We see this in all the translations of the Bible. Where the Bible says "God formed man dust of the ground" (Gen. ii : 7), it puts in Italics, and says, "God formed man *of the* dust of the ground." Where the Bible says, "Let the waters bring forth the moving creature that hath a living soul" (Gen. i : 24), it relegates the disagreeing stripe into the margin, and translates it "that hath life." Where the Bible says, "He shall come at no dead soul" (Num. vi : 6), it attempts an honest relief again, and translates, "at no dead body." Now this is what I would show by the Indian box. The doctrine that we are not immortal would tally easily with all real language. But the world has been setting on the lid the wrong fashion ; and this mark of the tool is one of the most striking evidences that could at all be calculated.

Let me add now a further number of examples. The Bible says, "And he that smiteth the soul of a beast shall make it good, soul for soul" (Lev. xxiv : 18). Our translation has it, "And he that killeth a beast shall make it good, beast for beast." Ecclesiastes says, "For that which befalleth the sons of men befalleth beasts ; even one thing befalleth them : as the one dieth, so dieth the other ; yea they have all one spirit" (Ecc. iii : 19). The translation has it

## Can the Scripture be Unmistakable? 67

"Yea they have all one breath." The next sentence is, "All go into one place: all are of the dust; and all turn to dust again. Who knoweth a spirit of man that goeth upward, and a spirit of the beast that goeth downward to the earth?" King James no longer translates "breath," but gives the word, as usual, "spirit," though it is precisely the same word; but now puts in the definite article, which gives just the opposite sense;—"Who knoweth the spirit of man"—as though there *were* such an essence, and it went upward—"Who knoweth the spirit of man that goeth upward, and the spirit of the beast that goeth downward to the earth?" Again, other instances. The apostle says, "Seeing we have lying around us so great a cloud of witnesses" (Heb. xii: 1). King James gives it to us, "Seeing we are compassed about with so great a cloud of witnesses." The verse just before is prejudiced worse. The original makes it, "These all, having been attested by faith, received not the promise; God on our account having looked forward to the something better, that they without us should not be made perfect" (Heb. xi: 39, 40). King James' men quite erase all that, "These all, having obtained a good report through faith, received not the promise: God having provided some better thing for us, that they without us should not be made perfect." Once more, in Leviticus, "For the soul of the flesh is in the blood, and I have given it to you upon the altar to make an atonement for your souls" (Lev. xvii: 11). Our version has it, "The life of the flesh is in the blood," just sponging out altogether the antithesis of the beast's soul with the man's soul. And further;—" Therefore I said unto the children of Israel, No soul of you shall eat blood ; neither shall the stranger that sojourneth among you eat blood. And whatsoever man there be of the children of Israel, or of the strangers that sojourn among you, which hunteth and catcheth any beast or fowl that may be eaten, he shall even pour out the blood thereof, and cover it with dust."—Now observe again, —" for it is the soul of all flesh. Its blood is in * its soul ; therefore I said unto the children of Israel, Ye shall eat the blood of no manner of flesh; for the soul of all flesh, that is its blood ; whosoever eateth it shall be cut off" (Lev. vii : 12–14). Our English by a sort of instinct turns it all round to what is orthodox, " For it is the life of all flesh ; the blood of it is for the life thereof." The likening of every creature's "soul" is utterly sponged out. " For the life of all flesh is the blood thereof: whosoever eateth of it shall be cut off."

Now, touching with a light finger any one such apparent prejudice, we are disposed to lay a strong accent upon it when it is one of many. And when it becomes almost a mannerism of exegetes, and their work is full of this turning aside of thought, the proof becomes overwhelming. It is stronger than Paley's coincidences in the Horæ Paulinæ, because, equally unconscious, it is greater in numerical extent, and recurring with the punctuality of light when any passage seems unfriendly to immortality.

* Or " as " (*bêth essentiæ*).

## CHAPTER II.

### THE FOURTEENTH CHAPTER OF JOB.

OUR first impulse was to deal with the elementary evidences of the Bible; for instance, to take the words, body, soul and spirit, and the phenomena of death, burial and resurrection, and see by a collation of the passages whether each of these things seemed to include all the man; or whether there was a separation of him under the names, and a separation of him also under these destined changes.

We mean to do all this yet.

But we remembered that such labored work gives the air of after-thought and special pleading; and that when it was done, there would be a sense of advantage taken; and that while we were fresh, it would be better to bring forward the more important Scriptures, and treat them in a more common fashion; that there might be no complaint that we had cooked up a set of solvents by which any passage might be made nought, and by which the strongest testimonies might be turned aside into the support of heresy.

We shall treat five passages therefore first, two of them witnesses for us, and three of them assumed to be the other way. We shall consider them in their simplest sense; and keeping religiously away all appearance of refining upon their drift, we shall show that the whole five match easily with us; and that only three appear to do so under the opposing theory.

The first is that beautiful passage of the Book of Job so often read on occasions of burial. It is the language of Job himself (Chap. 14). "Man that is born of a woman is of few days and full of trouble." Before we go on we need not anticipate a difficulty about Job being inspired, or stop to show that each text is, in view of the difficulty that the prevailing drift of these debates was in many points mistaken. Our readers will adjust all that. The men that will denounce our doctrine are not those that will be dissatisfied about the patriarch Job. We will treat this beautiful poem as though, in the required light, the word of God ; and will run the risk of any one rejecting it for want of inspiration. Now let us read its testimonies:—

"He comes forth like a flower, and is cut down; he moves across also like a shadow, and does not stand. And is it really on such a one that thou dost open thine eyes ? and wilt thou bring me into judgment with thee ? Oh that the clean might be put apart from the unclean that they be not one. Seeing his days are determined, the number of his months are with thee, thou hast appointed his bounds that he cannot pass ; look away from him and he will cease, so as to rejoice as a hireling in his day." Now this *ceasing* is on a par with all the testimonies of the inspired word as to the end of man. It is not that my body will cease, but the whole man : and this testimony is not a thing that we stop to accentuate as from this single text, but in all the Bible.

It is not the body that dies, or is buried, or rises again, but it is Abraham, or Christ. And in this sentence of Job the *ceasing* is peculiar. " Look away from him, and he will cease." It is one of those passages that present in the strongest light the dynamic theory of our being.

But now comes the main thought, " There is hope of a tree, if it be cut down, that it will sprout again, and that the tender branch thereof will not cease. Though the root thereof wax old in the earth, and the stock thereof die in the ground ; yet through the scent of water it will bud, and bring forth boughs like a plant. But the strong man dies, and is down ; yea the common man gives up the spirit, and where is he ? The waters roll up (evaporate) from the sea, and the river wastes, and dries ; and man lies down and rises not : TILL THE HEAVENS BE NO MORE THEY SHALL NOT AWAKE, NOR BE RAISED OUT OF THEIR SLEEP."

Now why is this testimony not quoted ? The Bible has been ransacked for the other view, and slender asseverances insisted upon ; but this square statement seems for nought. And if you carry it now, as we suggest it, and offer it to some friend, and ask, What are we to make of this passage ? he will cast himself at once upon the tide of his preconceived opinions. This ceasing, he will say, is the ceasing of the body. This sleep is the slumber of the body. And this waking and being raised up when the heavens are no more, he will tell you with a zest that will be a solvent for anything from Scripture, is the mere rehabilitating of our ashes from the grave, and the mere incarnating of the saint after an age among the blessed.

But now go on with the passage. "Oh that thou wouldest hide me in the grave, that thou wouldest keep me secret till thy wrath be passed, that thou wouldest appoint me a set time and remember me. If a man die, shall he live again?" What would be a natural reply to this, if it meant a death all over? Why certainly that he would have to wait. If the heavens be no more before he awake or be raised out of his sleep, he would naturally say that he must lie dead till he is called. And this is exactly what he does say. "If a man die shall he live again? All the days of my appointed time will I wait, till my change come. Thou shalt call, and I will answer thee. Thou wilt pine after the work of thine hands."

We count this strong argument. But if it is doubted, let us at least modestly ask that it be one stripe in our Indian casket. It fits solidly and well; and the rest of the chapter refers to second childhood. We cannot stop to sift it, but it is very striking. It is quoted by Papists for purgatory, but it refers to an old man. "His flesh upon him shall have pain, and his soul shall mourn over itself." His decay shall be like slow washings. "As the very mountain crumbling wastes down, and the rock wears by age out of its very place; as the waters wear the stones, and as its floods carry off the dust of the earth, so thou destroyest the hope of man. Thou bearest perpetually upon him, and he moves lower; thou alterest his looks, and sendest him further down. His sons grow great, and he has no knowledge; or grow small, and he understands nothing about them. Only his flesh upon him shall have pain, and his soul shall mourn over itself."

We must dismiss this passage. We beg that it may be treated fairly. There are four others that must be considered in their turn.

## CHAPTER III.

### THE FIFTEENTH CHAPTER OF FIRST CORINTHIANS.

IF any candid exegete were asked, what is the most detailed passage in the word of God on the subject of the resurrection, he would probably point to the fifteenth chapter of First Corinthians. Nobody can challenge us, therefore, for choosing that as an authority; and, in doing so, we have an instinct which forbids labored criticism of any sort, and claims as decisive the inevitable drift of the apostle, whatever may be our difference about minor difficulties.

In the first place there can be no question at all about the subject that the apostle is talking about. It is our rising; and, by a happy fixing of his sense, not a survival of the soul, but a resurrection of the believer, whatever that means, at the final day. This appears before he has finished a paragraph. "For I delivered unto you first of all that which I also received, how that Christ died for our sins according to the Scriptures; and that he was buried; and that he rose again the third day according to the Scriptures "(1 Cor. xv: 3, 4). This is his setting out. And now he binds the chapter to this beginning, by the most inseverable bonds. For he says, " If Christ be preached that he rose from the dead, how say some among you that there is no resurrection of the dead?" A resurrection, therefore, from an actual tomb, and on an actual day, and of an actual buried mortal, is the resurrection talked of all through this celebrated passage. Now for the question, Was it of the body merely, or of the whole man? We shall pretermit the evidence taken from the general expressions. That we shall deal with by itself (see future chapters). The Bible never speaks of the resurrection of the *body*. It speaks of the *man* rising again. This is one of the stripes of the box that is never noticed. Listen to this very opening of the subject ;—" Now if *Christ* be preached that he rose from the dead " (ver. 12). Let us not distract ourselves however. We wish, for the present, only the bold and more sweeping proof that the apostle has in his mind a resurrection from a total death ; and not a resurrection of the body to rejoin a soul that has been all the time immortal.

Observe his reasoning :—" Then they also which are fallen asleep in Christ are perished " (ver. 18). Again, " If in this life only we have hope in Christ, we are of all men most miserable " (ver. 19). Again, " Why stand we in jeopardy every hour? I protest by your rejoicing which I have in Christ Jesus our Lord, I die daily. If after the manner of men I have fought with beasts at Ephesus, what advantageth it me if the dead rise not ? " Now observe this argument all the way along. If the dead rise not, those asleep in Christ have perished ! Just think of the ungrateful heresy! And yet these are hard drawn lines of argument. Observe them again. "If in this life only we have hope in Christ!" Why Paul must be beside himself! According to our friends, hope never vanishes. The soul lives right on. Paul is reigning this very blissful moment; and yet, like a child crying for the moon, he has to remember that he was of all men most miserable because he could not have the matter of the body!

Now I do not deny for a moment the advantage of such a having; nor do I challenge the philosophy, nor the philology, nor the cosmogony, nor the theologic probabilities of thought, that make the body very necessary to the soul. On the contrary that is our great hinging fact. But we say, When Paul sums up, " Let us eat and drink for to-morrow we die" (v. 32), and makes that the alternative of there being no resurrection at the last; when he says, " If after the manner of men I have fought with beasts at Ephesus, what advantageth it me if the dead rise not;" and when he says, "Then they which are fallen asleep in Christ are perished,"—he is not thinking that they do " immediately pass into glory." If he does, he is the very heel of ratiocinators. We do beg a square treatment of this proof. Paul never could have believed that he was the possessor of an immortal spirit, if he made in this life only his hope toward God, and the alternative, " To-morrow we die," if debarred only of a bodily resurrection.

There is a text, " Else what shall they do that are baptized for the dead" (v. 29). It would not really affect us logically, no matter what might be its superstitious interpretation. Let us give the whole of it. "What shall they do that are baptized for the dead, if the dead rise not at all? Why are they then baptized for the dead?" If it were an old observance, as most commentators think, it would not decide our question; because, if it were a living friend getting himself baptized in behalf of a dead friend (as most people think it was), for the reason that that dead friend believed in Christ, and yet for some cause omitted baptism,—it would not show that that friend existed in the spirit, or was living somewhere in a disembodied state, but would only show that he needed baptism, leaving the whole question as to when or where, precisely as it would be without the passage.

But as the passage is a strange one, and might seem to disturb the smoothness of the chapter, and as its superstitious readings have been associated always with an intermediate state, we beg to suggest what is most simple. And though our solution is a new one, it is all the more fair; for it offers itself, without any prejudice in its defence, solely upon the evidences in the words of Scripture.

The Apostle, having appealed to the analogies of doctrine for his position, viz. to Adam, and to Christ, and to the victory of Christ over death, appeals next to ordinance, and to their own usages as Christians. And he appeals to baptism as one of the most comprehensive of ordinances, and a good type of all the rest. He says, "Else what shall they do who are baptized for the dead, if the dead rise not?" The superstitious solutions to which men have seemed driven, have all originated in limiting the meanings of the preposition which is translated "*for.*" That word in the Greek has all the ambiguities of which it is capable in the English. It is a word therefore that can mean *as.* We say in English, "I shall run for governor:" or we say, "Hang him for a thief;" or we say, "Trust him for a perjured villain." This, therefore, is a rendering that is possible with the apostle (see Thucyd. 1,141). We take it as the solution of the passage. Paul means, In all those ordinances that recognize man as "dead," what are you imagining? Why are you baptized as being dead, if the dead rise not? Your ritual images of death, are they not hopeful with the light of resurrection? This is his meaning. And it gets rid of all puerile conceits? There is no trace of a baptism for dead persons: and when at length such usages appeared, it was like the Chinaman imitating to the very patch. It was a usance built on this text. And it was like washing one another's feet (Jo. xiii: 14), like the kiss of Sandeman (Ro. xvi: 16), and like regeneration in baptism (Jo. iii: 5), a running into the ground of the words of Scripture.

So much for this little *soupçon* of an intermediate state. The words of the chapter, in all other respects, present a solid front against our immortality.

## CHAPTER IV.

### THE TWO ADVERSE PASSAGES

BY far the most serious passages against our doctrine are those in the fifth chapter of Second Corinthians, and in the first chapter of Philippians. One speaks of being absent from the body and being present with the Lord (2 Cor. v: 8), and the other of departing and being with Christ which is far better (Phil. i: 23).

We are bound as honest men to say that if they were really just as they are translated, we would not be moved by these single passages away from that vast array of proof that crowds the Word. We would neglect them, even if we could not explain them; just as we would neglect the passage, " This is my body," even if we could not expound it so as to yield to the enormous mass that presses against its being taken as it is.

If we thought these passages were to be translated as they stand, we would say that for all practical purposes they were true, because we do depart and be with Christ, the ages that might come between being quite unconscious nothings in our path to our Redeemer.

But fortunately for our prejudiced position, it does not ask from us such a boldness. The passages correct themselves; and we desire to show how the same apostle that wrote the chapter in First Corinthians, could write these also, and yet be steeped in

## The Two Adverse Passages. 79

the idea that we pass into an unconscious state, and that the soul is not immortal.

And lest it should be imagined, as a matter of course, that we must begin now a destructive criticism, and do that which men are too prone to do, viz., abate at all hazards an antagonist revelation, we state what the most prejudiced will be arrested by, viz., that the world's ablest evangelical commentators have expressed their wonder that their favorite doctrine of immortality should be so strangely left out from these very passages, which seemed most to teach it.

For example, Lange;—"It may be alleged that the intermediate state between death and the resurrection is entirely lost sight of in the Apostle's mind, inasmuch as we know that he looked upon it as altogether temporary, and hence that the perfection to be obtained after the resurrection was the absorbing object of his attention in this passage" (2 Cor. v: 1). Dr. Hodge argues that the "building" here spoken of is evidently to be entered upon at death: therefore he denies that it is the body, and argues that it must be heaven itself (see Com.). Ellicott on the other passage would evidently qualify the right to "dogmatic deductions in reference to the intermediate state" (see his Com. Phil. i: 23). But in Lange such a reserve is much more pronounced:— "There is no thought here of an intermediate state" (see Lange on same verse): and in Alford on Second Corinthians the omission is apologized for,—"A difficulty has been raised by some commentators respecting the intermediate disembodied state,—how the apostle here regards it, or whether he regards it at all. . . . The intermediate state, though lightly passed over, as not belonging to the subject, is evidently in the mind of St. Paul" (see Alford, 2 Cor. v: 1). Could there be a stronger argument? The two passages which are the chief resort of theologians who would teach the doctrine of our immortality, are found under the most scholarly hands to be so disturbing to the commentators as to their own ground of an intermediate state, that they have constantly to be apologizing for Paul for seeming to teach the very opposite idea.

And now as to the passages themselves. That in the Second Epistle to the Corinthians begins to speak, in the fourth chapter, of our outward man perishing, and our inward man being renewed day by day (iv: 16). This sentence is certainly far from encouraging our separating a soul from a body; or our making either the outward or the inward stand clear the one from the other as literally flesh and spirit. But whatever cannot be distinguished there, cannot be distinguished certainly in the texts that follow. "For our light affliction, which is but for a moment, worketh for us a far more exceeding and eternal weight of glory; while we look not at the things which are seen, but at the things which are not seen: for the things which are seen are temporal; but the things which are not seen are eternal. For we know that if our earthly house of this tabernacle were dissolved, we have a building of God, an house not made with hands, eternal in the heavens" (iv: 17, 18; v: 1).

Now let us suggest three theories. A physicist, when he cannot unravel facts, suggests a theory. That is the triumphant theory which takes in all the facts. Such is really the way to study a passage: it is, to take up all the theories that different minds may suggest. That is the meaning of the passage which accords with the word of God, and embraces as a consistent whole the circle of its texts. (1) The first theory we reject. It is, that "our house of this tabernacle" means, nakedly and without any distinction in the least, the intelligent man, or the intelligent soul. We waste our thinking upon such a folly. The thought of a house, or, as we go further on, the thought of a garment, must have an eye to something that is covered; and, therefore, that the soul dies with the body in such a way as that the figure of a house has no force, is corrected by the very language. The theory, therefore, that would make all this mean that the house is the soul and the soul is the house, would be absurd past the possibilities. Paul, in speaking of the earthly house of this our tabernacle being dissolved, must be speaking of something that admits this idea of shelter.

(2) It might seem, therefore, that all that our adversaries asked for was allowed. Their theory is that the body is this shelter; that when Paul says, "that I must shortly put off this my tabernacle," he means the body; and that he means it in so distinguishable a sense as that the body can be dissolved and perish, and that the soul can live. This is the theory that we are combating. This is the theory that grows, so so many commentators think, so in-

evitably out of this passage. And this is the theory that we ourselves confess (grant it the prevalence that it at this day holds), seems to come naturally into this passage, and to take up its parts with scarce a challenge to any preconceived ideas.

(3) But now abandon this theory for a moment. Let me substitute another. Imagine the common one to be clean off the stage. Suppose the soul not separate, and life not to last, and the stage to be actually free, so that the mind of man could get up its images for that state of things which would supervene upon an intermittency of our being. Let us merely try that condition for our rhetoric. The bean would have no life outside of its matter, and yet, when this was granted, we might begin to speak of the life of the bean. We might image it as shut up in its matter. We might in figure talk of its departing from the bean. And we might most reasonably indulge in such an imagery for the plant as would make its stem and branches the " tabernacle " of its whole vitality.

Who would wonder at this as to a brute?

Now if I may speak of a brute as having his " tabernacle" in the body; and if I may speak of his soul as departing, when it does not travel one inch from the ashes of his tomb, why may I not do the same in respect to man? particularly if the whole stage is cleared, and there are no preconceived ideas to curtail the scope of this bolder and freer employment of the image?

For example, when Peter says, " Knowing that shortly I must put off this my tabernacle ;" if we were positively advertised that we had no surviving consciousness, we would have no revolting at any violence in the figure; but would simply understand that, as in the instance of the plant, the whole concentrated life was thought of as under the shelter of the body.

Now our argument is that the passage in Corinthians is more after this theory (3) than after the other (2).

Paul says, "We know that if our earthly house of this tabernacle were dissolved, we have"—what? An immortal consciousness? Noticeably not: but just what we would have if our life went out at death, and went in again at the resurrection. It is not even said, We shall have. But just as if there were no conscious experience between one tabernacle and another, " We have."

And now notice other points. If the soul perishes at death; that is, if life goes out altogether, and the soul is but the appanage of the body, the man never has an absolutely holy life till the resurrection. Consequently that resurrection is very great, and the soul, if it perishes at death, not simply gets back its body at the last, but gets its earliest perfectness. This corresponds with Paul speaking so much of "*that day*." In fact it unravels the puzzle of so much talk about the resurrection of the dead. If the soul dies out at death, it does not come in at our rising after ages of grace, but it comes in fresh from the ashes of the sepulchre; and therefore a great step upward is made, a great grace is given, on the morning of the resurrection. The soul that went out sighing, comes up a glorious inheritor. And, therefore, "the day of redemption," as that day of new life is scripturally called (Eph. iv: 30), is a most significant account; seeing that the soul, if our scheme be true, has never experienced before felicity or purity of being.

Now I beg that in this light the chapter before us be considered. If it be merely the dust that rises; see what exaggerated language. "A building of God!" And then comes a sentence that occurs twice before in the Bible. Circumcision is implied to be not "made with hands" (Eph. ii: 11; Col. ii: 11). The expression evidently means that which does not spring from preliminary causes.* A circumcision not made with hands means a purifying of the heart, out of the course and without the efficiency of nature. So Christ was not made with hands (Mar. xiv: 58) when, as a temple, he was destroyed one day, and raised up another. These things rise like an exhalation, without that preliminary cause the absence of which is made a cavil against our doctrine. So then,

* Paul actually explains what it means. He says, "Christ being come an high priest of good things to come, by a greater and more perfect tabernacle, not made with hands, that is to say, not of this building" (E. V. Heb. ix: 11.) We spring eagerly after the Greek, and this unveils itself—" Not made with hands, that is to say, NOT OF THIS CREATION." What a noble text for Huxley! He may carry back evolution as far as he please. There come at last things " NOT MADE WITH HANDS, THAT IS TO SAY, NOT OF THIS CREATION." Adam and Eve were such things, as to any previous universe. The widow's " oil" was such a thing, when it welled up to pay her debts (1 Ki. xvii: 14). The twelve baskets full of fragments were such things (Matt. xiv: 20). They were " NOT OF THIS CREATION." And the raised sinner will be such a thing, a something " not made with hands eternal in the heavens" (2 Cor. v: 1).

when this house is said to be " not made with hands," it is too grave a statement, along particularly with so many other that we notice, to be applied merely to the waking of the body; and means that total rising, that new creation at the last, which makes a new man so utterly, that the cavil has already been noticed that it destroys our accountability in the reckoning.

Now, notice other words. It is a house " from heaven" (v. ii): nay, it is a house " in the heavens" (v. i). Surely this is strong language for our dust. Again, no mention is made of spirit. Paul is comforting himself for death, and not a word is said about the years when he is in the sepulchre. He strikes right across the flood, and sets his comfort in the resurrection. He vests nothing in being disembodied. His commentators notice that. But he has now two pictures which seem to me well nigh decisive; one that he longs to be " clothed upon." The meaning in the third verse is a little clouded. Let me translate it strictly. " Earnestly desiring to be clothed upon with our house which is from heaven, if so be that we may be found clothed, not naked. For we that are in this tabernacle do groan being burdened; not for that we would be unclothed, but clothed upon, that mortality might be swallowed up of life" (vs. 2–4). Now it may do very well to say that Paul shrunk from being disembodied; but why? If that was our nature; if that was our well understood gift; if to be disembodied was to be for the first time perfect, and to be for a long time happy; and resurrection was after that, thousands of years,—it was impossible that Paul should labor to disgust the pious, and breed a fever for immediate resurrection; and should call that being clothed upon; and should put it in the strong shape of "mortality" being "swallowed up of life" (v. 4); and what is still more incredible, say that "he that hath wrought us for the self-same thing is God" (v. 5), as though they really should escape being disembodied, and as though they really should be clothed upon, and escape the long millenniums of an unclothed but rapturous felicity. Now all this is dangerously incredible.

And we add to it the other sentence. Paul speaks of the "earnest of the Spirit" (v. 5). Why did he need the earnest of the Spirit for a mere carnal rising? It seems that this is the strongest consideration that has been mentioned. If he was to rise as a total penitent, buried sinful and rising perfect, then the earnest of the Spirit is significant as showing him the proof that he had been sealed for that better resurrection. But that he was to be happy for thousands of years, and that the whole thing talked of was the mere resurrection of flesh, makes the whole comfort seem ridiculous. He was not to be clothed upon; he was not wrought for the self-same thing; he was not to escape being unclothed; and he was not to realize the earnest of the Spirit in any mere waking of the body, till ages after his admission into paradise.

And now the critical sentence! (v. 8).

Let me premise:—Paul seems to bend all feeling toward the tenth verse, which like many another

## The Two Adverse Passages.

closing announcement in the Bible (see Matt. xviii: 14, 35; xx: 16; xiv: 11), seems to be the pith of all that has been declared. He says, "We must all appear before the judgment seat of Christ." This seems to live in his memory as the great background of every picture. When therefore he says, "We walk by faith, not by sight" (v. 7), we understand him as we do in the fourth chapter (v. 18), "While we look not at the things which are seen, but at the things which are not seen." Paul was doing this very thing when he uttered the sixth verse, "Therefore we are always confident;" that is, Living, we keep up our confidence more like other men, but dying, we have these pictures before us,— "While we are at home in the body, we are absent from the Lord" (v. 6). And it is just here he puts in that sentence, "For we walk by faith, not by sight" (v. 7). And then comes the great text, "We are confident I say and willing rather to be absent from the body, and to be present with the Lord" (v. 8). Now, in the first place, if this means, when absent from the body like life out of a bean stalk he was immediately present with the Almighty, is it not strange he should be so shy of saying so all through the rest of the context? This was the very state he seemed to fly from,—to call it unclothed—to speak of it as naked—to beg concerning it that it may be clothed upon, and to long to skip over it, that in the language of the context "mortality might be swallowed up of life."

But, second, behold now the language. Suppose Paul had really believed as we do. Suppose he had thought about this intervening period, and too carefully to be willing to throw haze over it in the structure of his speech. Suppose he was bent upon the rising at the last, but not so as to forget the sleeping in the sepulchre,—how would he manage? Why, exceedingly well by using a very preposition that is employed in his text: he says not, " absent from the body and present WITH the Lord" (the very expression that makes the passage in Philippians more formidable, for there he does say, " depart and be *with* Christ"), but he says " *towards* the Lord," or on the way to Him, or *as pertaining to* Him (" things *pertaining to* God," as the word is translated, Heb. v: 1): and under all the circumstances of the passage it gives the most undoubted right to insist upon the difference, as lying smooth with all the other peculiarities that have been before us. " We are confident I say and willing, rather to be away from home as to the body, and at home *in the direction* of the Lord." For, mark you, he has just said, " We walk by faith, not by sight" (v. 7). And then to show how this prognostic of his is really the home in which he is living in the direction of his Master, he puts it beyond doubt: " For, we must all be manifested"—that is the expression. It is not the mere word "appear" (E. V.). It is, " We must all be manifested." And how can that be if we have been known as saints for thousands and thousands of years? " We must all be manifested," that is at our rising again ; " that every one may receive by the body"—why not by the soul, and long ago at our death?—" that every one may receive by the body things according to what he hath done, whether it be good or bad" (v. 10).

" Knowing *therefore* the terror of the Lord" (v. 11). Disembodied states he builds no warning upon at all.

Now we appeal to all the fair-minded, whether the passage, thus winnowed, does not fall from its high estate ; and whether it must not cease to be one of the two great pillars of our immortality.

But let us look at the other passage (Phil. i).

Paul is speaking of the same subject, viz., his death: only he is speaking of it with even more discrimination. He is speaking of it in view of the great doctrine that God loves the church; and he is pressing it into a corollary that is seldom thought of, and is never noticed in the exposition of his epistle. It is the corollary that, as God withholds nothing from the church, he would not withhold Paul from the church, if his living or dying could be useful to its kingdom.

This then was the crisis with Paul. If it was best, he would live: if it was best, he would die. And this best meant, best for the church. " To me to live is Christ, and to die gain" (v. 21). That is, If I live, it will be that Christ needed me, and worked in me, and actually *was* I, for a living gracious up-building of some of his people. And if I die, it will be because it was gain for somebody that I die. This was his doctrine ; and he pursues it strikingly from the beginning. " That in nothing I shall be ashamed" (v. 21). He alludes to so unpromising a thing even as his bonds (v. 13); and says that all his things were falling out "rather unto the furtherance of the gospel" (v. 12). He showed *how* his bonds had done good ; that they were manifest as for Christ in all the palace. He said, some had waxed bold by them (v. 14). And then he speaks of actual sin in preachers ; as for example preaching Christ of contention ; and boldly cries that even that will be overruled ; uttering that eloquent passage, " Nevertheless, Christ is preached ; and I therein do rejoice, yea and will rejoice" (v. 18). " For," says he, " this shall happen to me for salvation," that is for the general salvation ; and how? For any merit in wicked men? No; but "through your prayer, and the supply of the Spirit of Jesus Christ" (v. 19). And then he announces his " earnest expectation and hope that in nothing shall [he] be ashamed ; but that with all boldness, as always, so now also, Christ shall be magnified in [his] body whether it be by life or by death" (v. 20).

And now it is on this plot that we are to begin the consideration of the passage.

We will translate literally.

We have already considered the next verse. " For to me to live is Christ, and to die gain" (v. 21). " But if to live in the flesh that is to me to be fruit of labor and what I shall choose, I do not declare it" (for the best reason in the world, because he does not know it), his meaning being that if living was the most useful, it would be what he would choose to do, and what he actually would do, for he chose to do that which would be most useful, and what he chose to do therefore would be accomplished, for that would be accomplished which would be most useful, only he could not tell whether it would be life or death. " For I am held back" (he goes on) " from either" (that is, on account of the above entire uncertainty), " having the desire, as to the departing, to be also with Christ, which is the far better thing" (that is, with all the certainty that, if that turns out to be the lot, it will be the useful lot, on the principle already announced, and then " *also*" the happy lot, making it " far better"); " nevertheless to abide in the flesh, in case that be the more necessary for you. And once made sure of that" (viz., that to abide is more necessary for you), " I know that I shall abide, and continue with you all for your furtherance and joy of faith " (22-25). This last has been missed by everybody. The reading has been " Having this confidence." Paul would then say, " Having this confidence, I know that I shall abide." In the next sentence he would make it stronger. He would imply that he will come to them again. Whereas the whole thing is conditioned on his knowing that it would be for their good. The fact is he never did come to them again,—so most people believe; * and it is only on the rendering that we propose (and see warrant for it, in English as well as in Greek, in the use of the participle) that the passage can be redeemed from the most pitiable confounding on the part of

---

\* Conybeare and Howson teach a different idea ; but the evidences are, to say the very least, obscure ; and they do not in the least relieve the difficulty of their making Paul to say that he had " confidence " in a thing which he had said a moment before that he knew nothing about.

the apostle of his own confession of entire ignorance (v. 22).

Regarding this, therefore, as the whole drift of Paul, and considering him as alive with the thought that what was best for them that was the thing that was to override his murderers, can we give emphasis to the side thought, having the "desire, as to departing, to be also with Christ," to make it determinate of the fact that when we depart we shall be *immediately* with Christ, and that in the sense of his conscious kingdom?

I think no fair mind can say that we can.

And luckily, we can appeal to precedents. Take the passage in Corinthians (2 Cor. v: 1). Our opponents read, "If this earthly house is dissolved, we *have*"—the verb is in the present. Of course the inference must be that the heavenly house follows *immediately*. Does any one reason in that way? We are said in Scripture to sleep in Jesus (1 Thess. iv: 14). And we are said in the Confession to have our "bodies still united to Christ" (Sh. Cat. Qu. 37). Is there association with Christ in our very dust when it has been scattered, and shall Paul be impeached of carelessness when in the rush of a quite different thought he speaks of being happy in death, when it has been determined on high that that will be most useful to the cause, and when there is but an unconscious interval between death and the resurrection?

Samuel says, "Why hast thou disquieted me to bring me up?"\* (1 Sam. xxviii: 15). We take it

---

\* Will the reader please make a mark here? We will avoid the trouble of quoting again. Samuel does not say, Why hast thou dis-

that, but for this disquieting, the dead saint would have been dreamless in decay, and like the flash of the cable line, he was fleeting across the centuries, having departed to be with Christ with none but an unconscious interval.

### CHAPTER V.

#### THE SPIRITS IN PRISON.

WHATEVER may have been the meaning of Peter in the last part of the third chapter of his earlier Epistle, the vast majority of commentators believe that it alludes to an actual visit of Christ, and therefore that it sets at rest the question of our spirits.

Let me beg however one favor.

We are so unfortunate as to have our particular reading. It differs seriously from every other. We can hardly discuss this passage without giving it in full. And yet it makes one feel singularly foolish, when shoals of expositions have been given, to attempt to fight our battle with one which no mortal has ever honored by so much as conceiving in the study of the passage.

The favor is this.

It would be awkward to confront the chapter without letting our thought run in the lines of our entire belief. But there are great features of our

quieted me to bring me down? but, Why hast thou disquieted me to bring me up? These are the smaller stripes, which nevertheless all fit perfectly in the Indian casket.

belief, which have the main polemic value, which could be imprinted on other theories.

For example the "prison." We do not believe it is the grave at all, but only our impenitence. And "spirits!" We do not believe they are the dead at all, but all the impenitent. These points could be admitted into other readings. We will, therefore, go boldy into all our theory, believing that while the ninety and nine may reject our comments as a whole, they may be struck with them in part; or at least that we may show that we are helpless to meet this passage at all, seeing that we have grown committed to a sense which none other of the students in the case could think of or venture to defend.

Now for a beginning, we utterly deny the reading in the eighteenth verse (1 Pet. 3),—"being put to death in the flesh, but quickened in the Spirit." That would allude to the crucifixion, and refer only to that date, and fix the epoch of Christ's setting out, or departing, to the day of his resurrection: and though we might go on with what remains, even if we gave this its usual significance, yet we prefer to make it all complete. This sentence does not refer to the crucifixion or to the rising again, but a word is employed which has been singularly lost sight of in its beautiful determinations as to the passage.

That word means "made a dead man."

Paul says, "For thy sakes are we killed all the day long" (Rom. viii: 36), meaning, "as good as dead men." Christ also uses this word, "The brother shall deliver up the brother to death, and

## The Spirits in Prison.

the father the child: and the children shall rise up against their parents, and *cause them to be put to death*" (Matt. x: 21), meaning, give them over to death. So the Pharisees; " They sought false witness against Jesus to put him to death." It never means killing literally. And though it occurs eleven times in the Bible (Matt. x: 21; xxvi: 59, xxvii: 1; Mar. xiii; 12: xiv: 55, Lu. xxi: 16; Ro. vii: 4; viii: 13; viii: 36; 2 Cor. vi: 9, 1 Pet. 3: 18), it always means delivered over to death, and never in any actual sense killed at the time.

Now we believe that this whole passage means that Jesus Christ was as good as dead as to the flesh; that is, would have succumbed to temptation like any other man (see Heb. v: 7); but that he was made the living Saviour that he was, by the Spirit; and that, in the Spirit, long before he was made flesh at all, he set out and preached to the spirits in prison; that is, as the Great Prophet God, preached to poor sinners.

And how general this was, appears by the next expression, " Who *at any time* were disobedient." (That is the meaning of the particle in numerous passages, 1 Cor. ix: 7; Eph. v: 29.) And yet though he has preached in this way in the Spirit even before and after his incarnation, yet the chance for each mortal man was but " once." Notice how he brings in the case of Noah. " When once the long-suffering of God waited." This means to characterize all the impenitent that ever lived. They are waited for but once. In the rush of speaking Peter brings in a favorite case. Syntactically he trespasses a little, for it is the way with these apostles (Rom. i : 7 ; Eph. iii : 1) ; but trespasses with method. He does not say, " when once the long suffering of God waited in the days of Noah" (E. V.), but "in days of Noah," flinging, in his excitement, before their minds a certain case before the flood : " They did eat ; they drank ; they married wives, they were given in marriage " (Matt. xxiv : 38) ; and thus, like Christ himself, making the instance of Noah a fine warning to our whole impenitence.

Let us recapitulate the Apostle therefore. Even Christ is quickened in the Spirit. In the Spirit, before and since his incarnation, he has preached to imprisoned sinners. They are the men who at any time have been disobedient. And God has waited for them " once," viz., in their single life-time, in days of Noah. And having thrown that picture before the eye, he notes the likeness. They were like Noah as to an ark. They were like Noah as to the number saved. There was a resemblance really in the more shadowy emblem of the " water." Let us go over it on these points, hiding a little the eruptive rhetoric of the Apostle. " Long suffering,"—great and patient, and yet critical, viz., " in days of Noah" : and yet in Noachic days in other respects, that an ark was a preparing—sadly alike equally in another respect, that so few were saved ; in Noah's case, only " eight ; " and sadly alike too in this, that the very waters that wrecked the earth saved the ark, and that the very death that destroys the people saves us, when inflicted upon Christ, and raises us again through his blessed quickening.

It may be imagined, if it seem necessary, that this interpretation of ours is aside from the possibilities of the passage ; but here is precisely where we will press the difficulties of every other. It will be seen that we make the words a mere continuance of the didactic gospel of the apostle. We deny every thing ghostly. The spirits are merely the impenitent. The preaching is merely the usual work of the Divine Prophet, for sinners. The waiting is merely the gospel respite. And Noah with his days of crisis, the ark and the eight souls and salvation by water, all mere picturings, examples for the race, because actual instances of a divine redemption.

If any one says that he cannot admit this sense, then choose one that is preferable. A capital way to strip this passage of mistake is to demand its unravelment. Tell what your meaning is. If you say, It is Christ preaching in Noah, I say, No, for by your theory it was at the time of his resurrection. If you say, It was Christ preaching after he was risen, I say, No, for it was at the time of Noah. If you say, It was Christ preaching to the dead ; I say Why then speak of Noah? And if you say, as many do, It was Christ preaching to dead antediluvians in Hades, I ask, Why? And I beg you to give a consistent account of what message he could bring ; and whether you dare distinctly to assume that there is yet mercy for the perished after they have rejected it, and when for two thousand years they have cursed in the bitterness of perdition.

This is the treatment that seems to be fair. We give a meaning, and it is consistent with the common gospel. We expound it, and bring it into strict connection with the text. If it be denied, we have a right to demand another. If that be given, we have a right to insist upon it, and make it the final appeal. Now of all the expositions of this passage we beg to be informed of one that can so stand its own ground under the difficulties that it presents, as to be an unblushing arbiter in a question like immortality.

## CHAPTER VI.

### What Might We Expect of Scripture?

ACCUSED, as we naturally must be found to be, of trying to fit Scripture to a preconceived infidelity, of course it will be infinitely just to expect of the old faith that it shall purge itself of that suspicion too; not bringing in a theory to be tried, but finding its theory obtruded upon its belief by the plain announcements of the Holy Word.

More especially is this to be the case because the doctrine that they teach has at least three very bold annunciations.

In the first place, it announces two separate essences so independent in the nature of man that if one lies dead upon the earth, the other lives on perpetually. It must be like a bat in a cavern, astonishing every body by the skill with which it grazes what it meets, if the Bible can utter so many booksfull of human histories, and yet not speak in the most pronounced way of the soul and of the body if the theory of what they are is not to be brought to

## What to Expect of Scripture. 99

it to be tried, but actually to be carved out of it by its distinct expressions.

In the second place, if the soul is to be perfect at death, that is to say if the Christian at that date is immediately to pass into glory; and if therefore the hour of death is the most important time of life in the one respect of giving us our first enjoyment of absolute blessedness, it is impossible that such a bold faith should be gotten from a certain writing, and the writing give it so languidly forth that it shall seem brought to it from without, rather than like a clear bold fact taught by it as its own revelation. Let us think of this carefully. Here is a wonderful faith, opposing all the analogies of our animal existence. It is to cover the whole ground of centuries. It is to apply perhaps to-morrow, bringing us into the presence of our Maker, and describing our first joy, which is to last with us through unnumbered ages. And here is the book out of which this faith is to be gathered. I say, It must abound in it. If we are to get it from no other source whatever, then the exegetes who merely show that it is not *contradicted*, show nothing. It pretends to come from no other source. If the Bible does not *reek* with immortality, the design has failed. It is not a doctrine like infant baptism. It must be the great imagination of our lives; and that the Bible, speaking of our interests, should be like the bat flying through the cavern, avoiding these interests, and grazing when we should think it impossible these main pillars of the place, would really defy belief, especially as it is not a doctrine that we are to get from abroad, but to get solely and just as it is from divine revelation.

In the third place, if resurrection is taught, the whole temper of the teaching must be different, if it be a merely bodily resurrection, from that which must be expected if the whole man is raised from the darkness of death. We insist upon this. If life has never gone out, resurrection is a mere secondary thing, bringing back to us at best the matter of our frames. If we have been living centuries in heaven, we shall show, when we come to array the passages, that they speak far too little of death, and far too much of our rising; that this comparative test is decisive : we might explain away many other things, but that the Bible should harp so little upon our glory, and so much upon our return to flesh ; speak so often of the vivification of our dust, and so scarcely or not at all of what befalls whole millenniums before, is shockingly impossible ; and the expressions that we shall heap up of "redemption" (Eph. iv: 30), and "glory" (Col. iii: 4), and "*parousia*" (2 Pet. iii: 4), and surprise (Matt. xxv: 37), and remorse (Lu. xiii: 28), and disappointment (Matt. vii : 22), which we shall pile together as of the last day ; and the thinnesses and nothings that we shall exhibit upon our real coming to glory, as our adversaries would teach,— present in our view an overwhelming form of argument; offer the stripes in the Indian casket all awry ; and obtrude the one theory of the two under such singular straits, as to make the one ground of its strength the prejudices and preconceptions of the heathen.

And now, as to the other theory. If the Bible teach it, we should expect such things as these:—

We should expect many a passage in the Bible to speak as though man were nothing but body. If the one thing and the other thing were constitutionally inseparable, we should expect the Bible also to speak as though man were nothing but soul. If the soul and the body were indissolubly mixed, we should expect many a passage to speak of them interchangeably, with but little apparent care to separate them in the less vital passages.

On the other hand we should expect them to be separated. Just as the life is separated from the bean-stalk, though the life *is* the bean-stalk numerically or *qua essentia;* just as the soul is separated from the carrion (Ec. iii: 18–21), though the carrion *was* the soul such and so far as that nothing floated away from the carrion but the power of the Almighty,—so the soul can be separated from the body. And now the immortal soul having been abandoned, there is room to talk of these separatenesses. The life did not survive the bean-stalk: nevertheless it was additional to it in such a sense that the matter for a thousand years in just such proportion would not have produced the bean-stalk; and the life was additional and a new efficiency, and a new dose if you please above that which had been given in the efficiencies of matter.

And so the brutes. We may count three things, —matter, life and soul. Matter may have every particle there, and not have life; and soul may infuse every particle of matter, and yet never be the progeny of material molecules. It may be an additional and divine efficiency.

So when we climb to man, there are four things to think of. Let us look at this very narrowly. If there are four, why say two? In other words if the *usus loquendi* of man justifies his speaking of his body and of his life, and then separately of his soul, and then separately of his spirit, for these last are really spoken of as pitted against each other in certain passages (1 Cor. xv : 44-46), why may not soul and body be treated similarly? Why should the Bible speak of soul and spirit, and yet they be regarded as interterminally mixed, and yet not speak of soul and body without the suggestion of an independent essence?

To return, therefore, to the matter of theory. If there be a theory of a certain kind, what may be expected of the Bible if it embrace it? If there be a theory for example like this, that man has a body, but that the particles of that body would never give themselves life by being laid together ; that man has life, and therefore that life is additional to the mere endowment of matter : moreover that man has thought, and as thought is not life as life belongs to a bean, therefore man has soul also, a still higher gift, but still intermixed (for that the theory must be), as it is in the instances of brutes, with the life and with the efficiencies of matter : and lastly, that man has spirit, —the Bible must comply with all these seemings : and if spirit be the abode of conscience ; that is, if it be reason as a whole and mind as a whole, but reason where it has broken down, and mind where it has been specially injured under our fall from God,—the

Bible will be found especially obsequious to all these changes of thought. It will speak of man sometimes as all body. It will speak of man sometimes as all soul. It will speak of life and soul by terms that are interchangeable together. It will speak of man as dust. It will speak of him just as confidently as spirit. It will speak of Abraham as a dead body. It will speak of a carcase in the wilderness as a dead soul. It will be *careful* to mix expressions, so as to forbid superstitiousness. Nevertheless it will feel free to distinguish, and that, in bold instances, *ad unguem*. "Fear not them that kill the body, and are not able to kill the soul." And yet it will do the same thing as to the spirit. Trusting that no one will imagine that the spirit is a separate essence, it boldly pits it against the soul. It speaks of a "soul-body" and a "spirit-body" (1 Cor. xv: 44), when all that it means is, that the body is at last to have a spirit, that is, a spirit thoroughly infused by the grace of conscientious living.

Now our task in the chapters that remain is in this way laid open. We are intending to show that the soul is not immortal: that it is not immortal, or the Bible would speak more of its independent being; that it is not glorious at death, or the Scriptures would erect there its flaming bonfires; that it is not acquaint with bliss at the resurrection, or it would not be surprised so; and that that cannot be the date of the mere retaking of the body, or it would not be such a red-lettered date, so redolent of bliss— standing in such sharp comparisons with the slumbers of the sepulchre.

Then on the other hand, that the soul is not immortal because all the stripes of the bark casket match in a different fashion. The body is talked of as though it personated the soul, and the soul is talked of as though it decayed with the body. The life is talked of as though inseparable from both, and the spirit as though the complement of either. The soul is talked of as independent of the spirit, just as much as the body is talked of as independent of the soul: the spirit being all that a man would be if he were holy (Jo. iv : 23); the flesh coming to mean mind, heart, even our refined and more elevated nature when dead in spirit (Rom. vii : 18); and the whole being no more capable of being used when they have grown into their rhetoric shapes for a dyad or a triad of man, than " body " and " soul," to be a division of the Almighty (Dan. x: 6; Lev. xxvi: 11).

We set out, therefore.

Allow us one caution.

Matter is an efficiency; so say some scientists. Soul is an additional efficiency: so say we. Now if matter continues, though it be but an efficiency of power, why may not soul continue? And as matter continues slumbering in the grave, why may not soul be somewhere; and why may not it have a dreamless sleep? and why may we not get rid of the horror of thinking of it in utter annihilation?

One might.

Any man impressed that way had better.

We ourselves have spoken of this shadow of efficiency. We have suggested efficiency, and something more. What that more is who can tell? We are really arguing from the Bible. And while the Bible does not tell us what that efficiency is that is additional to the bean-matter, or what that efficiency is that is additional as the brute-soul, it does tell us that the two are inseparably together. And while the matter and the mind are both efficiencies, they differ in this. The matter is *not* "slumbering in the grave." It is as *alert* as it ever was, saving that it lacks life. It is needed in the circle of efficiencies. But the soul is not needed. The Bible gives us plenty of reason to understand why matter should be kept up. But the soul need not be. It may die in its efficiency, and rise again at the judgment of the just.

## CHAPTER VII.

### THE WHOLE MAN, BODY.

THERE is nothing left now but to arrange separate classes of Scripture as they bear upon the question before us. Our procedure will be understood. We do not quote any passage with a view of laying much weight upon it. We do not approach any chapter with a view to make the Scriptures that it employs bear all the weight, or indeed do more than their part in the general array. Our view is to unite all the chapters. If the whole man has body, and the whole man dies, and the whole man is buried, and the whole man rises; if the whole man awakes to judgment, and the whole man enters then for the first time among the blessed,—our proposition is proved. That is, no one of these points might appear conclusive; yet if they all combine, it betokens a habit of thought on the part of the Bible which puts beyond doubt the question of our being mortal.

Now in this chapter we are to quote where the whole man is spoken of as body.

In the first place he is said to be formed out of the ground. In the second chapter of Genesis the brutes are said to be "formed out of the ground, and then, a moment afterward, they are called "living souls." The English Version helps us a little by seeming shy of this latter expression. Let me quote the whole passage. " And out of the ground Jehovah God formed every beast of the field, and every fowl of the air, and brought them to Adam to see what he would call them: and whatsoever Adam called every living soul, that was the name thereof" (Gen. ii: 19). And yet in the same chapter this is the account of man,—" Jehovah God formed man dust out of the ground,* and breathed in his nostrils breath of life, and man became a living soul." Nor are these uncommon similarities. They occur often. "And God said, Let the earth bring forth the living soul after his kind, cattle and creeping thing and beast of the earth after his kind" (Gen. i: 24); and then in the third chapter,—" In the sweat of thy face shalt thou eat bread, till thou return unto the ground; for out of it wast thou taken" (v. 19). Solomon is infinitely bolder ;—" That which befalleth the sons of men befalleth beasts ; even one thing be-

* King James' men again modify the Hebrew, and say "*of the dust of the ground.*" The difference may be very slight, but the inclination, on that very account, very obvious.

falleth them: as the one dieth so dieth the other; yea, they have all one spirit; so that a man hath no preëminence above a beast: for all is vanity. All go unto one place; all are of the dust, and all turn to dust again" (Ec. iii: 19, 20).

But not only is man said to be "out of the ground," but he is called directly "dust." "God made man dust of the ground" (Gen. ii: 7). This is asserted with absolute boldness: "Dust thou art, and unto dust shalt thou return" (Gen. iii: 19). It is turned about with varied expression; — "He knoweth our frame; he remembereth that we are dust" (Ps. ciii: 14). "All go unto one place; all are of the dust, and all turn to dust again" (Ec. iii: 20). "All flesh shall perish together, and man shall turn again unto dust" (Job. xxxiv: 15). "His breath goeth forth; he returneth to his earth" (Ps. cxlvi: 4): and once more, "Then shall the dust return to the earth as it was, and the breath\* shall return unto God who gave it" (Ec. xii: 7).

Now, sentences that speak of us as "flesh" are still more striking. In the arguments of the apostles, flesh is made to answer to the whole unregenerate part of man. It is actually embodied as everything but the "spirit." And as the "spirit" is the conscientious part of our nature, the "flesh" must be the whole of the rest; and therefore must be the whole man in such a sense as to include thought and accountable activity. So the body is talked about. "The body is dead because of sin" (Ro. viii: 10). "I keep under my body, and bring it into subjection"

\* We shall recur to this last passage (see Chap. XII).

(1 Cor. ix : 27). " That ye present your bodies a living sacrifice" (Rom. xii : 1). Again, " Thy whole body shall be full of light" (Matt. vi : 22). Again, " The tongue defileth the whole body" (Jas. iii : 6). Again, " It is sown a soul-body ; it is raised a spirit-body" (1 Cor. xv : 44). " Having our bodies washed with pure water " (Heb. x : 22). Or once more, as some translate,—" Who shall deliver me from this dead body?" (Rom. vii : 24).

Now, when we return to the earlier part of the Word, and see " flesh" spoken of as though it were the whole of man ; as when we hear Job say, " All flesh shall perish" (Job, xxxiv : 15), or the Psalmist, —" He remembered that they were but flesh" (Ps. lxxviii : 39), or Moses,—" They shall be one flesh" (Gen. ii : 24), or the sixth chapter, throwing all animals together,—" destroy all flesh" (v. 17),—it does not settle indeed that such words shall never be used figuratively ; but it does throw the *onus* of the kind and degree of their figurative use upon those who gratuitously assume that the body, even when animate, is a brutal essence in such a sense that it may have living in it or living out of it, as the case may be, an immortal and separably existent thinking spirit.

We might add a paragraph about the " blood." The " blood" is said to be the " soul" (Lev. xvii : 14). We might speak of such expressions as, " This is now bone of my bones, and flesh of my flesh " (Gen. ii : 23). We might speak of woman as derived from man, and of children derived through sixty centuries from a single pair. But these things will be adverted to under other heads. It is enough for us to observe that the stripes, fitted thus far, fit better with our view than the other; that even when there are figures, the figures fit best in our arrangement of the box ; and, most graphic of all, that when we search through the *margins* of King James, we find whole sentences put off there, proving by their position in the margin that they are more faithful to the text : and giving us this honest and artlessly rendered testimony,—that they agree with our view of the soul, and not with its being independent in essence, and continuous in immortality.

## CHAPTER VIII.

### THE WHOLE MAN DEAD.

SUPPOSE the whole man does die at death, how would we prove it?

1. One proof would be if he is represented as becoming unconscious ; and this we have of the very strongest kind. " His spirit goeth forth ; he returneth to his earth : in that very day his thoughts perish " (Ps. cxlvi : 4). Lest any one should say, This means merely his counsels, we can fairly pile up kindred expressions. " In death there is no remembrance of thee. In the grave who shall give thee thanks ?" (Ps. vi : 5). " For the dead cannot praise thee ; they that go down into the pit cannot hope for thy truth " (Is. xxxviii : 18). " For the living know that they shall die ; but the dead know not anything " (Ec. ix : 5). " For there is no work, nor device, nor knowl-

edge, nor wisdom, in the grave, whither thou goest" (Ec. ix : 10).

2. Another form of proof is the absence of expressions about the death of the body. If this were the actual shape of the occurrence, it would cast language that way. And yet it would require the most patient searching, to find three passages in the word of God that speak distinctly of the death of the body.

3. On the contrary there are hosts of passages that speak of the *man's* death. " It came to pass that the beggar died" (Lu. xvi : 22). Is it likely that we would always hear of Abraham's dying (Gen. xxv : 8), and Ishmael's dying (Gen. xxv : 17), and how Rachel died (Gen. xxxv : 19), and how Christ died (Rom. xiv : 9), never venturing even in theologic passages to discriminate : and how they killed the Prince of Life (Acts iii : 15) : is it likely that there should leap to Jacob's lips the expression, " It is my son's coat ; an evil beast hath devoured him : Joseph is without doubt rent in pieces" (Gen. xxxvii : 33),—if there were saturated into men's minds the confidence that it was only the body that had died, and that the spirit had sailed joyously away to begin its superior existence ?

It may be said, *We* talk that way : we speak of the man dying. For good rhetorical reasons we think of him as living, and yet speak of him as dead. And the attempt might be made to obviate entirely the peculiar appearances of revelation. And yet it must be remembered that to a large degree we derive an imprint *from* revelation. When we speak of Joseph dying, and Joseph being buried, and Joseph being embalmed, and Joseph rising again from the grave, we follow the Scripture language even against our preconceived ideas; and yet we have fabricated sufficiently a language of our own, to show our difference from Scripture. We speak of the dead corpse, and of our mortal part, and of the relics of the dead, and of our mortal remains; and we speak of the rising of the body; *when it is not possible to match those words in Scripture.* Eschatology delivers itself in our day differently from the Holy Ghost. And I do not mean, in merely variant speech, but in difference of creed. The Bible keeps the soul in constant union with the body. Theology, in just such unconscious ways, implies their separation.

4. How astounding this becomes when passages, such as we are asking for, are forged by a false translation. Leviticus furnishes one, " Nor shall ye go in to any dead body "(xxi: 11). Numbers furnishes six, " He shall come at no dead body " (vi: 6). " There were certain men who were defiled by the dead body of a man " (ix: 6; see also v. 10). " He that toucheth the dead body of any man " (xix: 11; see also v. 16). We could increase the list. Now these might be triumphantly obtruded, and the great fact fancied that the Bible *does* speak as though the body were separately dead. And yet it is the mere translation-Bible. How surprised many an English reader will become when he understands that the simple Hebrew is, " A DEAD SOUL." Let me insist upon this. We have declared that the Bible no where contains any serious instance at all where the

body can be conceived of as separately dead. And here, where a sharp eye might suppose that there is one, it turns out singularly opposite. The body is not talked of, after all, as dead; but the soul is so talked of. And we shall see, when we come to devote a special chapter to the soul, that there is a world of similar speech; that that which dies at death, is specially the soul; that that which comes up at the resurrection, is specially the sleeping soul; that that whose sleep is death, is the soul even more than the body; and that that which is precipitated into hell, is the soul in its first surprises; along with the body in which it has just arisen from the darkness of the sepulchre.

We must not anticipate, however.

Our points are these:—

First, that death is spoken of as an unconsciousness: (if there are any difficulties in this, we shall speak of them in the next chapter:) second, that the body is not spoken of as separately dead: third, that the *man* dies according to the testimony of Scripture; and fourth, that if there be any difference it is on the side of the soul; we do most distinctly hear of "a dead soul:" " Nor shall ye go in to a dead soul" (Lev. xxi: 11). "He shall come at no dead soul" (Num. vi . 6). " There were certain men who were defiled by the dead soul of a man:" other passages, that speak of "dead bodies" (2 Chr. xx: 21; Ps. cx: 6; Jer. xxxi: 40; Am. viii; 3), using indeed not the same expression, but not at all the words dead body; using only a single vocable, as for example, " something faded" (Ps. lxxix: 2), or as for example, "*dead one*" * (2 Ki. viii. 5), or in another instance," *exhausted ones*" * (2 Chr. xx ; 24), expressions common to the whole man ; or, in the New Testament (Rev. xi : 8), a noun meaning wrecks or things fallen, having no distinct application, of course, to anything but the perished or exhausted sufferer.

Much of the argument suited to this chapter will, however, appear in the next.

## CHAPTER IX.

### THE WHOLE MAN BURIED.

IF we chose to take advantage of the dissensions of theology, on the principle *Divide et impera*, we might insist that whoever opposes us should state his theory, and then we might unsettle that, and so evict, in turn, each possible hypothesis.

For example, Turrettin, assuming what it would puzzle him immensely to conceive, that the soul, disembodied, can still have place, makes that place heaven, and makes the soul occupy the same place before and after the resurrection (Tur : Vol. 2 ; Quaest, 9, p. 281). Now the beggar's soul (Lu. xvi : 22) either did or did not rest in *hades* (see v. 23). If it did, Turrettin is mistaken. If it did not, then the whole scenic accuracy of the parable must be given up as a proof of immortality.

We might multiply the instances.

We are so clear, however, that we will not ask this advantage of segregation. The point shall be,

* Simple adjectives without nouns.

Is the soul immortal or not? And if the affirmative shift a little in their theorizing plans, so be it. It is a symptom of mistake. But we will not tax each separate conceit with more than its generic difficulties.

Now the difficulties common to every theory of immortality are, first, that our burial is spoken of as of the whole man; second, of the whole man not in such a sense as that a part can continue to live, but, that the whole sleeps; third, that that sleep is dreamless and entire; and fourth, that all the Scripture that might seem to imply that we are awake, is insignificant in extent, and easily manageable, on the other theory.

1. In the first place, the whole man is spoken of as buried. Now do not let us misunderstand this. I do not say that one such passage, or that ten such passages, would prove anything as against opposite texts: but I wish to crush by weight of column. I wish to show that all the idiom, like the current of the Nore, flows in but a single route. Like the pile on velvet, the Scripture can be smoothed down one way, and resists, the other. Take some instances. "Miriam died and was buried" (Num. xx: 1). "Aaron died, and was buried" (Deut. x: 6). Christ was buried (1 Cor. xv: 4). Or, taking the active verb, "They buried Abraham" (Gen. xlix: 31). They "buried Saul" (2 Sam. ii: 5). "I buried Leah" (Gen. xlix: 31). "I saw the wicked buried" (Ec. viii: 10). "David is both dead and buried" (Acts ii: 29). Suspecting some idiosyncrasies in this, try other expressions: try the whole weight of necrological detail. They killed him (2 Ki. xv: 25). They "embalmed him" (Gen. l:

## The Whole Man Buried. 115

2). "They put him in a coffin" (Gen. 1 : 26). They tore him in pieces (Gen. xxxvii: 33). They buried him (2 Chr. xxi: 20). Or try grammatic equivalents. See if some more distant idioms cannot hint at the body. "I will go down into the grave" (Gen. xxxvii : 35). Or read a little farther, "I will go down .. unto my son." So are many expressions. He was gathered to his fathers (Judges ii: 10). " He was gathered to his people" (Gen. xxv: 8). There is no hint that they were not all dead and buried. " He that goeth down to the grave shall not go up" (Job vii: 9). "If I wait, the grave is my house" (Job, xvii: 13). "They shall go down to the bars of the pit, when our rest together is in the dust" (Ib. xvii : 16). "Yet shall he be brought to the grave, and shall remain in the tomb" (Ib. xxi : 32). " They shall lie down alike in the dust, and the worms shall cover them" (Ib. v : 26).

2. Now, to preclude all idea of immortality, the Bible speaks of these people under the image of sleep. "Till the heavens be no more," Job says, " they shall not awake, nor be raised out of their sleep" (Job. xiv: 12). "Lighten my eyes," cries out the Psalmist, " lest I sleep the sleep of death" (Ps. xiii : 3). " The stout hearted are spoiled," he says ; " they have slept their sleep "(Ps. lxxvi : 5). The dead are said to sleep with their fathers (1 Ki. ii : 10; xiv: 20 ; 2 Chr. ix: 31). Stephen " fell asleep." " Many that sleep in the dust," prophecies Daniel, "shall awake, some to everlasting life, and some to shame and everlasting contempt" (Dan. xii : 2). We must not load our page. With the apostles it became a

usance. "Part remain, but some are fallen asleep" (1 Cor. xv: 6). "They which are fallen asleep" (v. 18). "Them that are asleep" (1 Thess. iv: 13). "For since the fathers fell asleep, all things continue as they were" (2 Pet. iii : 4).

3. But says some one, following each sentence as I quote it, and blotting it out,—That is but the sleep of the body. It is like the rising of the sun, or like the falling of the dew. The dew does not really fall, but it looks that way. Man does not really die, but beasts do. And the general look of our unconsciousness would fully account for the rhetoric speech. Grant all that. But then there is a difficulty. Would not the Holy Ghost come to our rescue? Would not the Holy Ghost, when he came to didactic utterances, set these things right? The sponging and the blotting — who more capable than God himself? Having left me sleeping in the dust, would he not paint again, and tell me, like the Shulamite, "I sleep, but my heart waketh" (Cant. v: 2). Now, unfortunately for my belief of immortality, he does no such thing. He follows this thought of "sleep," and prints it, and settles it: and this is our third evidence. I mean to note it rapidly. He tells us we are unconscious. He gives us no trace that we think in the grave. He tells us we do not: and leaves us, for the great purposes of mercy, only warned of a gracious resurrection.

"Why died I not from the womb?" cries the patriarch Job. "Now should I have lain still and been quiet; I should have slept: then had I been at rest." Is not the very idea here, of soul-rest, and thinking-

## The Whole Man Buried. 117

unconsciousness? "As a hidden untimely birth, I had not been; as infants which never saw light." Blessed be forgetfulness!—that is his idea. "There the wicked cease from troubling; and there the weary be at rest. The small and the great are there; and the servant is free from his master. Wherefore is light given to him that is in misery, and life unto the bitter in soul? Which long for death, but it cometh not; and dig for it more than for hid treasure; which rejoice exceedingly, and are glad when they can find the grave?" (Job iii: 11, 13-22). He says in another place, "I should have been as though I had not been"(Job x: 19). He speaks of the place as "a land of darkness as darkness itself, and where the light is as darkness" (v. 22). He speaks of the time as the whole period "till the heavens be no more"(xiv: 12). And he seems to take the ground of entire non-existence: that till the time of the blessed resurrection, even God shall not find us; "Thou shalt seek me in the morning, but I shall not be"(vii: 21). For "man dieth, and wasteth away: yea, man giveth up the ghost, and where is he?"(xiv: 11).

And lest any one say, Job was not inspired, let us appeal to the Psalms. "In death there is no remembrance of thee. In the grave who shall give thee thanks?" (Ps. vi: 3). They put it in still more methodic light;—" What profit is there in my blood, when I go down to the pit? Shall the dust praise thee? Shall it declare thy truth?" (Ps. xxx: 9). " Wilt thou show wonders to the dead? Shall the dead arise and praise thee? Shall thy loving kindness be declared in the grave? or thy faithfulness in destruction? Shall thy wonders be known in the dark? and thy righteousness in the land of forgetfulness?" (Ps. lxxxviii : 10–12). And then the refrain long afterward ; " The dead praise not the Lord, neither any that go down into silence" (Ps. cxv : 17).

Solomon is even still stronger;—"The dead know not anything" (Ec. ix: 5). "There is no knowledge in the grave" (Ec. ix : 10).

4. And now, in the fourth place, we are to consider those passages that seem to contradict all this; and first the parable of Dives.

We are teaching that man is unconscious in the grave. This parable is speaking as though death were alive with history. Let us listen, " The rich man also died, and was buried ; and in hell he lifted up his eyes, being in torment, and saw Abraham afar off, and Lazarus in his bosom" (Lu. xvi: 22, 23). This cannot be after the judgment, for he distinctly says, "I pray thee, therefore, father, that thou wouldest send him to my father's house ; for I have five brethren; that he may testify unto them, lest they also come into this place of torment" (vs. 27, 28).

Now there can be nothing fairer, as to this parable, than to reply, that if the favorers of immortality will say what this parable means, and choose an interpretation for it, we will meet them on their own ground. Is it a parable at all? Some say, No ; because a man's name is given. Let us choose, therefore, two grand methods of interpretation ; one as fable, and the other as fact ; in other words, one as the Unjust Steward, commended solely at a single point ; the other as the marriage of Cana of Galilee, true throughout, and responsibly told, as a strict detail of an accomplished history.

Our blessed Lord had been insulted. He had been told, " This man receiveth sinners and eateth with them" (Lu. xv : 2). He began a series of parables. The point of the parables was, The True Believer. He begins gently. We have, pictured first, the hundred sheep. He does not denounce the ninety and nine. He hovers only over the lost one, and brings him forth as rescued—the true Christian Believer. So the lost money ; as, in another chapter, the publican (xviii : 13) ; though there he begins to reflect more upon the pampered Pharisee. So the prodigal (xv : 11); but now with still bitterer reflections, making the self-righteous more and more ungodly; so that the elder brother stands out in the baseness of impenitent life. And so at last, Dives. The whole group is painted to convict the Pharisee. And when at last we are told of the purple and fine linen, it is infinitely far from Christ to be speaking of the luxury of rich men. He is speaking of the ascetic Jewish worshipper. The " purple" is a false royalty. The " linen" is a vain righteousness. And the " faring sumptuously" is the condition of the ninety-nine just persons. And Lazarus is the Eleazur of the Old Testament ; not a real man at all, but *Eleazur*, the Lord my help ; just the very picture, in his poverty, and rags, of the true believer—of that illustrious line, the Sheep, the Money, and the Publican, the Prodigal, and the Unjust Steward, all of whom picture in common forms the contrition and the up-waking of the gospel.

Now let our opponents choose. Shall this narrative, like that of the Unjust Steward, be confined to a single point; and shall that point be a trust to the blood of Abraham? Shall all the dressings of the fable be a mere device; and the main lesson be, that when Dives died, Abraham was afar off, and the beggar-man reposing in his bosom? or shall we bring in all the hard accessories? In one way the meaning is complete. The Unjust Steward can be taken in his allegoric point, viz., making friends in his life-time of the gifts and the grace which in his ungodly state are to him "another man's": and so Dives can be treated solely in his disappointed state of disinheritance from Abraham. But let our opponents choose. As to the verity that is actually meant we insist upon a choice being made. Is the whole an accurate fact? Or is it, like the tale of the Bramble (Jud. ix: 14), a free-wrought fable?

If it be an accurate fact, let there be no trifling, of course. If Dives lifted up his eyes, where did he get his eyes? Or if that may be thought to be a figure, let us notice how much need there is of figures everywhere. What are we to think of the "torment"? What are we to think of the "flame"? What are we to think of the "water"? What are we to think of the "tongue"? and of the cooling of the tongue? and of the "gulf fixed"? and of "Lazarus afar off"? and of the "bosom of Abraham"? If these things, on account of all three men being spirits, must be relegated into the realm of figure, where is the limit? and why may not all be? especially as there are parables of Christ that are not even allegorically just, except in one single phase (Matt. xx: 10, Lu. xvi: 8).

Our account, therefore, of the Pharisee is, that he is unconscious and dead; and that this scene in his sepulchre is of high rhetoric fiction. It merely brings out his dire mistake about the blood of Abraham, and about the publicans and harlots that would get into his bosom sooner than he. It is merely a notice of what he would see and know if he were to wake up in the dead grave and understand his history. To speak of the liberties taken, I would mention the very word *hades* as nowhere else spoken of as a place of torment. Gesenius, therefore, argues that it may mean such a place, but has the significant word *semel*, and a reference to this single passage. Moreover, the word itself ought to be looked at. I notice the active form *unseeing*,\* rather than the word *unseen*; and, therefore, boldly teach that the parable of Dives is the waking up of dead ghosts, to put on the cerements of their clay, and stalk the stage in religious fiction.

If any one begs that we bring forward anything else that will match it in the Holy Bible, we hurry on now to other passages. "Hell from beneath is moved for thee to meet thee at thy coming: it stirreth up the dead for thee, even all the chief ones of

---

\* This is worthy of study. If the Greek word *hades* means *unseeing*, and the Hebrew word (*Sheol*) means nothing to the contrary, it would require great ingenuity to show that the testimony of the name is not quite on the side of unconsciousness.

the earth; it hath raised up from their thrones all the kings of the nations. All they shall speak and say unto thee, Art thou also become weak as we? art thou become like unto us? Thy pomp is brought down to the grave, and the noise of thy viols: the worm is spread under thee, and the worms cover thee. How art thou fallen from heaven, O Lucifer, son of the morning!" (Is. xiv: 9-12). In the Revelation, " I saw under the altar the souls of them that were slain for the word of God, and for the testimony that they held" (Rev. vi: 9). See now how difficulties cluster. Understand all this as an allegory, and everything lies smooth. " Under the altar" means under the hope of blessed immortality that the altar has achieved. " White robes" means the same thing —laid away and buried with them to be put on at the last day. *Crying* means the impatient appeal of the blood of dead saints for speedy justice. *Resting* means unconscious death: and the date, precisely our date: for now read the whole. " And white robes were given unto every one of them; and it was said unto them that they should rest yet for a little season, until their fellow servants also, and their brethren that should be slain as they were, should be fulfilled" (v: 11). But now quote all this of their immortality, and what do we behold? Why first, we *behold* dead souls, just as Dives must behold Lazarus, though he was a disembodied spirit: second, they are under the altar; third, they cry; fourth, they speak about their blood, though they are disembodied spirits; fifth, they have white robes; and sixth, they *rest*, as though they were in durance vile, though they are in receipt of their felicity!

Job says, " Dead things are formed from under the water, and the inhabitants thereof" (Job xxvi : 5). We pass it as though it were trivial, but I happened to dig into the sentence, and there comes up another case. " Dead things" are *shades*. " Are formed" means *tremble*. The language reads, " The shades tremble under the waters, and under the inhabitants thereof" (Job xxvi : 5) ; the meaning being, that the whole universe bows homage to its Creator ; and, as in the other cases, bold rhetoric art makes even the dead join the spectacle, and down deep below the very monsters of the sea (Jon. ii : 5, 6) the Oriental *hades* tremble in its dark inhabitants.

Escaping, therefore, from rhetoric, which may linger more in doubt, our opponent may bring forth the celebrated case of the Thief (Lu. xxiii : 43).

But that we will not linger upon, because it is disposed of by the single remark, that the passage is *absolutely* ambiguous.

If I say in English, And Jesus said unto him, Verily I say unto thee to-day thou shalt be with me in paradise, it is a positive *équivoque* as to whether " I say to-day," or " thou shalt be to-day ;" and ten thousand years would not settle it as a point of grammar. But the question may be asked, Will the Greek help us ? or will the logic of the passage afford any solution?

As to the Greek, it has *like* ambiguity with the English, as may be learned from the fact that men like Hesychius (see Wetstein and Grotius *in loc.*), with no point to gain, have made Christ mean, " I say to-day." It may be set down as prejudice on our part, but we think the Greek has *less* ambiguity than the English. For example, Christ says, " Verily I say unto thee, This day. . thou shalt deny me thrice." Here, though the expression " this night" following immediately after, makes mistake more impossible, the word "that," as will be noticed, is put carefully in :—I say unto thee that this day," etc. (Mar. xiv : 30). The same guard is used in Luke iv: 21, and in Luke v : 26 (see also other passages, e. g. Lu. xix : 9). Moreover, the adverb is moved to a less exposed position (Lu. xxii : 34), and there are other marks (Lu. xiii : 32 ; Heb. v : 5). But we will not insist on the grammar (see also Acts xxvi : 29), nor much on the logic. We only think that the instinct that approaches a sufferer, and says, " I will not trouble you now ; but when you come to think of this scene, Lord remember me" etc. (v. 42),—might consider itself gloriously answered, if the Great Sufferer exclaimed, Thou *mayest* trouble me now ; I will settle it at once : " I say unto thee to-day" etc. etc. The Greek is, to say the very least. ambiguous ; and is therefore perfectly worthless to withstand on either side great evidences against it.

We grapple, therefore, with another sentence :— " Now that the dead are raised, even Moses showed at the bush, when he called the Lord the God of Abraham, and the God of Isaac, and the God of Jacob. For he is not a God of the dead, but of the living (Lu. xx : 37, 38).

This will be a grand sentence ; for it will be plain and positive which ever way the victory turns. It is not that it is a sentence of our Lord's: for that, past all peradventure, makes not a particle of difference. " All Scripture is given by inspiration of God." It is, that there is here no poetic flight, or flash of a dreamy rhetoric. It is all prose. It is in the tread of a grave debate. It is under the weight of a national question. It is under the spur of a grave opportunity for truth. And it is under the eye of a large assembly of the people, waiting eagerly for the expected answer.

Now, how possibly can I maintain my theory? I say, Abraham is dead. And not only so, but he is extinct from thinking. If he has a soul, it is a dead soul, committed to the keeping of God who gave it. He is in no manner of sense, as a present patriarch, alive. And yet our Saviour does most distinctly teach, as against the thought of the Sadducee, first, that there is a God of Abraham, and second, and in a way that is a reason in the case, " He is not a God of the dead, but of the living."

How possibly can we survive such a distinct ratiocination ?

It is fair to ask, What *is* the ratiocination ? In fact, can anything be fairer ? What was our Lord attempting to prove ? How if it turns out that this passage can be swept into the list of proofs for us ? *Our Lord is defending the resurrection.* Imagine a case. Suppose our Lord was not defending the resurrection. Suppose he were defending immortality. Suppose he were to argue, " I am the God of Abraham, and the God of Isaac, and the God of Jacob." Those patriarchs must every one of them be alive; "for God is not the God of the dead, but of the living." And suppose the answer came, Not so, Lord ; but there is a glorious resurrection; and the promise, " I am the God of Abraham" is incontestibly fulfilled ; not by his hovering like a sprite, but by his ascending among the blest ; not in this passing age, but in that glorious period when we are to be assembled beyond the tomb. Could Christ's argument stand out against such a reply?

But suppose it were different. Suppose it were for the " resurrection" (v. 33). Suppose it were just what it was. How complete, then, like all the pregnant ratiocinations of our Master (see Matt. xxi : 23, 24 ; xxii : 21). " Few and evil have the days of my life been," says the patriarch Jacob. Now, says our Lord, God was the God of Jacob. What is the use of having a God, if that was all the record of the ancient patriarch ? God is the God of every man, rectorally. But God, to be the God of any one as his good Father, must provide him better than Jacob had. And, therefore, there must be more of Jacob. Instead of an argument for immortality, it is an argument the other way; for it argues that there would be no chance to give Jacob a better life unless he rose again, which would be palpably untrue. Jacob, according to our opponent's plan, is now enjoying more than enough to balance all his misery ; and I will, in parting, give this slight touch too to the passage, that in the third account of the scene, viz., that of the philosophic Luke, he remembers another clause that he had heard reported, viz., this gloss of Christ himself upon what he was saying,—that the life he was speaking of was a life that we had, treasured in God (see Jo. vi: 57; Col. iii: 3); for, as he chooses to express it, "all live unto, i. e., *in reference to* (see Greek particle), Him" (v. 38).

One passage more. The risen Samuel (1 Sam. xxviii: 11). This also is quoted as proving that we can listen in our tombs.

We have already remarked that Samuel says, " Why hast thou disquieted me to bring me up?" (v. 15), which agrees, in all its cast as a sentence, with the proprieties of the speech in Acts, " For David, after he had served his own generation by the will of God, fell on sleep, and was laid unto his fathers, and saw corruption" (Acts xiii: 36).

But neglecting that; what does the passage in any other way conclude? Has any one denied that the dead can be raised up? Why, our very doctrine is, that all will be brought up alive at the final judgment. Was it a ghost that Endor saw? She says, Not. The language is, " An old man cometh up;" and she says, " He is covered with a mantle. And Saul perceived that it was Samuel; and he stooped with his face to the ground, and bowed himself" (v. 14). That the old man stirred in his grave one moment before he was lifted up, is no more apparent than that the millions of the earth must be awake, or they cannot hear the final trumpet. No text can be tortured, in all this narrative, to say one word for immortality.

But on the contrary, Why did not Samuel say something about his glorious state? *There* is an argument that has not been enough considered. There have been a room-full of the departed, that have gone and come again; and many of them have lived long lives, like the Shunamite's son, and told nothing. There is Jairus' daughter. Why did she not testify to her Deliverer what she had heard of him in Hades? It may be said that they were forbidden. Then why was not that mentioned? Moreover, scores of men that were healed, refused to be bound by any secrecy (Lu. v: 14, 15). Why not some resurrected one? And Eutychus and Lazarus and all those lifted out of *hades*—why are they as silent as their sepulchres? And why did the Widow's son, spending long winters in his village, tell to an inquisitive world no grand facts of his immortal living. The very idea is impossible.

Gathering up our train, however, we must prepare for the next step. If the whole man is dead, and the whole man is buried, we will look with keen avidity to the next fact, viz., a like uniformity in revelation as to the whole man rising again.

CHAPTER X.

THE WHOLE MAN RAISED FROM THE DEAD.

IN arraying our argument here, we will speak first of the single expressions of Scripture, like those we have already noticed of death and burial; we will consider, second, the accent laid upon our rising; we will consider, third, the fact of judgment; we will consider, fourth, the surprises in that event; we will consider, fifth, the picking out of a DAY, the Judg-

## The Whole Man Raised. 129

ment Day, and emphasizing it so much ; and we will consider, sixth, those serious sentences in which men are entered *together* into heaven or into hell.

I. In respect to what is first, we have but to match the sentences which we quoted at large in respect to our dying. It appeared that, for some cause or other, the Holy Ghost never talked of the body. We could balance that now, if we found He did talk of it in the instance of resurrection. Jacob died. Jacob was embalmed. Jacob was buried. We could carry that much rhetoric speech, and still believe it was the body, if there was a change in the description when He came to speak of our rising. But, instead of that, the habit is repeated.

No mortal ever comes up by miracle without coming up as Samuel (1 Sam. xxviii : 14), or Moses (Matt. xvii ; 3), just as he comes up at the resurrection in the last day. If he were conscious in his sepulchre, why not bring Moses up, and let him talk to the Lord disembodied, or like that ether that floated before the eye of Eliphaz? (Job iv: 16). Why create a body? And why ALWAYS—and I beg that may be noted as the point of my argument—is the whole machinery of Scripture framed on the notion of an undivided man?

Especially, why evermore speak of the *man* as rising? " Now if Christ be preached that he rose from the dead, how say some among you that there is no resurrection of the dead ? " (1 Cor. xv : 11.) Notice the striking uniformity ;—" The dead are raised up" (Matt. 11 : 5). " Whoso eateth my flesh, I will raise him up at the last day" (Jo. vi : 54). Lazarus is raised

(Jo. xii: 1). "Christ both died, and rose, and revived" (Rom. xiv: 9); and again, "died, and was buried, and rose again" (1 Cor. xv: 4); or, a little differently, "must be killed, and must be raised again" (Matt. xvi: 21). "Women received their dead raised to life again" (Heb. xi: 35); and "all that are in their graves shall hear his voice, and shall come forth" (Jo. v: 28).

Let it be distinctly understood:—The whole force of our evidence here is not exhausted even in these combined quotations. But a man breathes by his lungs. There may come a time when he may lose too much of his lungs to breathe at all. Immortality is a question of Scripture. We may cut off so much of Scripture as to stop its breath. We have cut off necrological speeches about the grave. We are cutting off necrological speeches about our rising. And we are to complete our task. The roots of the whole dogma are possible only in the Word. We are cutting them off, one by one. And as we reach the last, there is no atom of sap that can be pleaded from outside tradition.

II. Again, if resurrection be only of the body, why is it so constantly harped upon as everything in our history? Death is never alluded to. If resurrection be only of the body, then death was my great birth. I leaped at once from shame to blessedness. Why does not all this appear? If death be only of the body, I shoot up, when that falls, into the life of Jesus. Who does not long for that? If resurrection be only of the body, it finds me an old citizen: I have lived and reigned with Christ millenniums of years. And yet I am to be told, that, though I have never lived otherwise scarce at all; though the life I once lived in the flesh was not a century; though it was wretched; though it seems to me like an ugly dream; though it flew by me like a vision; and death bore me out of it, and I became perfect at the grave; yet that is not my " great day" at all; but the whole oil of exultation is to be poured out on the resurrection of my clay.

Will any one solve the riddle?

What mourners men have been at the idea of glorification! " Man lieth down, and riseth not: till the heavens be no more, they shall not awake nor be raised out of their sleep. O that thou wouldest hide me in the grave; that thou wouldest keep me secret until thy wrath be past, that thou wouldest appoint me a set time, and remember me" (Job xiv: 12, 13). " Thou wilt not leave my soul in hades; neither wilt thou suffer thy Holy One to see corruption" (Ps. xvi: 10). Even the Messiah seems to have no love for the grave. " But God will redeem my soul from the power of the grave: for he shall receive me" (Ps. xlix: 15).

Now why is this?

And why, though the body is important, yet bear down upon it with so much accent, when none has been allotted to the more giant upstarting of the soul? " If a man die, shall he live again?" Why certainly, in the twinkling of an eye. But, poor Job!— " All the days of my appointed time will I wait, till my change come" (Job. xiv: 14). And listen to David,—" But God will redeem my soul from the power of the grave: for he shall receive me" (Ps. xlix: 15).

And all this becomes still more decisive when Paul speaks of the resurrection as the great "hope" of the believer. "Looking for that blessed hope" etc. (Ti. ii: 13). "And now I stand, and am judged for the hope of the promise made of God unto our fathers. Why should it be thought a thing incredible that God should raise the dead?" (Acts xxvi: 6, 8). And again, —" have hope toward God, which they themselves also allow, that there shall be a resurrection of the dead, both of the just and of the unjust" (Acts xxiv: 15). Again, "What advantageth it me if the dead rise not?" (1 Cor. xv: 32). "If in this life only we have hope toward God, we are of all men most miserable" (v. 19). "They also which are fallen asleep in Christ are perished" (v. 18). And again, that almost blasphemous sentence, "Let us eat and drink, for to-morrow we die" (v. 32). I say, almost blasphemous: for if Paul really believed that we are glorified at death, and yet spoke of our unblameableness (1 Thess. iii: 13), and our confidence (1 Jo. ii: 28), and our redemption (Eph. iv: 30), and our sanctification (Eph. v. 26, 27), and our adoption (Rom. viii: 23), and our joy (1 Thess. ii: 19), and hope (Ti. ii: 13), and comfort (1 Thess. iv: 18). and our glorification (Rom. viii: 17, 18), and our entire reward and perfectness (Rev. ii: 18), as all waiting for us in our sepulchre, we would turn against the apostle as an intellectual puzzle, and judge it to be a light verdict, that gay reply of Festus, as he "said with a loud voice, Paul thou art beside thyself; much learning doth make thee mad" (Acts xxvi : 24).

III. Again, another very plain consideration :— What is the use of judgment, if men have been living scores of centuries in heaven?

If I am unconscious in the grave, and the clangor of the trumpet supervenes upon my dying memory, I can understand the Great White Throne, as an apparition strangely natural, and the Grand Assize as in the highest degree to be expected after the confusions of my earthly living. If my neighbor, when he dies to-night, has his whole case left resting through the ages of the sepulchre; if there be, therefore, the necessity of a seal, by which he may be known at last (Eph. iv : 30); and an earnest (Eph. i : 14); and a life hid with Christ (Col. iii : 3); and an attesting by his earthly faith (Heb. xi : 39); I can understand how all this must be looked into, when he comes to rise, and how the hurrying thousands may be spoken of as before a solemn judgment. But how unspeakably does all this puzzle us, if it be our body! If it be our body only that is missing, and Jehovah's trumpets are sent out only for our dust; why make a court for that? And why, after we have been ages in hell, summon us up by a herald to meet a Grand Assize, simply when we are putting on our body? The idea of any judgment, therefore, when we have been fixed in our awards for ages, puzzles our whole thought; and though our thought is not the test, still, as against the proofs that have been brought, it will serve to give confidence to men, as against phantasies that have so long possessed us.

IV. But, fourthly, there is to be a waking in surprise (Matt. xxv: 11). How is that to be considered possible?

I lie down to sleep, and friends, who saw me sink into dissolution, know that I died in hope. I had a hope full of immortality. But suppose I was under a grand mistake. Scores of instances, coming up at the last, might fill the judgment spaces with terrible amazement. And this would plainly seem the nature of the Bible picture. But suppose I have been in hell. Here really comes in sight the dignity of a Scriptural refutation. Suppose I have been glorified. Nay rather this—Suppose that I never died. Suppose that I lived right on; and what was called death was the mere dropping of my frame. Suppose that I knew last night as much of fate as I shall know for a thousand years. What is meant by my surprise? And why do I cry out in remonstrance (Lu. xiii: 25); and tell how I prophesied (Matt. vii: 22); and ask, "when saw I thee naked" (Matt. xxv: 44); and call, in sudden tones, and in an agony of anguished disappointment, "Lord, Lord, open unto us?" (Luke xiii: 25).

All this has to be taken in under the "immortal" theory.

V. Fifth, why is "*that day*" (2 Tim. i: 18) so noteworthy?

When I died, I became glorified. I had never been perfect before. I had always sinned against my Redeemer. When I died, 1 became perfect. There then, if anywhere in the calendar, I must expect to see my Red Letter. Why is the Bible so twisted? The day I die seems sponged out of the account; and the day I rise, when by these "immortal" notions bliss is an old tale ; when I have been glorified for thousands of years ; when death was my nativity, and life lies behind me like a speck in the past,—"that day" (2 Tim. iv: 8), or "the day of Christ" (Phil. i: 10), or the day of mercy (2 Tim. i: 18), the day of hope (Tit. ii: 13), and the day of redemption (Eph. iv: 30), the declaration day (1 Cor. iii: 13), and the coronation day (2 Tim. iv: 8), and the inauguration day (2 Thess. i: 10), "the day of wrath" (Rom. ii: 5), the unknown day (Matt. xxiv: 36), "the great day" (Jude 6), or, as one apostle expresses it, "The Great Day of His Wrath" (Rev. vi: 17),—is greeted with a blaze of ornament; and my dawn of glory stands so unmentioned as to be almost forgotten. Why is this? The judgment, which would be indeed our life-date if our theory be true, treated as though it *were* our life-date, and death, which is our adversary's birth, scarce ever mentioned?

VI. Lastly; why are the paradise-gates opened as though for the first time? Paul says, " These all, having been attested by faith, received not the promise (see 2 Pet. iii: 4; 1 Jo. ii: 25), God, with reference to us, having looked forward to a something better, that they without us should not be made perfect" (Heb. xi: 39, 40). "With reference to us;" that is, that Paul may not enter late to heaven, and find Lot centuries in advance. This seems the plain meaning: that the souls under the altar may rest yet for a little season, till they and their fellow-servants, and their brethren also, who should be slain as they were, should have their numbers filled up (Rev. vi: 11). This seems the sole meaning. No Scripture ever speaks of an earlier entrance into paradise. And as we can see a plain reason for all starting evenly in heaven and in hell, we see the probableness that it should occur at Judgment; in fact, the whole beauty of the scene, if the Judgment at the last actually consigns the object of it either to pain or glory.

Now seven quotations more. " The wicked is reserved to the day of destruction" (Job xxi : 30). Again, " They shall be brought forth to the day of wrath" (ib.). " Many of them that sleep in the dust shall awake, some to everlasting life, and some to shame and everlasting contempt" (Dan. xii : 2). " He shall separate them one from another, as a shepherd divideth his sheep from the goats" (Matt. xxv : 32). " But rejoice, inasmuch as ye are partakers of Christ's sufferings; that, when his glory shall be revealed, ye may be glad also with exceeding joy" (1 Pet. iv: 13). " Henceforth there is laid up for me a crown of righteousness, which the Lord, the righteous judge, shall give me at that day" (2 Tim. iv : 8). " The Lord knoweth how to deliver the godly out of temptations, and to reserve the unjust unto the day of judgment to be punished" (2 Pet. ii : 9).

CHAPTER XI.

THE WHOLE OF MAN, SOUL.

IF soul has an analogy with life in the bean-stalk, we might expect that, in a long document like Holy Scripture, if dust and flesh were spoken of as the whole man, so soul and spirit would be ; and this we everywhere discover throughout the revelation. The attempts of the translators to conceal it, only show the unconscious prejudice which is a help to our position. It would be impossible, if soul and body were separate essences, and if, as a subsidiary fact, the body died on a certain date, and the soul continued animate, to find the Holy Ghost, and that as His literary habit, representing the soul as dead, and the body not so in any single instance. What are we to augur, if this actually comes out in the Hebrew? and if, when we find it so, we find the translators apparently shocked with such a discovery, and smothering it up in their translation? For example, what are we to think if we read in Leviticus, " Neither shall he go in to any dead soul"? (xxi : 11). What are we to think if there are scores of such expressions? (Num. vi: 6 ; xix: 11 ; Hag. ii: 13). What are we to think of smiting the soul (Lev. xxiv: 17, 18), and killing the soul (Num. xxxi : 19), and slaying the soul ? (Deut. xxvii : 25). What are we to think of metamorphosing this (E. V.) into slaying "persons," or smiting the " life" (Lev. xxiv: 17, *marg.*) of anybody? What are we to think of the expression, " Doeg slew eighty-five souls ? " (1 Sam. xxii : 18). Or what are we to think of the Bible enumerating men by their souls, and speaking of " thirty and two thousand souls" (Num. xxxi: 35), and of the translators changing this usually into persons (Num. xxxi : 35 ; Gen. xiv : 21), but of its occurring so often that they feel the monotony of the change, and sometimes keep in the more literal word? Nay, what is to be thought of this having stolen into classic English, and that we ourselves should speak of so many thousand souls? letting the soul stand for the man, just as the dust does (Ps. xxx: 9), and just as the flesh does (Lu. iii : 6), in other corresponding expressions?

Do not let it be said, We can overcome all this: for what are we to overcome it with but the Bible? These adverse appearances are in the Bible. All those other are in the Bible. And if life and death and burial, and rising again, and judgment, all offer themselves in idioms, and all in ways idiomatically alike, where are we to go to correct everything? and where get proof of immortality except in some other texts, which in some way, idiomatically or not, will furnish us with a different impression?

Look at another fact. The translators introduce the very word soul as though it were a human adjunct. They associate it with Adam. They say not one word about soul till man comes to be created : indeed, not there, in the first chapter (Gen. i : 26); for there is no word that would answer to it. It is not till the second chapter (Gen. ii: 7), that we hear a word about it; and there it is made to start, as though it were the appanage of man. We have this distinct rendering;—" God formed man [of the] dust of the ground, and breathed into his nostrils the breath of life ; and man became a living soul." Who would ever dream that the word was first applied to fish? We turn to the first chapter and read, " Let the waters swarm with swarms of living soul" (i : 20). We look a little further, and " God created great whales, and every living soul" (v. 21). We glance down the page, "And God said, Let the earth bring forth the living soul"(v. 24): a little further, "And God said, To you it shall be for meat, and to every beast of the earth, and to every fowl of the air, and to everything that creepeth upon the earth, in which is a living soul"(vs. 29, 30). We come to man, and no use of that word for him occurs in the first chapter. The word animal (*anima*, Lat.) seems, at the start, to assert its whole right to the name. I charge no unfairness; but I charge unconsciousness. I charge unconscious prejudice. And I charge that no Englishman would know of these facts, or would suppose that beasts had souls, save only in an accommodated sense, or in a form that would be set down as secondary.

To resume ; I am alluding in all this to the fact, that the translators, before they come to speak of man in the second chapter, smother the word soul under a false or indifferent translation.

Now, abandoning these bolder points, let us do what we refused to do first, i. e., treat the soul more radically. We would not do it first, because those bolder things would serve best, *in limine*. When we begin to refine, men stop their ears. We wished to get it uttered that the Bible talks of dead souls ; and that it treats the whole man as though he were dust, and also as though he were soul; and that it mixes him irreparably with brutes (Ec. iii: 19); that is, that, unless there is a resurrection, the Scripture so endows us like brutes, that we have, as Solomon states it, all one spirit (Ec. iii: 19) ; and such inseparable unity, that as the brute dieth, so dieth also the man (ib.). This seems shocking doctrine; but so much more glorious the resurrection of the dead; and so much more intelligible the treatment of the Bible, when it lays such awful stress upon the wrath (Rom. ii : 5), and upon the glory (1 Pet. iv : 13), of that final day.

Let us go back, however. Soul is too seminal a word not to be looked into radically; and, therefore, we will treat the original image, that breeds the word in so many of the languages of the earth.

And I begin by saying, that it would be a great outrage upon truth, if a trope were seized upon to express all the great realities of being, and there were nothing in that trope, so fondly gone for, to express in eligible detail the idea that gendered it.

*Breath* is the trope we are thinking of.

There is a strange tenacity with which thought has refused all other expressions.

Let us inspect but two languages.

There was needed a trope that should become the name for *living*. We hardly think of tropes in such a connection. And we turn to the Hebrew, and find the word *hayah;* and turn to the Greek, and find the word *zoe;* and we hardly think of them as any but original words. But the least touch of a dictionary reveals the image. *Hayah* means life, and *zoe* means life; but, when we penetrate to the root, we find in both of them the idea of *breathing*. Now that might be thought enough. Breathing is a very tolerable image. When a child is born, breathing announces that he is alive; and when the man is dying, breathing announces that he is not dead. It is the ocular insignia of life. But one would think that that might end it. And yet, with wonderful tenacity of gripe, all nations seem to love that figure. There comes up an idea of *soul*. How it originates, may be perhaps best claimed from the word. But delaying that, there comes up a need for an expression; and we turn to the Lexicons, and find, no longer indeed *hayah* and *zoe*, for they are already appropriated; but we find other and similar vocables that mean breath. Why is this? What is there in souls, whether of animals or men, that implies breathing? And yet no other trope is thought of. We have *nephesh* in the Hebrew, and *psuche* in the Greek. And all through the weary way, these words come up. Now it is an outrage upon thought, that men should stick to a figure so closely, and yet that there should not be some prevailing feature to make it such a desired expression.

But now further! Thought rolls on, and there is need of another explication. What shall it be? There is need of something higher. Life is subtile enough, but there is life in a bean. Soul is dignified enough, but there is soul in a brute. I do not mean anything outside of soul; but it would be convenient to speak of *conscience*, and the higher thought; and that which the soul possesses above the range of merely sensuous ideas. Soul moral we would like, as well as soul rational and fleshly. How shall we call it? How strange if the speech-builders should go with a bee-line to the old figure, and search whether there be not another word which means nothing in the world but breath, but which is thus far unoccupied; and which will leave the delicious image, which seems to have attracted everybody, free and unspoken, as now quite a different word for higher and still more ethereal being.

The word has risen to the lips already; *ruah* in the Hebrew, and *pneuma* in the Greek; translated out of both languages by our word *spirit;* borrowed, as being our nobler title, and applied to God; and yet nothing in the world but *breath;* that trope, for reasons that must have been singularly express, following our race through all the higher conceptions of their created being.

Now what are those reasons?

Let me pause, however, to say, that it would be an idle chapter if I filled it with typological conceits. The reader can build those as well as any one. If I went nakedly to the trope, and said,—Breath acts so and so, and therefore soul, by reason of the name, must be so and so, and that against the current of popular persuasion, men would laugh at me; and, therefore, let it be distinctly understood;—I do not mean to prove that the soul is not immortal by mere lexicon proofs of what the breath is, and, therefore, of what the soul must be to have bred the figure. Far otherwise. I mean to resort, as before, to Scripture. I mean to be firm within it. But, as Scripture talks of the soul under no other similitude than breath, I mean to talk so also; and on this thread of a tropical sense I mean to string the thoughts that are to be derived from the Holy Ghost.

1. In the first place, breath is evanescent. It is so with the bean stalk. It dies; and its *hayah* just

ceases, and perishes like a dream away. Now, listen to the Scripture :—" His breath goeth forth ; he returneth to his earth ; in that very day his thoughts perish" (Ps. cxliv : 4). We look into the Hebrew, and the word translated " breath" is just the common one, *spirit*. The answer, then, echoing back, Yes, but it also means breath, places us in just the position in which we wish to stand. A word means breath, and that same word, falling under the Hebrew eye, means also spirit. Breath is known to be evanescent. In spite of its evanescent character, it is the favorite word for spirit. Now, if this were all, the inference would not be so complete. But, presently, we are thronged with passages which either (1) seem utterly careless whether we translate breath or spirit, or, what is far higher proof, (2) oblige us to translate, spirit ; but imply a kindred evanescence to that which is included in the idea of breath.

(1) Of the former class is the text just quoted, " His breath goeth forth" (Ps. cxlvi : 4). It would answer just as well to say, " His spirit goeth forth." We can multiply the instances. Job says, " In whose hand is the breath of all mankind" (Job xii : 10). It might just as well be translated, " In whose hand is the spirit of all mankind." " Thou takest away their breath, they die" (Ps. civ : 29). " Thou takest away their spirit" : it would have been just as well. And so in Solomon, " Yea, they have all one breath" (Ec. iii : 19). " Yea, they have all one spirit." In the Greek, King James' men often hesitate. Witness an instance in St. James :—" For as the body, without the spirit" —They throw immediately into the margin, " The

body without the breath" (Jas. ii : 26). And how could they decide?

Now I say, This negligence of speech is thoroughly venial, if the soul is a breath. If when Jesus cries, "Father, into thy hands I commit my spirit," it would create no confusion of speech if it were translated, "Father, into thy hands I commit my breath"; if, in other words, spirit were figured by breath in the precise sense in which Christ was using it : if Israel gave up the ghost (Gen. xlix : 33) in that perishing sense in which he gave up his breath ; then it would make little difference,—this negligence of use as between the breath and the spirit. Driven for our proof entirely to the words of Scripture, that man will be an unfair polemic, who, when we touch the Scripture language here and there, entrenches himself in imagined proofs ; when we are literally cutting away all his evidences.

(2) Then again, the Bible justifies the figure. It not only uses spirit and breath indiscriminately ; it not only uses soul and life with utter negligence ; but it does not hesitate an instant to speak of a dead soul.

Here is the place to notice that enormity.

Abraham speaks constantly of his soul living (Gen. xii : 13). Lot seems to have no other idea of his escape from peril (Gen. xix : 20). The patriarchs seem to have no other idiom so present in their language. And, when the converse comes up, and we hear of smiting souls (Lev. xxiv : 17), and of smiting beasts' souls (v. 18), and of cutting off souls (Ex. xii : 15), and of that strongest of all expressions, "dead souls" (Lev. xxi : 11 ; Num. vi : 6), as answering entirely to the idea of the loathsome corpse (Num. ix : 10) by touching which the Israelites might be defiled,—we have certainly gone a good deal farther than the negligent mixing of soul and breath; and have reached that other point, namely, that the whole man is talked of boldly as though he were evanescent spirit.

2. Let me speak of this under a second head.

That the soul is figured under the name of breath, requires a word of explanation before we can teach thereby that the soul is therefore inseparable from the body. That the breath, in a certain intelligible way, is also inseparable from the body, does not forbid the speech that the breath has left the body. We say that the life has left the palm-tree. But what do we mean? We mean that the two things, body and breath; or the two things, viz. life and the palm-tree,—are inseparable in the very highest way; that is, not only cannot the breath go out, and exist, or similarly, not only cannot the life leave the palm and continue to be,—but the palm cannot exist either. The life has gone out like a spark; and the man and the tree have lost their being. Now till the Bible taught us differently this is what we would infer from the departure of the spirit. The spirit goes out (Ps. cxlvi : 4); the spirit is given up (Job xi : 20); the spirit is departing (Gen. xxxv : 18); or, in a rare case or two, returns (1 Ki. xvii : 22) ; or comes back (Lu. viii : 55), after returning to God who gave it (Ec. xii : 7); and if left to ourselves, we would treat that like the oak tree, and regard the departure of life like the departure of breath from the living animalism.*

But, luckily, the Bible is very communicative. It does not leave us to guess, but favors this very supposition.

In the first place, it makes soul inseparable by dignifying it often as the whole name for the person. "Seventy souls" (Jud. ix : 5). "Thirty souls" (xx : 39). "Eighty-five souls" (1 Sam. xxii : 18). Our translators smother the idiom (Num. xxxi : 35) : sometimes, however, it is allowed to come out (Gen. xlvi : 15, 18, 22, 25–27). It is a favorite expression of the Bible. Just as animals are called lives (Gen. xxxvii : 20 ; Ps. civ : 25), so men are called souls. And, as a further step in the investigation, soul is a favorite name for self (see Gesenius). Indeed there is no other expression in the Hebrew to answer at all to this personal idea (Job ix : 21 ; Ps. iii : 3 ; Is. li : 23).

But further ; soul is ever on the lips when inspired men need a word for life (Lam. v : 9, Job ii : 4, Jo. x : 11). This puzzles the translators. In our view the thing is manageable. If soul is answered to by the expiration of breath, then it is the essence and whole of that subtile thing called living. In fact all these terms are interchangeable. Spirit is soul, and more. Soul is mind, and more. Soul is life, and more. And life is more than vegetable life, and different from dust, though we cannot conceive of life but as dwelling in a body. To us, therefore, all the Bible *équivoques* become matter of instruction. " Take no thought for your soul (*psuche*), what ye shall eat

* Judg. xv : 19 ; 1 Sam. xxx : 12 ; 1 Ki. x : 5.

or what ye shall drink" (Matt. vi : 25). The translators drop the word, of course. And they dislocate sentences. Our Saviour, in a brief context, declares, " For whosoever will save his soul, shall lose it ; but, whosoever shall lose his soul for my sake and the Gospel's, the same shall save it" (Mar. viii : 35) ; and immediately adds,—" For what shall it profit a man if he shall gain the whole world, and lose his own soul ? Or what shall a man give in exchange for his soul ? " King James translates differently in one clause and the other.

Let us not be misunderstood : we are not sure we would not translate some of these clauses as they have done. We would, but for certain specialties of exegesis.* But that is neither here nor there. What we are protesting against is, such a popular belief as sways languages, and has erected such barriers of thought as between the soul and the life of the mammal.

The Bible boldly says, The soul dies (Jud. xvi : 30 ; Job xxxi : 39 ; Ps. lxxviii : 50). It says that it goes down into the grave (Ps. xxx : 3 ; lxxxvi : 13 ; Acts ii : 31). It vacates it of all its consciousness (Job x : 22 ; Ps. vi : 5 ; cxlvi : 4). And if it says that it departs, it is as the breath departs. God is the former of our bodies because they are framed of dust, and give back the dust again after they are dead. But he is the father of our spirits ; not only because they

* We are inclined to the belief that wishing to save one's soul means having no higher motive ; and that losing one's soul means, as by contrast with a higher and nobler object ; and that the doctrine of the passage is that a man is not saved till he catches sight of something higher than mere salvation.

possess his likeness, but because they go back into his hand ; that is, because there is nothing to survive that we know of, but His hand's efficiency.

So much for the second point. Let me conclude it in the words of Scripture. "If He set his heart on Himself; if He take to Himself His spirit and His breath, all flesh would breathe out (expire) together, and man would return to the dust" (Job xxxiv: 14, 15).

3. Now, we have but to imagine that all animals were brutes, to bring out a third point, viz., that, taking the document of Scripture as it is, all mankind would be perfectly reconciled to the belief in souls as though they were evanescent like the breath. I am sure that it would be impossible to have any other idea. We have seen that souls begin with fishes (Gen. i: 20). Swarms of living souls are our first notice of this great anti-type of breath. The word is never idle. It occurs four times in this very chapter. It occurs never in this first chapter of Genesis in connection with man. It occurs just as it would occur if the animating principle that makes the brute, were, just as that word *animal* declares, a soul under the image of breath. And as it is an unnatural conceit that that soul should float off, and live separate after the animal dies, I think everybody would assent to the belief that, if man were out of the way, the soul, wherever it is mentioned, might be likened to our breathing life, a thing hanging upon our breath, and a thing that might be conceived as vanished, when the eye glazes, and we breathe out our life into the air.

## The Whole of Man, Soul. 149

And why should man stand in the way?

I beg it may be noticed that all the Israelitish books speak of the brutes as having souls. There is never a hesitation. If there is any halting of a verse to give beasts this exalted gift, it is found to be by the translators. "Any living soul that is in the waters," says Leviticus (xi : 10). "And with every living soul," says the Almighty, "that is with you ; of the fowl, of the cattle and of every beast of the earth with you ; from all that go out of the ark, to every beast of the earth" (Gen. ix : 10). The cases are many (see Gen. ii : 19). "This is the law of the beasts, and of the fowl, and of every living soul that moveth in the waters, and of every soul that creepeth upon the earth" (Lev. xi : 46).

The position, let it be noticed, is, that if these broad passages, that seem to introduce the very idea of soul for the first time, were unincumbered with the instance of man, the verdict would be an easy one. We would all exclaim, The soul departs like the breath ; and it is its ceasing like the breath, that has made the expiration from the lungs so favorite a type of what is animate in creation.

But now for the easy retort, that man is not out of the way. Man is the great mammal. Man is heaven-wide from the brute. And it is reasonable that this nobler animation should be endowed with a great soul that does not succumb to the changes and chances of mortality.

But let it be considered. Is not this mere philosophizing? Notice what we have said. Our appeal is to the Bible. Man, Scripturally, is a wonderful chief. But we get that out of the word of God. Man, Scripturally, is to live in Paradise. But must we not get him there in a Biblical way? Man, Scripturally, is to be raised again. Now we have said all along, We insist on what is said in Scripture; and, as Scripture does not say we are immortal, we insist that the soul of man shall be confounded with the brute, except in those precise respects in which we are taught otherwise in the word of God.

And that perishableness is not one of those respects, we prove by showing how the Bible delights to mix men with brutes in speaking of their spirits. "One soul of five hundred" says the Almighty; "of the persons, and of the beeves, and of the asses, and of the sheep" (Num. xxxi: 28). These blendings occur on great occasions of divine administration. "Behold I destroy all flesh wherein is a spirit of life," says God, (Gen. vi: 17). And we learn that "All in whose nostrils was the breath of a spirit of life, of all that was in the dry land, died" (Gen. vii: 22). "This is the token of the covenant," says God, " which I make between me and you, and every living soul that is with you, for perpetual generations" (ix: 12). "And the bow shall be in the cloud; and I will look upon it, that I may remember the everlasting covenant between God and every living soul of all flesh that is upon the earth" (v. 16). Now hold, if you please, that there is nothing positive in this treatment of the *genus* soul; I beg you to observe how much negative there is in it—that just where of all the world we would expect to find some disseverance of the beast's soul and the man's soul from each other, they are thrown, on solemn days, remorselessly together; and, indeed, in moral enactments. Man is enjoined not to smite the soul of a beast. "He that smiteth the soul of a man shall surely be put to death. And he that smiteth the soul of a beast shall make it good, soul for soul" * (Lev. xxiv : 17, 18).

Now here we might rest. But I beg to say that the inspired writers go further, and absolutely deal with what is positive. Not only do they say that like sheep we are laid in the grave, and that Death shall be our shepherd (Ps. xlix: 14); not only do they say that we are "born like the wild ass's colt" (Job xi : 12); not only do they affirm that we are "like the beasts that perish" (Ps. xlix: 12); not only do they ask, " Who knoweth a spirit of man that goeth upward, and a spirit of the beast that goeth downward to the earth?" (Ec. iii : 21); but they say in this very last chapter, "I said in my heart concerning the estate of the sons of men, that God might manifest them, and that they might see that they themselves are beasts. For that which befalleth the sons of men, befalleth beasts; even one thing befalleth them : as the one dieth, so dieth the other ; yea they have all one spirit : so that a man hath nothing left of him† more than a beast: for all is vanity.

* The translators say " beast for beast ;" and that doubtless is the meaning. But the universal care to throw out the word soul, and put in something else, shows how thought has been saturated. " Killeth a man " is the translation of the first clause, and " Killeth a beast," of the second ; giving nothing in the margin for the second ; and giving another word than soul for its account of the first.

† Not " no preëminence" (E. V.). That could not be said. The word is *mothar*, from *yather*, to *leave* or *have over*.

All go unto one place; all are of the dust; and all turn to dust again" (Ec. iii: 18-20).

Now, as we have all along said, we do not trust to these texts, or to a thousand such texts. But let it be observed, we are going through the whole of the Bible. I do not trust to one lung, or especially to one part of one lung. But I beg to ask, Where are my antagonist's lungs? We have sounded from side to side, and cannot discover for him any breathing spaces.

4. But fourthly; men may ask, Do *you* not distinguish the soul from the body? And here will be our fourth argument. Breath also can be distinguished from the body. We may go down as low as the lily. The dust in the lily's stalk, and the life of the lily, are plainly distinguishable. And if we ascend to animals, the dog, with his fine intelligence, is to be looked at in different endowments; his matter first, his life afterwards; and his intelligent life after that: and let it be distinctly understood; we believe these to be different gifts, and different efficiencies, from God who made us. But does that at all prevent that they be inseparable? Molecules might be related a million of years, and yet might never climb a pole; and, therefore, we believe in motions of life which must be by energy of heaven, which enables the bean-dust to sprout itself upward, and to draw in surrounding molecules, and to become unitary as one climbing vine upon the earth. Soul, therefore, may be thoroughly distinguished from molecules of matter; and yet may not be separable in the least degree. Animals afford a still stronger analogy. If life may

be distinguished from the lily-dust, so may soul from the dust of the cat and the dog. And yet, if we do not separate the vital oak from the tons' weight of leaf and branch, and if we do not separate, except in thought, the mind of the bison from his material molecules,—why should we do it in the instance of man? I mean, why should we do it unless there is that in the language of Scripture that ordains a difference? that is, that asserts the fact that man, different from the tree, has a separate essence, independent of the body?

But, now, the Bible's distinctions of the soul are just as ours are in the tree and in the bison. It begins with vast indifference. It speaks of the body as though it included the soul, and it speaks of the soul as though it included the body. This is just as it might better be, if each were interlinked with either. It speaks of the soul as though it included every thing; and, therefore, we have the soul for self (Ps. ciii: 1; Ho. ix: 4); and, therefore endlessly, we have the soul for person (Num. xix: 18; Ez. xxvii: 13); and, therefore also, we have the soul indifferently for body (Lev. v: 2). We hear of dead souls (Num. vi: 6), and of souls physically smitten (Lev. xxiv: 17), and of souls sensuously eating and thirsting and touching and crying out, which are functions of the animal frame. In other words, we have the Spirit speaking expressly in ways in which we are accustomed to speak when we mix, in ontological respects, life and matter. At the same time, we have the two distinguished. Beginning back at the beginning, we have the soul *acting*, and that in ways that involve the body. "Make me savory meat," says the patriarch Isaac, "that my soul may bless thee" (Gen. xxvii : 4). "When a soul will offer a meat offering," says Leviticus (ii : 1). We need make no discrimination. It may be eating. It may be smiting. It may be touching. There is a perfect carelessness of division. "Soul take thine ease" says the rich sinner, "eat, drink and be merry" (Lu. xii : 19). These are the sentences which mix the oak with its vitality. Then there are sentences where the soul is said to *feel*. There the vitality separates a little. "His soul clave unto Dinah," says the narrative in Genesis (xxxiv : 3). "Ye know the soul of a stranger," says Moses afterward (Ex. xxiii : 9). "Our soul loatheth this light bread" (Num. xxi : 5). "If your soul abhor my judgments" (Lev. xxvi : 15). And then, "anguish of soul"(Gen. xlii : 21), and "bitterness of soul" (1 Sam. i : 10), and grief of soul (Job xxx : 25), and affliction of soul (Is. lviii : 10), drift us away from what we ever dream of as connected with the body. Nay, we have sins of soul (Lev. iv : 2), and, finally God's soul (Jud. x : 16),—which seem to make audaciously wicked the linking of soul with the brutal chemistry of our bodies.

And here, indeed, is the grand rally of the appeal. Is it not, it will be said, past all decency of doubt that the soul does and the body does, nay that the soul is and the body is, a very different thing? May not these travellers together get mixed in many a sentence? May not the soul eat, and may not the soul smite and touch and slay, just as the body may "serve" and be "holy," through the mere tasteful mingling of important metaphors, and yet, when it comes to sin (Ez. xviii : 4), and to love (1 Sam. xviii : 1), and to faith (Lam. iii : 25), and above all to God (Jer. xiv : 19), can there be the same conceivable essence in both soul and body ?

Now here is the place for making our grand final distinction.

There is not the same conceivable essence of life and a bean-stalk. We assert of life what we cannot assert of the mere molecules of the bean. The mere molecules of the bean have a certain efficiency. The mere life of the bean-stalk has another efficiency. The mind of the bison and the dog has an efficiency still different. These are energies of God. They are piled up still heavier in the case of man. Now, they are so different in faith and in hope and in love and in sin from what they are in moving the body, that there are no limits which we will not concede in the ennobling of thought beyond the molecules of the body : and yet, with the precedent of life so far beyond the bean-particles, and with the precedent of soul so far beyond the dog-particles, we cannot mix the dog's soul with his body, and then refuse, except on the distinct basis of Scripture, that the soul of the man shall follow, as the dog's does, the natural history of the animal frame.

The soul, as a distinct appellative, becomes so common, that the Bible does not hesitate, in one passage, to link with it all the highest interests of our eternal claim. "Fear not them," says our blessed Redeemer, " which kill the body, but are not able to kill the soul" (Matt. x : 28) : but not only does the passage itself correct itself by immediately linking one with the other, " Fear him who is able to destroy both soul and body in hell"; not only does our Saviour put a gloss upon it by modifying the like sentences,—" And I say unto you, my friends, Be not afraid of them that kill the body, and after that have no more that they can do" (Lu. xii : 4); not only does he throw away the idea of our being disembodied, by leaping, as in other passages (2 Cor. v: 1), across the gulf, and saying, " Fear him which, after he hath killed" (that is, the body, v: 4), " hath power to cast into hell" (Lu. xii : 5); not only is the same leap characteristic of Paul :—" It is appointed to all men once to die, and after that the judgment " (Heb. ix: 27); but the case itself is of no particular moment when we come to remember that, like the life of the oak (Ps. lviii : 10), or like the soul of a fish (Gen. i : 20), or like the spirit of a saint (1 Jo. iv : 2), the soul does, most of all, describe the man. It is not at all unnatural that we should hear of the salvation of the soul. It would be highly unnatural if that word were not preferred, to speak of the raised man, when he is to be immortal. And just as Stephen says, " Receive my spirit" (Acts vii : 59); and just as Christ says, " I commend my spirit " (Lu. xxiii : 46); and just as the parable says, " Thy soul shall be required of thee" (Lu. xii : 20),—so the phrase, " And are not able to kill the soul" (Matt. x: 28), is so naturally accounted for without, that it cannot overcome the weight of the aforequoted antagonistic revelations.*

---

* God's soul of course, on any theory, is a mere metaphor.

It remains only to note another fact, viz., that the blood is said to be the soul (Lev. xvii: 14).

Now I am not going to run away with this, or to teach the doctrine that it is a scientific inspiration. It may have been a creed in Egypt; and the argument may have been, With this profound association with blood, ye shall not eat it. I do not care scientifically to expound the passage. It may have been a wise incorporation by God of the deepest science about our life with the respect due to our history; but no doubt the blood of Christ is the metaphor for atonement for all our sins, because of some ancient thought that blood was the soul: a thought that must be largely metaphoric; but which, by passing by brain; by saying nothing of that cerebral part which must very early have appeared to man as the secret of his consciousness; by passing by nerve and lung and liver and sense, and all our vital members; by coming to such a senseless thing as blood; by coming nevertheless to that which modern discovery does put at the very fountain of our being; by singling that cell-germ which does begin in the blood, and which does grow from the very fœtal cellules on, like a coral reef—I say, this profound hypothesis:—
"Flesh in the soul thereof, which is the blood thereof (Gen. ix: 4): "For the soul of the flesh is in the blood" (Lev. xvii: 11); "No soul of you shall eat blood" (v. 12), "For it is the soul of all flesh. Its blood is in [or as] its soul: for the soul of all flesh is its blood" (v 14: see also Deut. xii: 23–25),— *does* show that the inspired Author of the Bible had no earthly aversion to encouraging the belief

that the soul was inseparable from our bloody tissues.

## CHAPTER XII.

### SPIRIT.

SPIRIT has been spoken of almost enough; because much that should be said of it could not be separated, conveniently, from the soul.

There are, however, some aspects that must be treated specially.

Spirit is a higher word; more recent, probably, than the soul. Soul comes to the lips of the chronicler, as of reptiles and in the very first creation (Gen. i: 20). Soul, therefore, has lost its early sense, and is seldom used for wind or breath: we might almost say, never (*see Gesen.*). Spirit, therefore, seems the newer word, and naturally more extreme, in this, that, first, it has not failed out of its earlier sense (Job ix: 18), and yet it has been chosen to mean what is the very highest and noblest. Accordingly, as we might expect, it has some meanings that are lower and plainer than are found for the soul; but most, a great deal higher.

Let me illustrate.

" His spirit came again," we hear in the inspired history (1 Sam. xxx: 12), when " they gave him a piece of a cake of figs and two clusters of raisins." So it was with Samson (Jud. xv: 19). And it was expressed with even a commoner word when a person actually died. " There was no breath left in him" (1 Ki. xvii: 17); and Elijah went and prayed, "and the soul of the child came into him again"(v. 22). Spirit, also, is spoken of beasts; and, in fact, of man and beast; for all are thrown together in whom are the spirit of life (Gen. vi: 17); and Solomon declares, " For that which befalleth the sons of men befalleth beasts; even one thing befalleth them: as the one dieth, so dieth the other; yea, they have all one spirit" (Ec. iii: 19).

But, needing a name for conscience and the higher part, the Scriptures have fallen upon this; so that, as we have said, spirit is the name, not only for the common breath or life of man (Ez. xxxvii: 8), but, more theologically, for his conscience (Gal. v: 17). This last is erected into so distinct a notion, that the Apostle calls it the " inner man " (Rom. vii: 22), and plainly implies that it belongs to all men, saints and sinners. He speaks of it as in himself. He represents the *pneuma* as pleading for the law, even when he was carnal, sold under sin. He represents this *pneuma* so strongly, that modern exegetes break away from the old patristic understanding, and think he must be speaking of the regenerated man. And yet the very strongest expressions, as for example this,—" I delight * in the law of the Lord after the inward man" (v. 22); or, for another example, this,—" What I hate, that do I" (v. 15); or, for still another, this,—" With the mind I myself serve the law of God" (v. 25); however much they may have been seized, in modern times, as describing the believer, do really describe the impenitent;

* This English is too strong: the Greek is *sunedomai*, " I am pleased with."

the idea being the old and common one, that man has an imperial conscience ; that that conscience is on the side of law; that that law is spiritual (Rom. vii : 14) and the mind of the Almighty; that that mind is liked by the inner nature of man (v. 22) ; that that nature is decaying in the lost ; that that nature is renewed in the believer (Ps. li : 10); and that that nature, which ever way it is going, whether as being renewed or as being grieved away, is the spirit of man, for which that name has been decreed which we are now considering as among the words of Scripture.

This spirit is so distinctly set apart, that it is antagonized to other powers, which nevertheless can think and reason ; as, for example, to the flesh. The flesh is said to feel (Rom. xiii : 14) ; and also, without hesitation, it is said to desire (Eph. ii : 3) ; and we are to understand that it thinks and reasons (2 Cor. i : 17): and yet, in the same narrow realm of man, we are to suppose there is room for spirit. " The flesh lusteth against the spirit" (Gal. v : 17). I beg that it may be noticed how didactic the expression is. The apostle is dealing in the soberest reflections. And yet he hesitates not a moment ; " The flesh lusteth against the spirit, and the spirit against the flesh : and these are contrary the one to the other, so that ye cannot do the things that ye would." Our point, therefore, is, that spirit is used to describe the moral faculty of our nature.

But not only is it antagonized to flesh, and that ruder form of our carnality ; but to soul, and that in ways injuriously smothered by our translators. Paul makes it color the risen body. He says, "Some will say, How are the dead raised up?" (1 Cor. xv: 35). And after a good deal of preliminary writing, he comes to this striking expression, " It is sowed a soul-body ; it is raised a spirit-body" (v. 44). He is not afraid to descant upon it :—" There is a soul-body, and there is a spirit-body": and then winds up with the asseverance, " Howbeit that was not first which is spiritual, but that which is *psuchical*, and afterward that which is spiritual" (v. 46): the meaning of all which is, that we are born into this world with a body that is under the dominion of the soul; that is, of man in all that part of his nature that has least of conscience and of the fear of God ; but that we will be born into another world, spiritual. There is no thought of etheriality of flesh, or of spirituality, in any sense of there being no grossness or avoirdupois solidity of our persons ; but it is an intimation of our holiness ; that, whereas, in this world, we had bodies subject to our souls, in a better world they shall be subject to our spirits ; the mere conclusion being, that spirit is a higher name for the soul; that is, that it is the conscience and the moral part, at the Great Day become regnant in our nature.

With this understanding, we have no trouble with " spirit, soul and body" (1 Thess. v: 23), and the mad trichotomies preached up in our day. Body contains the whole. Soul is inseparable from the body. And spirit is but another name for it in its grander and more conscientious leanings. The three borrow and diffuse their lights. The soul need not be separated from the body, if the soul is not to be separated from the spirit. I mean, the very use of this trinity, throwing the soul into the same category with the body, and then throwing the soul with the evidently inseparable spirit, leads to the imagination that all are inseparable, and are only to be distinguished in those natural ways that are common even to the brute creation.

But now, further! God becomes mingled with this language. What is the meaning of spirit? Breath. Whose breath? Man's. Nay but who breathes it? God. There is a delight in Scripture in attributing to God subjective presence in the work of man. Paul, magnifying prophecy (and he meant prophecy in the wider sense), says, " Thus are the secrets of his heart made manifest; and so, falling down on his face, he will worship God, and report that God is in you of a truth" (1 Cor. xiv : 25). Christ says, " The Father that dwelleth in me, he doeth the works" (Jo. xiv : 10). And breaking out in a still grander strain, Paul declares, " I am crucified with Christ : nevertheless I live : yet not I, but Christ liveth in me : and the life which I now live in the flesh, I live by the faith of the Son of God, who loved me, and gave himself for me" (Gal. ii : 20).

It is not a violence, therefore, that Scripture, having this tendency of speech, should take the word breath, and apply it to Him who breathes it. And we should predict that, if one word breath was higher than another word breath; that is, that if one word breath was applied to soul, and another word breath was applied to something higher, namely conscience, —God would be especially described by that higher

# Spirit. 163

and nobler breath. Hence God is very rarely called soul, and is very constantly called Spirit; sometimes as breathing into matter (Job xxvi: 13), but oftener as breathing into our higher part, and working the very renewal that we need in our heart and conscience.

Now, so inseparable is our breath from God's breath,—I mean *pneuma* or breath as the trope for conscience,—that in many a passage it makes no difference which is thought of. For example, where Paul says, " They that are after the spirit, do mind the things of the spirit" (Rom. viii: 5), it makes no difference which we understand, unless indeed it does make a difference, and we should understand it of *our* spirits, seeing that, in the ninth verse, the Spirit of God is separately mentioned, " Ye are not in the flesh, but in the spirit, if so be that the Spirit of God dwell in you." We can multiply these *équivoques*. " If we live in the spirit, let us also walk in the spirit" (Gal. v : 25). " He that soweth to the spirit, shall, of the spirit reap life everlasting" (Gal. vi : 8). " Sanctification of the spirit" Paul talks of, when writing to the Thessalonians (2 Thes. ii : 13). " By the spirit that he hath given us," says the apostle John (1 Jo. iii : 24). And that no one may be horrified by this raising of a doubt, let him examine the work of our translation, and he will see the most painful confusion in supplying the capital letter, where God's Spirit or man's spirit is the thing in question (see for this Jo. iv: 23, 24 ; 2 Cor. iii : 6; xii: 18; Eph. vi : 18 ; Phil. i: 27 ; 1 Tim. iv: 12; 1 Pet. iv: 6; 1 Jo. iv: 2).

I say, therefore, that it makes no difference, in many a passage, whether the word *pneuma* is the spiritual breath that God breathes into man, and, therefore, that glorious efficiency in the soul of the sinner, or whether it is the spiritual breath that that efficiency creates, i. e., the higher conscience or moral part of our humanity. And, now, I go further and say, that there is a splendid passage that says that the one thing and the other thing are distinguishably and with reverent significance the same.

Let me proceed carefully.

When I say that God is in me, I mean modest and easily defended truth. The Bible is full of such things. It says we are "partakers of the divine nature" (2 Pet. i : 4). It can only be because some instance is new, that it can shock us in the least degree.

Now, we introduce such an instance. Our Lord speaks to the woman of Samaria. He has been sketching the realities of worship. He says, " Ye worship ye know not what: we know what we worship : for salvation is of the Jews" (Jo. iv : 22). He goes on to say, " But the hour cometh, and now is, when the true worshipper shall worship the Father in spirit and in truth" (v 23). And then follows this strangely misrendered aphorism—" SPIRIT IS GOD" (v. 24). I know of nothing so confidently thrown into mistake in all our criticism. The meaning of our Saviour is evident. Man, he says, must worship the Father in spirit. And then, as an obvious consideration why spirit must be the region of worship, he says, " Spirit is God."

Nor need we be shocked at such an asseverance. The Apostle repeats it. " Now the Lord is that spirit" (2 Cor. iii: 17). The last sentence in which the word "spirit" had been mentioned, it is spelled without a capital even by the translators (v. 6). And, yet, here comes the bold echo, " The Lord is that spirit." And it puts beyond difficulty the words of Christ when he speaks in awful earnestness to the woman of Samaria.

"Spirit is God."

Now, I know, grammar will be appealed to to refute us. But take this sentence,—" Gain is godliness" (1 Tim. vi: 5). Precisely the same grammar reigns in one passage as in the other. Old Middleton has ruled another case (Jo. i: 1) through the Article. But Glassius and Rambach have entirely refuted him (see Winer). There are no grammatical difficulties. The meaning of our Lord is plain. We recur to our idea. Spirit is so the breath of the Almighty that it gives a name even to Him. And our blessed Lord would teach the doctrine; not that God's Spirit and man's spirit are one and the same thing,—but that, in Oriental speech, as life in us is Christ in us (1 Jo. v: 12), and as miracle in us is God in us (1 Cor. xiv: 25), and, hence, as piety in us is the Holy Ghost in us (1 Cor. iii: 16), so, and more definitely, the spirit or higher part in man is God's Spirit; as the old heathen expressed it, the voice of the Almighty; and in very literal ways, the work of his power: like the life in the bean, a divine efficiency; like the mind in the ox, the light of the word of God; in the instance of man, a higher word, warranting the speech of Christ that the spirit or higher part of man is God's Spirit, not altogether in metaphoric sense, but in that efficient way in which God is our light and righteousness.

Then, firstly, the passage is lost to them who would build on it, in any way, helps to the doctrine of the separateness and essence of the spirit. There is no such passage as " God is a spirit."

Secondly, we understand the sentence, "Whether in the body or out of the body" (2 Cor. xii : 2).

If God is our upholding Breath, he could carry Paul, in the spirit, altogether away from any other efficiency of his nature. He could make Paul *be* on earth, and *see* in heaven. He could work any miracle. And, therefore, this conscious uncertainty of Paul is no more decisive of his two estates, than his yet more mere shadowy speech, " absent in body, but present in spirit" (1 Cor. v : 3). We may pass these things.

Thirdly ; spirit, therefore, is not disembodied. It parts, never a moment, with its metaphor of breath. Even God's mixture with it betokens the same idea. " If we live, it is not we that live," but there is no sign of living outside of either soul or body; and " the life that we now live in the flesh," must be so a pattern of the embodied life beyond, that, unless Scripture is a mistake, we settle that as our faith from its plainest revelation.

## IV.

## THE IMMORTALITY OF THE SOUL A RELIC OF PAGANISM.

THE most intolerable burden that our doctrine has to carry, is the weight of the world's belief: and I confess that the church is so far infallible, that all the great teachings of the gospel cannot be supposed to have been lost or hid or misunderstood among believers.

But our very statement is, that our doctrine is not a vital one.

Far more vital is the doctrine of the sacraments. If the sacrament is of the very body and blood of the Redeemer, to disown it, when our Saviour says, "This is my body" (1 Cor. xi : 24); to denounce it, in the face of that earnest speech, "As the living Father hath sent me, and I live by the Father, so he that eateth me shall live by me" (Jo. vi : 57)—a speech repeated, and redoubled, and wrought in, even when according to our Protestant thought it was seen to be misunderstood,—then the Papist is right, and it is a horrible impiety ; and yet all this was the belief of the world, scarcely broken until three hundred years ago.

It will not do to plead precedents.

Galileo shocked the faith of the whole of Christendom.

And yet it will be said, Take the common sober

arithmetic. Where are the probabilities likely to preponderate? Are you certain to be right, and the whole family of believers of crass intellect, and pitiably and, as you would have it appear, shamefully and with scarce any argument asleep and wrong? That is the strong appeal. What ought we to do?

It will be right certainly to pare down the opposition, and to show that the court of Christendom has had offered to it some notable demurrers.

I. In the first place, Augustine, in his earlier writings, showed wonderful vacillation, to say the very least, and though he recalled various evidences of this in his Retractions, yet the very pause and hesitation of such a mind as his is full of genuine significance.

II. In the second place, the Fortieth Article of the Episcopal Church read in this way, " They who say that the souls of such as depart hence do sleep, being without all sense, feeling, and perceiving, until the day of judgment, or affirm that the souls die with the bodies, and at the last day shall be raised up with the same, do utterly dissent from the right belief declared unto us in the holy scripture."

This article not only showed the prevalence of such conceits by its adoption, but it showed, either first, their innocence, or second, their revival and obstinacy, or respectable continuance, by its rescission ; for in 1562, ten years later than Edward's reformers, the Articles were reduced to thirty nine ; and this was one of the three that were bodily excluded. The remark of Archdeacon Blackburne may be noted:

## a Relic of Paganism.

"By allowing separate souls to have sense, feeling and perception, the doctrines of purgatory and invocation would naturally follow" (Blackburne's Works, vol. iii: p. 85).

III. In the third place, I appeal to Luther.

Now Luther's testimony has been wonderfully debated.

Bayle denies that he believed in our being mortal.

Luther certainly hankered after invocation. It filled his fancy. Moreover, in the broil of a reform, just such as Luther would be thrown back upon many an expression of his old belief. Besides, he was taxed with this inconsistency, and beyond all manner of doubt paltered and hesitated. We do not defend him. We only say, He taught our doctrine: and no twisting of his speech can work out of it any other expression.

Let me quote.

On Eccles. ix: 10 he says, " Therefore Solomon thought that the dead utterly slept, and were quite unconscious. They lie there dead, not counting days or years; but when raised up, shall seem to themselves scarce to have slept a moment." * On Gen. iv: 9 ;—" We gather from this place the very strongest showing, that, if there were no one that had a care for us after this life, Abel slain would not be again sought after. But God seeks after Abel taken away from this life ; wills him to be not forgotten ; keeps memory of him ; asks where is he."†

One of the apologists of Luther says that " the

* *Opera Wittcomb.* vol. iv. p. 36.　　† Ib. vol. vi. p. 64.

origin of the calumny," for so he chooses to call it, "is in a letter he wrote to Amsdorf in the year 1522, in which he appears much inclined to believe that the souls of the just sleep to the day of judgment, without knowing where they are, etc. He does not pretend to say that they are dead in this interval" [What can be *meant* by that?], "but only lay in a profound rest and sleep, *in which opinion he followed many fathers of the ancient church.*"

Let it be observed, these are the words of an *apologist*.

Look again:—"When he shall rise again," says Luther, speaking of the Elector who died on a return from the chase, "it will seem to him as though he had just come from the forests, where he was hunting."*

Luther seems to have conceived it right to speak of the soul as living though dead (Col. iii: 3); but this is about his account of it: "True it is, they have peace in faith," says he, speaking of Rom. v: 1, "but the same peace is invisible and surpasseth all human conceit: insomuch that, being even in death, feeling no life at all, we must nevertheless believe we live."†

There can be no doubt of Luther's leaning; and Sleidan, telling us of his death (which of course precludes the idea of his having recanted), gives us this sequel:—"At supper he spoke of various matters, and asked this among the rest, whether in the eternal life we shall know each other? and when the desire was expressed to know his opinion, What, he

* *Seckendorf Hist.* B. iii; p. 30.　　† *Coll. Mens.*, p. 402.

## a Relic of Paganism.

asked, happened to Adam? He had never seen Eve: but, when God was forming her, he was *wrapped in the profoundest slumber*. Nevertheless, roused again to life, he did not ask, when he saw her, Who is she? or, Where did she come from? but says, she is flesh of his flesh and bone of his bones. How, though, did he know this? unless, filled with the Holy Spirit, endowed with the knowledge of God, he so pronounced? In the same manner we, in another life, shall be renewed by Christ; and parents, wives, children and all the rest, we shall know much more perfectly than at that time Adam knew Eve." \*

So much for intermediate unconsciousness as incontestibly an idea of Luther.

4. Now Tyndal; what are we to say of him?

I will transcribe at length.

He is replying to Sir Thomas More. "And ye, in putting them [departed souls] in heaven, hell and purgatory, DESTROY THE ARGUMENTS WHEREWITH CHRIST AND PAUL PROVE THE RESURRECTION.† What God doth with them, that shall we know when we come to them. The true faith putteth the resurrection, which we are warned to look for every hour. The heathen philosophers, denying that, did put that the souls did ever live. And the Pope joineth the spiritual doctrine of Christ and the fleshly doctrine of philosophers together, things so contrary that they cannot agree, no more than the spirit and the flesh do in a Christian man. And, because the fleshly minded

\* *Sleidan*, B. xvi : p. 488.
† The capitals are ours. Let us recollect ; this is William Tyndall.

Pope consenteth unto heathen doctrine, therefore he corrupteth the scripture to stablish it. Moses saith in Deuteronomy, the secret things pertain unto the Lord, and the things that be open pertain unto us, that we may do all that is written in the book. Wherefore, Sir, if we loved the laws of God, and would occupy ourselves to fulfil them, and would, on the other side, be meek and let God alone with his secrets, and suffer him to be wiser than we, we should make none article of the faith of this or that. . . . If the souls be in heaven, tell me why they be not in as good case as the angels be ? And then what cause is there of the resurrection ?" On More objecting,— "What shall he care how long he live in sin that believeth Luther that he shall after this life feel neither good nor evil in body or soul until the day of doom ?" Tyndal answers, " Christ and his apostles taught no other, but warned to look for Christ's coming again every hour ; which coming again, because ye believe will never be, therefore have ye feigned that other merchandise."*

Could I with any wisdom continue the list ? Locke and Dodwell and the Bishop of Carlile and the Archdeacon of Cleveland and Coward and Layton might add more signatures to the opinion, but could they add more influence ? What pious saint could give a weightier judgment in the Bible than its martyred translator ? "The peculiar genius," says Froude, speaking of a later version,—" The peculiar genius, if such a word may be permitted, which breathes through it ; the mingled tenderness and majesty ; the Saxon

* *Tyndall*, p. 327.

## a Relic of Paganism. 173

simplicity; the preternatural grandeur, unequalled, unapproached, in the attempted improvements of modern scholars,—all are here, and bear the impress of one man, William Tyndal. Lying, while engaged in that great office, under the shadow of death, the sword above his head, and ready at any moment to fall, he worked under circumstances alone perhaps truly worthy of the task which was laid upon him: his spirit, as it were, divorced from the world, moved in a purer element than common air. With the reward which at other times as well as those, has been held fitting by human justice for the earth's great ones, he passed away in smoke and flame to rest." \*

He was attacked for his belief; but nothing was wrested from him but this. " I protest before God and our Saviour Christ and all that believe in him, that I hold, of the souls that are departed, as much as may be proved by manifest and open Scripture, and think the souls departed in the faith of Christ and love of the law of God to be in no worse case than the soul of Christ was from the time that he delivered his spirit into the hands of his Father, until the resurrection of his body in glory and immortality. Nevertheless I confess openly, that I am not persuaded that they be already in the full glory that Christ is in, or the elect angels of God are in. Nether is it any article of my faith: for if so it were, I see not but then the preaching of the resurrection of the flesh were a thing in vain. Notwithstanding

---

\* *Hist. of Eng.* (Lon. Ed.) vol. ii : p. 498.

yet I am ready to believe it, if it may be proved from open Scripture."*

We have broken the force of the severest animadversions upon our belief; for the church and the world will not upbraid us so bitterly, if they see men like Tyndal yoked with us in our forth-putting of the intent of revelation; but we have not broken the force of this damaging appeal, viz., that it is to the highest degree incredible that the immense *mass* of catholic belief, within the range of more recent history, should have coined such a thought as that we are immortal, with no foundation in the least but what may have been forged for it in the brain of man.

The bold polemic, too, will make a demand of us. He will say, Explain this prodigy. He will be right. Universal thought demands some origin. That which *semper, ubique, ab omnibus*, has been believed, cannot grow up out of the vapors of the night, but must have had an intellectual source, commensurate with the boldness of its presentations.

What is this source?

Our doctrine, let it be perceived, is the resurrection of the dead. Man, to have fulfilled his duty, should have grasped what he could of that, and held on to the light as it was bestowed, until life and immortality were brought to light in the Redeemer. He fell from this knowledge. Immortality in some shape he could not relinquish. Immortality in ghost and spectre; nay, in just what shape he could dream, after all that was visible was put away in the sepul-

* *Tyndal's Works* (1573), Pref.

## a Relic of Paganism. 175

chre, would be just that shape of the belief that heathen would be apt to have. Resurrection was too unlikely. It was distant; nay, had been but partially revealed. At any rate, it had been lost; and no matter what had been the cause, we may search all the books, and not a trace of it can be found, except a slight syllable or two among the dead in Egypt. What was to be done? Give up our living again? Never. The mind yearns after immortality. The *manes* of ancient Rome, with just the least possible of dress or form; immortality, with scarce any substance; our thought and our feeling busily kept on with but little account of *quo* or *quomodo*,—would be the natural device, and, beyond all doubt, the actual one. The world peopled itself with shadows, and that as the natural scheme, when the doctrine of our rising had faded, or had not yet been revived into view.

But, now, when it *was* preached, what would be natural? When I give a boy an apple! Suppose he has one. His little chubby hand holds it; but I give him a brighter and a better! What is the result? He grasps both. This is the simple history of immortality. Man is a composite animal, made up of different faculties. There is not a trace of revelation that he lives divided. When he dies, the Bible seems to say, He dies. When he lives, it seems to be by rising. And yet that doctrine unquestionably was lost. Refusing to be mortal, he conjures up the idea of spirit. Spreading over the earth, he builds that faith into his monuments. Becoming a writer and a sage, he sings it, and weaves it into his speech. Becoming imbedded in his literature, it is seated in the very heart of man. Christ comes, and brings another resurrection: but the little boy clutches both apples. This is our account of immortality. And let it be remembered,—if it have a shadow of the truth, we are not the rationalists: we are not the novices, greedy for something new: we are not the dotards, grubbing into the past: we are not infidel, determined upon change; but we are just the plain men of the Word of God, restricting ourselves to texts, and showing where a Pagan flood broke in upon the fountain of the Gospel.

Now, that all this is not mere impudence, look at some facts that may be noted:

First, these very testimonies of Tyndal. "The heathen philosophers, denying that, did put that the soul did ever live." And again, "The Pope joineth the spiritual doctrine of Christ and the fleshly doctrine of philosophers together; things so contrary, that they cannot agree, no more than the spirit and the flesh do in a Christian man." And then, "Because the fleshly minded Pope consenteth unto heathen doctrine, therefore he corrupteth the Scripture to establish it."*

Second; worldly men have taken the same view. Let me quote from Macaulay. "At length the darkness begins to break; and the country which had been lost to view as Britain, reappears as England. The conversion of the Saxon colonists to Christianity was the first of a long series of salutary revolutions. It is true that the Church had been deeply corrupted both by that superstition and by

* *Tyndal's Works* (1573), p. 324.

## a Relic of Paganism. 177

that philosophy against which she had long contended, and over which she had at last triumphed. She had given a too easy admission to doctrines borrowed from the ancient schools, and to rites borrowed from the ancient temples. Roman policy and Gothic ignorance, Grecian ingenuity and Syrian asceticism had contributed to deprave her. Yet she retained enough of the sublime theology and benevolent morality of her earlier days, to elevate many intellects, and to purify many hearts." *

Thirdly; as reasoned out by any competent reader of the past, this vivifying of the old life into the new can be plainly exhibited. It was so in sacrifice. The old Astarté lived again on the hills of Benjamin. It was so in ritual. The lustrum bewitched the sacrament. It was so in calendar appointments. The Saturnalia bestrid the feast day.

Nor is it uninteresting that God Himself set certain examples that were perverted. He burrowed into what was Egyptian. "I shall be that I shall be" has been uncovered on the Nile.† He measured temples. The court and sacred places had their patterns over the flood. There is no jealousy of this sort with the Almighty. And when our Saviour came, he borrowed for the Sermon on the Mount. Paul took all he could from what was Greek (Acts xvii: 28). And Christ, in all these ways, has taught the lesson, that nothing is to be despised, and that what God has cleansed, that no man is to call common.

* *Hist. of Eng.* vol. i: p. 5.
† At least, it is said so. We doubt it.

8*

But, then, an imitating world has gone too far.

What a good thing it would be if all the borrowings from Paganism were set down in a chart. The world will learn more of these things. Such men as Aristotle have been teaching from their urns. Such men as Plato have colored the very books of Scripture. And though, blessed be God, they have made these more full, and, for the ages of time, more bold and more useful to the Church, yet no one can read the Evangelist John without seeing, that Plato helped to shape him; that Philo, or his predecessors, helped to choose for him his points; and though all under the influence of the Spirit, yet the Spirit moving the Apostle to resist those frauds that were being imposed by the men who were the expounders of these great philosophies.

Now, what John did not fence off, broke into the Church. It is horrible to see the ravages of Platonism. We are occupied with it yet. And it has furnished so much example of the world dominating over the faith, that I need but mention my plea, which is, that it is the commerce with the past that has made men sink into the rut of the soul's being immortal.

THE END.

II.

# WAS CHRIST IN ADAM?

# PREFACE.

I KNOW of no authority, ancient or modern, for the doctrine I am about to promulgate. I have heard of something of the kind in Vinet: but I have searched his writings, though not, I confess, all of them, and find adverse, rather than favoring, intimations.* It makes one shiver to go on so exposed a road, without any company; but there are certain mitigating circumstances which it is fair to quote.

1. In the first place, this book would not have been so much as thought of, but at the suggestion of the Bible. Philosophy, for the person of Christ, seems vain and impertinent. We cannot employ it even afterward, when our faith has been revealed. We confess nothing of research or venture in this direction. It certainly soothes a timid scruple to know, that, even if this work were a mistake, the promptings to it have been altogether Scriptural; I mean by that, it has been in reading the Bible, that

---

* While going through the press, a friend sends us a volume of Irving. We are not in time thoroughly to study his belief; but find him accenting the peccableness of Christ; speaking of the graciousness of His being kept holy; but not accounting for it by federal descent; and, therefore, receding too much away from it again, when arraigned for it as heresy.

the suggestion has come, of the mistake of the prevailing Christologies. There, too, we invite the debate. We suspect that what is old has been a philosophy; and we offer the new to be settled entirely by revelation.

2. In the second place, we are cheered by great simplicity of the texts.

3. And in the third place, we hope to make this appear. The very newness may be one harbinger of hope. There having been no trial in the church, and no statements opposite recorded in the world,— who knows what may happen? What seems so plain to us, may seem plain, in the same texts, to others. There may be a healing, as the surgeons say, " by the first intention ;" especially, as we reach a much warmer faith; making Christ more our Christ; bringing him a great deal nearer to the curse ; seating him a great deal closer to his people ; and lifting a great deal higher, that righteousness of the cross, by which humanity must obtain redemption.

JNO. MILLER.

PRINCETON, Sept. 5th, 1876.

# CONTENTS.

|   | PAGE |
|---|---|
| INTRODUCTION | 9 |

## I.
REASONS FOR THE OLD DOCTRINE ............... 13

### CHAPTER I.
CHRIST ONE PERSON ................................. 13

### CHAPTER II.
CHRIST BORN OF A VIRGIN .......................... 24

## II.
REASONS FOR THE NEW DOCTRINE .............. 28

### CHAPTER I.
CHRIST AND MAN ..................................... 28

### CHAPTER II.
CHRIST AND WOMAN .................................. 33

### CHAPTER III.
CHRIST AND DEATH ................................... 35

### CHAPTER IV.
CHRIST AND LIFE ..................................... 43

## CHAPTER V.
Christ and the Spirit.................................... 50

## CHAPTER VI.
Christ and Ransom..................................... 56

## CHAPTER VII.
Christ and Justification ............................... 70

## CHAPTER VIII.
Christ and Adoption ................................... 73

## CHAPTER IX.
Christ and Sanctification............................... 76

## CHAPTER X.
Christ and Ordinances ................................. 79

## CHAPTER XI.
Christ and Glorification................................ 83

## CHAPTER XII.
Christ and God ........................................ 86

# III.
CONCLUSION ........................................ 91

# INTRODUCTION.

THE sixteenth question of "The Shorter Catechism" is as follows,—" Did all mankind fall in Adam's first transgression?" The answer is, " The covenant being made with Adam, not only for himself, but for his posterity, all mankind, *descending from him by ordinary generation*, sinned in him, and fell with him, in his first transgression."

It would be hazardous to pause upon the meaning of the doctrine, for it would delay and confuse us. Men have differed about the sense of imputation. Some have thought it natural. Some have thought it federal. All have thought it real: but have been entirely at variance as to the nature of the hereditary result. The writer thinks it both natural and federal, and that it is stated so to be, in the two lists of texts that are quoted by the different polemics. He thinks it natural, like the descent of a bad plant from a bad seed. He thinks it federal, to justify such a descent. He thinks God has arranged the universe so that like produces like, but that, when it comes to moral intelligences, there must be law, as well as nature: there must be the fact of a moral adjudication. It will not do to wave the hand, and say, All perish, by a fiat of nature; but there must be a forensic cause:

that is, the seal of heredity, in the instance of man, must be applied by juridic rule, that God may be just, though he breed hereditary bondsmen out of all mankind.

Not positing, however, the justness of such a view, we give it merely as an example, and fall back to the more universal ground, that *some* effect has been transmitted, of Adam upon man ; and state, now, the universal thought, that that effect has not been a heritage to Christ, or in any way natural to him by blood relationship. He has been thought a new man, foisted in upon our race ; or, if that word is connected with the idea of falsehood,\* then, grafted in upon it, with no hereditary descent, but able to begin, with quite unimplicated nature, to take *our* guilt, and to cut off our hereditary taint, by his own independent sacrifice.

Now, our object is to point out the opposite doctrine as the doctrine of the word of God.

We believe that Jesus Christ was an elected man ; and, with reverence be it spoken, that you or I might have been the chosen one for the incarnation of the Most High. We believe that this is taught laboriously, in plain terms, under both the dispensations. We believe that he was a child of Adam, and an heir to him, like you or me. And, inasmuch as this would have brought him into sin like you or me, we believe that his birth of the virgin, and his conception by the Holy Ghost, was to cut off this taint of nature. He was " holy, harmless, undefiled, SEPARATED † from sin-

\* Fr. *Fausse*.
† " *Separate*" (E. V.). It is the Perfect :—" *that had been separated;*"

ners, and made higher than the heavens" (Heb. vii: 26). We believe, further, that, inasmuch as he could not be cut off from sin, except as the effect of ransom, Daniel and Job and Abraham were saved no otherwise than the humanity of Christ. Daniel and Job were saved retroactively; and so the person of Christ, being made up of God and man—of God, quite unimplicated by guilt,—and of man, quite implicated by it, that is, to the full extent of a descent from Adam,—we believe that the divine nature saved the human; that is, that the glory of the God (Rom. vi : 4) and the obedience of the man (Rom. v : 19) worked an entire emancipation; and that the effect of it was, not simply to save the dead Daniel and all the millions of the saints, but the millions and One; that is, the Head of the Church, and all the millions of his believing brethren.

May I beg that this may not be considered a philosophic venture? It was suggested to me by a singular look of passages of Scripture.

Let my doctrine not be misunderstood. I believe Christ to be very God, and, as such, Jesus, that is God a Saviour. But I believe him also to be very man. And I find him in the Bible, not taking refuge behind his birth of Mary, but standing out as though a dead man had he been left to the flesh (1 Pet. iii: 18), and owing his life, by ten thousand asseverations of the fact (Is. lxiii: 5; Heb. ix: 12), to that ransom from death, when he offered for himself and for the errors of the people.

*i. e.*, not separated after being one of them, but, that, *a parte ante*, had been separated.

Let me be very precise, therefore. Jesus Christ was a child of Adam. Being such, he was guilty, as being in the loins of his fathers ; or, in whatever manner all are guilty before they are born into the world. As such, he was a dead man according to the flesh. As such, he needed a ransom ; and won it, when he broke the bands of death for himself and his people. As such, he must antedate the purchase, like Job or Samuel. As such, he must be perfect, and must be regenerated from the womb ; nay, never regenerated, because never fallen : and as such, therefore, gloriously born ; not needing a father; but wrapped, before the possibilities of sin—before his very conception—in a birth of the Spirit.

Christ, therefore, was of guilty parentage, though only of a woman : he was of a wicked nature by right of descent ; its wickedness, though not its infirmity, being cut off from him by the Holy Ghost : nevertheless he had to keep that holiness, and win it further, by hard trials of temptation : and herein lay his torture : He resisted even unto blood (Heb. xii : 4) : and, being " obedient unto death," (Phil. ii : 8), he was made " perfect through sufferings" (Heb. ii : 10), and obtained, even for himself, " eternal redemption" (Heb. ix : 12).*

---

* " *For us*" (E. V.) is in Italics. Such liberties shonld not be taken.

# I.

# REASONS FOR THE OLD DOCTRINE.

## CHAPTER I.

### CHRIST ONE PERSON.

WE tried the experiment, once, of offering our doctrine of Christ to a distinguished and very judicious theologian. We were curious to see what would be his first impulse of thought in taking up an objection to our idea. We were not long in suspense. His mind seemed to strike at once upon the thought, that the God and man in Christ were one person, and that, therefore, it was impossible to suppose, that one was glorious and divine, and the other under bonds and guilty.

Let us state this in dialectic form.

1. Jesus Christ is God and man. The God in Christ is too unspeakably perfect to unite himself in eternal Sonship with anything guilty or accursed. Such is the first difficulty.

2. Second; Christ has a forensic unity. He is a person in court. The name is above every name; and it must have a distinct personal acceptance, or else it could never serve to stand in the place of a

deceived and accursed people. This is the second obstacle to our thought. If Christ be condemned and accursed himself, the Vicar needs some substitutionary victim; and how can God arrange, himself to save, if, in the very person of his Son, the court holds him as himself amenable?

3. Thirdly; as to mediation. The parties are, the King and the rebel. The theory has always been, that a free substitute steps between. If Christ is guilty, what mediatorship can we conceive? Not his divinity, for that it is that has been offended; and not his humanity, for that is condemned itself. Where is our resting place for thought, if the daysman that comes in, himself requires reconciliation, and a sacrifice to save him?

Now, as to the whole argument, we beg to say, that it has a confession which we will not admit. It holds to a rational appeal. What claim is there that we should be called into such a court? We have stated that, in reason, we have been children; that we did not travel that way; that we were waked up by the inspired oracle; that we were ready with a bundle of texts; and that we were afraid that it would be imagined that we had been seduced by reason, and by the decoy lights of some favorite scheme of heresy.

We had thrown ourselves, therefore, with uncommon care upon the mere dogma of the Book; and, therefore, had gathered up all our part of the discussion upon assorted texts, the bundles of which were to mark the chapters, and give shape to our discussion.

Let me lodge the plea, therefore, that it is the old doctrine that offends by rationalism. So seemed it when this learned friend first struck upon his reply. We propounded to him texts of Scripture. *Our* reasoning was the mere mortar that coupled together the assertions of the text. But his was a rationalistic appeal. To appear in court, there must be a person. To appear effectually, he must be responsible and free. To be One Person with God, he must be worthy of such a seat. And, to be Mediator, he must be his own independent actor in the field, exempt of all personal debt, and entering, as an untrammelled substitute, upon the enfranchisement of his people.

We protest, therefore.

But, premising that, we meet the arguing, destitute as it is of any inspiration.

1. In the first place, who is to decide who the great Jehovah may, or may not, unite with, as One Person? It seems, he does unite with a man; and that man has great infirmities of attribute. He is tempted (Heb. ii : 18). He is weak (Matt. xxvi : 41). He is timid (Matt. xxvi : 39). He is mortal (Heb. ii : 14). He shrinks from the lot that he encounters (Lu. xxii : 42). He is tempted in all respects like as we are, yet without sin (Heb. iv: 15). Moreover He is despicable (Is. xli : 24). He is ignorant (Mar. xiii : 32). He is finite (Jo. v : 19). He grows in wisdom and favor ; and if he is not accursed by heritage and by covenanted oath, it is almost the only weakness that has been debarred by the decree that brought him into being. Now, what exactly is the objection

to the view we take? It will be said, God cannot be incarnated in a sinner. But our view is, Christ was not a sinner. He was kept from being so by his own redemption. In his first embrace of his Godhead he was sanctified, and that perfectly. In fact he never knew taint, because, by the effect of his atonement, he was created sinless, and God never came into unity with a transgressor.

But it will be said, He was guilty; or, with a little difference, he would have heired guilt if he had not been ransomed; nay, he may be counted to have been implicated, till his work had saved him; and it was incompetent for the Great I AM to yoke His person with an heir of Adam.

Well, let us look at that. There is certainly a boldness in it that looks like rationalism. Let us drive it to be precise.

What is it? "The temple of God is holy" (1 Cor. iii: 17). There can be no communion between Christ and Belial (2 Cor. vi: 15). God could not be tempted of evil (Jas. i: 13); and, therefore, he would not have linked his life with that of an apostate who had descent from Adam. But we claim that he was not an apostate; that he was redeemed from apostacy. We claim that he was not sinful, but that he was redeemed. The gist of the objection, therefore, is, that he needed redemption; that, before all time, he was contemplated as guilty; and that, as much as you or I; he had inculpation from Eve, and would have been both sinful and accursed, but for the effect of his own redemption.

Then, let us move still closer.

## Christ One Person.

If guilt is the point, let us know distinctly when and how. He never became personally guilty, for he was enfranchised from it before he was born. But just there, where is the reasoning? Was it that he was by nature guilty? See then how much is arrogated for reason! Here was a man that was born to be accursed. He was decreed to be guilty for the sins of all mankind. Such was the structure of his person. He was conceived of as one to be accursed. And, centuries before he came, he had been levied on, and men had gotten into peace on the faith of the curse to be laid on their Redeemer. He was, therefore, guilty in a most shocking way; for there came crowding upon him, by decree, the sins of all that might be forgiven. Now, that must be a bold intellect that shall attempt to decide,—God may become incarnate with a man who is covered over with guiltiness; but it must be of one sort, and not of another. There is no question of personal guilt as the result of personal transgression, for no one impeaches him of that. But, of the two sorts that remain, God may become incarnate with man, if he sustain superhuman guilt, be it only of the men whom he is to redeem; but God may not become incarnate in man, if he sustain Adam's guilt; that is if he be born of an ungodly line, and must expiate his measure of hereditary inculpation.

Such, then, is our answer. It is not an argument, but a mere unveiling of the facts. If our adversary will admit our exhibition, we appeal from the court, and refuse to be tried. We are going to bring texts of Scripture: and, as to the points *in thesi* in the case, we deny the competency of reason to declare that God may become incarnate with man when he has the guilt of millions, but may not become incarnate with man when impended over by his own guilt, that is, the guilt of the act in which all mankind stood together in a federal relation.

2. And so, disposing of the difficulty that a guilty heir cannot be one person with the Almighty, we advance to the second, which is that a guilty heir cannot be a free sacrifice.

Now, let us inquire into this, with the necessary thoroughness.

A free sacrifice, as a notion to be applied to Christ, must imply a freedom in either of two particulars; first, in its being unincumbered; and second, in its being voluntary; and, in both of these respects, our doctrine would be opposed, as denying the freedom of redemption.

But let us look at both. In the first place, what is meant by being unincumbered? If Christ were a sinner, all parties would agree that he could not atone for sin. But that he should be guilty, all parties agree. In the days of Adam, Abel left upon Him guilt. Christ was not yet born, and yet Heaven had settled that; and Abel was redeemed, solely on the faith that Christ should become guilty. It soberly appears, therefore, that Christ was a guilty man long before he came into the world. It appears that he was federally guilty; and, though all agree that he never was, and never was to be, personally sinful, yet, under one covenant, he certainly was involved, and the only question is, was he so under the other? Under the covenant of grace he was born with millions of guiltinesses. Under the covenant of works, was he an heir of Adam's guilt? To say, He decidedly was not, and to argue it on the plea of a free sacrifice, and to say, He never could have atoned for man, if by nature he was an heir to death, and to appeal to this as of the alphabet of the cross, is beyond all question rationalism; for it pretends to say, Christ could buy me off, if all mankind were upon his shoulder, but not if Adam were; or, to speak more plainly, he could be considered a free sacrifice if encumbered with all the lost, but not free if incumbered for himself; that is, God, who knows no heritage or birth, could give price-availing value to the man with whom he chose to be incarnate, but it must be a price-availing value sufficient only for millions, and not for the one humanity, descended from Adam, which God has chosen to take into union with Himself.

Now, I say, This is rationalism.

And there is a plain victory in store for our side of the case, if we say, Our appeal is solely to Scripture: grant that Christ never sinned, and that he was redeemed, *ab ovo*, from all his guiltiness; and grant that we are successful with our Scriptures; and grant that the Scriptures show that he bought off the whole churchly body; and grant that they expressly teach that he broke the bars of the pit, and let himself out, as well as his disciples,—and we may laugh at the difficulties of the theorist. Grant only that he was born sinless, and that that escape from Adam was purchased, like yours or mine, and no mortal is such a practitioner on high, that he understands the law of the case, and can rule that the God Christ can buy off the millions of the church, but cannot buy off the man Christ, when the God Christ is unincumbered of descent, and is known to be the basis of all the liquidation.

And, in the second place, in respect to what is *voluntary*. It is known that Christ was incumbered long before he was begotten of Mary. God's share in the plan must be that which is chiefly looked upon as unincumbered and voluntary. God *was* free in all time, and yet not free in one particular, viz., free to do wrong; and it would have been wrong not to have embraced the methods of redemption. But, in all juridic views, in which we are now only to speak, God began this scheme long before there was any bond, and before there was any motive but the eternal wisdom which had embedded him in his whole decree. At that ancient time the true ideas emerge. God was voluntary. And God was utterly unincumbered. There was no Adam to implicate guilt. On the side of the Almighty, we get the fullest idea of an unincumbered and free Redeemer. But on the side of man it is different, a little. The *Man* appeared with centuries of steps taken for him, and no questions asked as to his will. The Man was born of the Virgin with a price upon his head. His leave was not asked, but millions of men had been born to life upon his guiltiness. This is not altogether voluntaryism. It *was* voluntary; and the Scripture makes much of that account. But it was voluntary *quo ad hoc*. *God* was in Christ. The eternal voluntaryness reigned, and was accepted in his nature. But it was not voluntary* as it had been in the beginning; for, already, millions had been bargained by it, and implications had been had, that would have made it a sin in the Man if he had not kept up to the bargain of the God.

So then, now, in the other respect. If Christ had his share in Adam, he was where he had been put by the will of the Father. He was no more implicated than by us. If he had to offer, first for his own guilt, and then for the people, it is but to show his shareholding under both covenants. And to say, Reason forbids it, is to uphold the sternest rationalism. Quit of all personal sin, we have carried the Saviour far enough for logic; and then, how he came so, whether by being a *novus homo*, or by being "the first born from the dead," must be a matter of revelation; and he is a bold rationalist who says, There is freedom and chance, if Christ had no guilt from Adam, but no freedom and no chance at all, if he had to be washed from his own guilt, and redeemed by his own ransom from his own share of the curse, and born of the Virgin, to secure retroactively entire quickening.

3. And now, one thing more; as to our Mediator.

\* Christ says, "I lay it down of myself;" but he immediately says, "This commandment have I received of my Father" (Jo. x: 18). The very bloodiest moment of his life he approaches in this way:— 'But that the world may know that I love the Father; and as the Father gave me commandment, even so I do"(Jo. xiv: 31). "For I came down from heaven, not to do mine own will, but the will of him that sent me" (Jo. vi: 38). The sacrifice was voluntary, therefore; but, like the worship of the blest, voluntary, yet commanded.

The argument here is, If Christ be one with Adam, and is himself, *quoad* the earlier covenant, bound for Adam's sin, he is himself of the party of the guilty. And what becomes then of the idea of a go-between? Being himself of Adam, and acting for himself, the idea of an inter-nuncial messenger seems mightily obscured. To all which we reply, by charging again a hardy rationalism. A days-man, in the instance of our race, is a third person. There is a king, and there is a culprit, and there is a third man who lays his hand upon both. Nobody pretends to this in the instance of our Redeemer. Paul specially demurs, and teaches that the whole thing is an imperfect illustration. And the difficulty lies here: God is one party, and man another, but the Mediator is obscured under any theory. The Mediator is also God, and the Mediator is also man; and, even though we were to throw him out as an actual heritor with man, he would still remain " one body" (Rom. xii : 5). He delights to speak of himself as the head with the members. And, therefore, he is really of both parties. He delights to speak of himself as God (our Confession phrases it "very God"), and he delights to speak of himself as man, and, therefore, under any supposable theory, he is not a mediator of any usual kind. And, therefore, the spell of any sharp rationalistic arguing is broken. Paul says, " Now a mediator is not a mediator of one, but God is one" (Gal. iii : 20). And demurring, therefore, to the idea of mediation as actually precise, he leaves us to canvass Scripture. If God is one, and therefore a mediation within his own substance must be of a peculiar kind, and man is one, because, as Christ claims, he is of one body with his people, then to call Christ a Mediator at all, is but an approach to the truth; and to go further, and say, Christ mediates for himself, does not so far increase the difficulty as to make any appreciable difference in the argument as based upon mediation.

We would mark Christ thus:—He is the offended God: he is also the offending man. He is the offended God, as being of the same substance. He is the offending man, as being a federal heir of our apostacy. He is a mediator in but a partial sense: first, as separated from God by his humanity; second, as separated from man by his divinity (a mediatorship, therefore, thus far, rather as compound than as simple); thirdly, from his being unlike man in obedience; fourthly, from his being unlike God in suffering; and fifthly, from his whole sacrificial work. See how this last unifies him. He could not do it as God, from its humiliation. He could not do it as man, from its atoning value: and, nevertheless, he did do it, and thereby stood out from his race. And it is this blended One, thus standing out from our humanity, that became the Mediator; God, on one side, and man, on the other; God, on one side, and, therefore, not a mediator there; and man, on the other, and, therefore, not a mediator there; but a mediator when united into one—a chosen member of our race, in whom the great God was to be incarnate; who was to stand representing all his people; who, though weak, was never to be lost by weakness, but was to be clothed with power; who, though peccable, was never to be allowed to sin, but was to be filled with the Spirit ; and who, though guilty, was never to be born in guilt, but was to be snatched from corruption before his very beginning, and was, in this way, to become mediator—not as God, for there he is one, and not as man, for there he is a party too, but as God and man, in that middle position in court, in which he brings into the case the representation of both natures.

Christ's being one with God, is not irreconcilable, therefore, in its thought, with Christ as being an heir of Adam.

### CHAPTER II.

#### CHRIST BORN OF A VIRGIN.

A READER, who shall have followed us thus far, will very probably throw off, with impatience, the charge of rationalism. Is not ours the old doctrine, he will say? and therefore, he will feel, as I always did, that the Scriptures must be full of it. Where did men get it, he will be ready to exclaim, unless it has been the burden, all the time, of the Christian revelation?

Now, Has it been? That is exactly what we wish to press. If the Scriptures be all full of it, mention fifty—nay, coming down as Abraham did, mention thirty—mention twenty—nay, mention ten—give us *five* simple Scriptures that make it at all to be understood that Christ was not of Adam when he came into the world. The pressure upon the mind of the reader, even though it be a thing altogether negative,

## Christ Born of a Virgin.

must have its effect. Where, in all the Bible, do you find a passage that testifies of a created Christ; of a Christ superinduced upon our line; of a Saviour cut off, by intention, from descent; an imitated man, rather than one hereditarily derived from our accursed ancestors?

There floats in many a mind the single sentence, " A body hast thou prepared me :" but, besides the singular fact that that is not the original; but that the original favors weakness and stupidity and deafness of nature as native to Christ, and reads, " Mine ears hast thou opened ;" in addition to all this,—the sentence, if it were correctly in the Hebrew, would be but a slender base on which to build such a substantial teaching.

In all the Bible, therefore, there remains but one other passage, and that is, The Birth from the Virgin. We had not advanced a page, before, beyond all doubt, every body thought of this imagined testimony to the separateness of the Redeemer.

We are to treat this argument in an after part of our book; but we cannot afford to postpone it. One fact about it now! There are four considerations that make it utterly inadequate to answer its end in the reasoning.

1. In the first place, there is nothing natural to answer to it. A mother's son is just as much a heritor as a father's son. Intellect, virtue, good looks, strength, and stature, are more often inherited, many men think, from the mother, than from the other side. But all that apart. The question was never made practical but once. Beyond all manner

of doubt there is not a farthing of value to the consideration that the man hands down the traits, beyond the thought that it may be done by the woman. So much for nature.

2. Now for Scripture. There is not a line of Scripture that explains the transaction this way.

3. On the contrary, thirdly; we are distinctly taught that Christ was a child of Adam—that he was a child of Abraham—that he was a child of David. His maternal birth was never for a moment federally dwelt upon. On the contrary, as we shall afterward see, the Scripture delights to call him a " Branch"—to speak of his growing up " from beneath" (Zech. vi : 12) ; to speak of his mortal flesh ; to speak of his " being a dead man according to the flesh" (1 Pet. iii : 18); and to talk of him in all those ways which never relax for a moment into any relief by showing what he gained from his mother.

4. Lastly, his miraculous birth is explained. It is necessary, considering him lost.

Reverse all the usual ideas. Consider him guilty. That is ; in the loins of his fathers, and as an heir like us, suppose him to be federally dead. Then suppose him to be elect, and to be chosen, before all time, to be the prophet of his people. Suppose that he is to be God ; that is, that he is to be the temple of God incarnate. Suppose that, on account of this amazing glory, he is a prince, and that what he suffers is as though all suffered, and that, as he obeys, that is sufficient as the obedience of all mankind—I say, His birth of a virgin is necessary to inwrap him with the Spirit : he must be holy, harmless, separated from sinners, and made higher than the heavens—to be all this, he must be redeemed—to be redeemed, his human part must get a share from his expiatory labor —to perform that labor, he must be perfect—to be perfect, he must be sanctified from the womb, nay, he must be perfect in the earliest conception of his being —and to be so, he must be born, not like you or me when we are born again, and not like Jeremiah if he was converted from the womb, but like his own blessed self, born as a "holy thing," in the womb of the Virgin Mary, under the power of the Holy Ghost, that, though inheriting weakness from his mother, he might be cut off from sin by that perfect shrouding of his nature, *ab ovo*, in the grace that sanctifies.

For these reasons we think this noted narrative to be less against us than in our favor, and wish to be distinctly understood ;—Our Christ is a Prophet like us (Deut. xviii: 15); infinitely far from us in his divinity; and infinitely better off than we, in that he was regenerated from the womb ; but perfectly at one with us in his descent from Adam, and liable to all our curse through his mother's guiltiness, were he not bought off by the work which he was yet to finish, through his glorious Godhead.

## II.

## REASONS FOR THE NEW DOCTRINE.

CHAPTER I.

CHRIST AND MAN.

IF Christ were a new creation, and grafted by a second covenant in upon the body of our race, care would not be taken to make all our humanity one, and to make Christ so distinctly as he is made, a part of the aggregate man.

This begins in the very first chapter of the Scriptures. They seem to delight to call men *man*, and to give no separate name to Adam but this name *man* (Adam), the name of all mankind.

Hence it is a puzzling thing to translate, in certain passages. " This is the book of the generations of man (Adam). In the day that God created man (Adam), in the likeness of God made he him. Male and female created he them; and blessed them, and called their name man (Adam), in the day when they were created. And man (Adam) lived an hundred and thirty years, and begat a son in his own likeness, after his image; and called his name Seth: and the days of man (Adam), after he had begotten Seth, were eight hundred years; and he begat sons and daughters. And all the days that man (Adam) lived were nine hundred and thirty years: and he died" (Gen. v: 1–5). Another fragment (if we adopt the idea of many good men, that Moses under divine inspiration selected from among these ancient annals), confirms in the most careful way this desire of unitizing humanity. " God said, Let us make man (Adam). . So God created man (Adam) in his own image, in the image of God created he him; male and female created he them. And God blessed them" *etc.* (Gen. i: 26–28). And again, " The Lord God formed man (Adam) dust of the ground, and breathed into his nostrils the breath of life, and man (Adam) became a living soul" (Gen. ii: 7).

This is one stage.

Now, another.

" Let them have dominion over the fish of the sea, and over the fowl of the air, and over the cattle, and over all the earth, and over every creeping thing that creepeth upon the earth" (Gen. i: 26; see also 28).

David, thousands of years afterward, repeats this, " Thou madest him to have dominion over the works of thy hands: thou hast put all things under his feet" (Ps. viii: 6). And Paul, a thousand afterward, lifts this quite out of the category of a common dominion, and ascribes it to Glorified Man. " For unto the angels hath he not put in subjection the world to come whereof we speak. But one in a certain place testified, saying, What is man, that thou art mindful of him? or the son of man, that thou visitest him? Thou madest him a little lower than the angels: thou crownedst him with glory and honor, and didst set him over the works of thy hands: thou hast put all things in subjection under his feet. For in that he put all in subjection under him, he left nothing that is not put under him. But now we see not yet all things put under him" (Heb. ii: 5-9). Why not? Christ was long since glorified. And Paul states that. "We see Jesus crowned with glory and honor." But see, now, his blessed doctrine! *All* saved humanity is to be crowned. That is the waiting consummation. We are to see the kingly Adam. And as MAN was to "have dominion," we see not yet all things put under *him* (Adam). "But we see Jesus," the Head and Prince and God: *He* is glorified; but not the entire man: the finest attestation we can dream of His being of the one humanity.

And not only so: the Bible is not only careful to make all humanity one, but it shows how. It does not leave us to those realistic follies which make all man sin personally, and by whimsical presence in the Garden of Eden, a conceit so brainless that it stains polemics, but it treats all hereditarily, and manages the unity of man federally, and by the matter of birth. Christ, in this way, holds of Adam all through the word of God. Paul, in his very comment on the Psalm, viz., that man is to have dominion, and that Christ, who now has dominion, is but a part of man, fortifies that conception by words that cannot be mistaken; for he says, "Both he that sanctifieth, and they that are sanctified, are all of one: for which cause he is not ashamed to call them brethren ; saying, I will declare thy name unto my brethren ; in the midst of the church will I sing praise unto thee (Heb. ii : 11, 12). And so of other passages. What we find proved is, that Christ is Adam-born, like Tamar, or like Amon, or like any other in the list of his progenitors. The Bible makes no difference. In settling for us a creed, Paul tells us that He was " born of the seed of David according to the flesh' (Rom. i: 3). Antioch is to receive him as "this man's seed," viz., David's (Acts xiii : 23). Isaiah discourses upon him as " out of the stem of Jesse" (Is. xi : 1); nay, as " a root out of a dry ground" (Is. liii : 2). Zechariah makes him " grow up from beneath" (Zech. vi : 12). And Moses (Deut. xviii : 15), quoted afterward by Peter (Acts iii: 22), gives it with almost startling plainness. It justifies the speech that Christ was elected (Is. xlii : 1), and anointed (Is. lxi : 1), and set up (Ps. ii : 6), and ordained (Acts xvii : 31), like Saul or David out of the multitudes of Israel. For listen to the language, " Jehovah thy God will raise up unto thee a Prophet from the midst of thee, of thy brethren, like unto me."

Boldness seems the last thing that the men of inspiration seem inclined to fear. Isaiah calls him an abomination (Is. xli: 24). He says, He made dust his sword, and driven stubble his bow (Is. xli: 2); meaning by that, that the human part of Christ, except through Him that raised up the righteous man, was like what Zechariah calls him, " a brand plucked out of the fire" (Zech. iii : 2). Hosea says, " I called my son out of Egypt" (Hos. xi: 1). And now, dwelling upon this, there can be no doubt that this is the whole gospel mystery. Matthew studs his chapters with these pregnant quotations from the prophets. "That it might be fulfilled," he says—(and surely he would not load his verse with mere puerile allusion): "He came and dwelt," he says, "in a city called Nazareth: that it might be fulfilled which was spoken by the prophets, He shall be called a Nazarene" (Matt. ii: 23). Now, what are we to understand? Nothing trifling, beyond all manner of doubt. What are we to understand by the fifteenth verse, "that it might be fulfilled which was spoken of the Lord by the prophet, saying, Out of Egypt have I called my son" (Matt. ii: 15). The thing to be understood is, that Christ was an "abomination" (Is. xli: 24); that he was "stubble;" that he was "dust" (Is. xli: 2), in his vile heredity: that he was a brand plucked from the burning as to his claim by birth; and that was what Matthew was seizing upon in the historic allegory. He came out of Egypt, just as all the rest of us come out of the iron furnace. And he was called from Nazareth, not only because Nazareth was an "abomination," but because Christ was the "Branch"* (Is. liii; 2; see Zech. iii: 8; vi: 12), fairly and actually derived from our dead humanity.

We would like to quote other passages. "Agur," an allegorical personage, is himself Christ's humanity;† and he wonders at his own relief,—"Because I am more brutish than a man of the better sort,

* Heb. *Nezer*—a branch.
† See the author's Commentary on Proverbs, pp. 506–509.

and have not the discernment even of a common man, and have not learned wisdom, and yet have the knowledge of holy things : who hath ascended up to heaven and come down " *etc.*, *i. e.*, who has ennobled such a humanity? (see the whole passage), the idea being that the man Christ, by any race-heredity, and by any tie of flesh, is literally "an abomination," and that this would have come out save for the intervention of the Most High ; but that from the emigrants out of the iron furnace there was to be raised up one who was to be chosen before all time ; who was to be lifted out of the miry pit ; who was to be known before he was in the womb ; who was to be sanctified before he came forth (Jer. i : 5) ; and who was to be so tabernacled in by God, as to become God himself; and who was therefore to be worshipped and adored, though but the worm Jacob (Is. xli : 14), and though effecting his triumphs on paths that he could not tread with his feet* (Is. xli : 2).

## CHAPTER II.

### CHRIST AND WOMAN.

OF course, if Joseph were the father, no difficulty would occur in Christ as the inheritor of Adam : but, as Mary was the mother, it still remains to prove that that makes the slenderest difference as to a true connection with our humanity.

* This is a peculiar expression, and means that Christ was so verily man that, like the man Elijah, or the man Paul, he could not follow the omnipotence, and actually feel it, and wield it, and tread in the path of it, in his mere humanity. His humanity did not raise the dead ; but only his Deity as his humanity willed it.

Notice this,—Woman herself is introduced to us in a careful presentation. She is not brought from a distance, as Christ is supposed to be, but she is bred of Adam. " This is now bone of my bones" (Gen. ii: 23), says our old progenitor. And the Bible seems careful to declare that " she was taken out of man" (ib.). Her very name in Hebrew (*isha*) betokens that (ib.); and the passage seems to delight to declare that the man and wife are " one flesh" (v. 24).

Now Targums are not more fabled and traditionary than our glosses of the text. I have searched everywhere. Men are called seed of man (Gen. xvii: 7) and seed of woman (Gen. iii: 15); and I can trace no difference. Eve seems to have imagined Cain to be the Messiah; and announces him,—" I have gotten possession of the man Jehovah" (Gen. iv: 1). If she had been taught that much, why had she not been taught that in an ordinary birth it was impossible? Tamar! was her blood less contaminating than that of Obed? And Rahab! and Bathsheba! It has often been remarked that Christ was brought nearer to man by the turpitude in some of his mothers. Has all that been folly? And, if so, why? Mary brought to the temple a sacrifice upon the birth of her child. And if " the days of her purification" (Lu. ii: 22) were for herself, why does the word " THEIR purification" linger about the old manuscript? and why, at any rate, in this particular instance *have* a sacrifice, if immaculate purity, even to the extent of their being no heredity from Adam, was to be the conception of the birth?

## Christ and Death.

Why, moreover, had Christ to pay a ransom as the first born?

### CHAPTER III.

#### Christ and Death.

IF Christ, though woman-born, was an heir of Adam, and, as Peter expresses it, of the fruit of the loins of David (Acts ii : 30), he is brought squarely under the curse, " In the day thou eatest thereof thou shalt surely die." But our attention was first excited by passages far more express than this. And what we wish to notice is the exceeding daintiness with which the inspired writers pick out their words. The subject is, of course, a delicate one. Christ never sinned. And should I select the title, " Christ Lost in Adam," my language would not be as happy as that which corresponds to it in the living word. When Paul says, " In Adam all die" (1 Cor. xv : 22), see how expert he is. He does not make his statement in the past tense, but with singular deftness tells us this,— that, ages after Adam (using the present tense), men who were in no sense in the garden, now " die," temporally and eternally, in consequence of his sin ; or, as it is tersely expressed, " in Adam." With like skill are those wonderful passages that I am about to quote. When I say, " Christ Lost in Adam," I instantly have to define. He is not lost, in many important particulars. He was never lost. I mean by that, Christ as God was never lost at all. And Christ as man, when he actually came into being, was already saved. He never saw corruption. *I* was never lost. That is, if I belong to Christ, I was covenanted for from eternity; and twenty centuries ago I was paid for: so that I could never have perished. But Christ was saved in a far more efficient sense. He never sinned. He never tasted actual apostacy. And, therefore if I were to call my book, "Christ Dead in Adam," I should have to show that he never died actually; it would have to be, that he inherited death; nay, that he actually incurred death, as one, by the earlier covenant, with the offending Adam; that he actually feared death, (Heb. v : 7), as we shall most particularly show; that he actually felt death, in an enervated conscience (Mar. xiv : 38; Heb. v : 2), and in the power of a supreme temptation; but that he never succumbed to death, simply because he was redeemed; the Holy Ghost meeting him in the very womb of his mother, and overshadowing him at the very first, and saying to death, "O Death, I will be thy plague," that death having the rights by heritage, and rights that would have been enforced, were it not for the identical ransom which expelled it in the children of his people.

Now, if there are sentences that come out that tell all this, and tell it in the most emphatic way, I beg you to notice how aptly they will tell it, and how the texts I quote tell it at the very first blow; how they frame it in a final shape; and though they provoke you to exclaim, How very strong they are! yet there is no room for wavering. I need not say, They are true in that sense, but not true in the other. But they have all that digested at the first. They have all said at a stroke, without the need of returning limitations.

## Christ and Death.

For example Peter says, "Being put to death in the flesh" (1 Pet. iii: 18).

Now, in our haziness, we shroud this under a trivial translation. We make it refer to the cross. Nobody dreams that this does not mean "put to death," at all.

The verb (*thanatoö*) occurs eleven times in the Greek. It never means slain, or killed, but always, "delivered to death," or "made as good as dead." Paul says, "For thy sake are we killed all the day long" (Rom. viii: 36). Three of the cases refer to religious persecution (Matt. x: 21; Mar. xiii: 12; Lu. xxi: 16); three others to the counsel of the scribes (Matt. xxvi: 59; xxvii: 1; Mar. xiv: 55); each of the six meaning to "cause to be put to death." Of the three that remain, one is the passage, "dead to the law" (Rom. vii: 4); another the expression, "chastened and not killed" (2 Cor. vi: 9); meaning "not delivered over to death:" and the only remaining one is that in Romans: let me read the whole of it;—"If ye through the Spirit do mortify the deeds of the body" (Rom. viii: 13); meaning, if ye give them over to die. This now is the skill I speak of. The apostle Peter does not say, Christ was dead; but he says, "Being made a dead man, or as good as dead." This is the exact limit of the purport of my book. Being made a lost man by the flesh, but quickened by the Spirit; which may be stated thus—dead federally, but never allowed to see death,—graciously redeemed in the womb of the Virgin Mary, and born of her, yet without sin: or, returning to the apostolic language,—"A dead man by the flesh, but quickened by the Spirit:' by which Spirit, we go on to hear, he was not only quickened, but went forth to quicken others. He went into this great "prison" house of earth, and preached to its dead spirits (1 Pet. iv: 6); not always as man, for he was not man always; but to spirits "who at any time (*pote*) were disobedient, when once the long suffering of God has waited in days of Noah," that is, in days like those of Noah, "an ark being a preparing." We are carried too far, however. A glance must be enough for the context.* Returning to the eighteenth verse, we will confirm it by another from the Apostle Paul. But before we do that, let us restate its meaning. It means that Christ was as good as dead according to the flesh; for that an old man would have been born within him by his fleshly nature, and that he would have fallen into sin; but that he was made alive, as a new man, by the work of the Spirit; and that the new man utterly destroyed the old; not its infirmities (Heb. v: 2); not, at all, its peccableness (Heb. v: 7); not, least of all, its tempted nature (Matt. iv: 1); but its actual sinfulness; not as in his glorified state, but by the naked power and overbalancing mastery of the Holy Ghost. This is Peter's testimony.

Now for another apostle.

When Christ was set up from eternity, he was decreed as the head of the universe (Ps. 2). "For him were all things created" (Col. i: 16). He was not created first, but created centrally. All things

\* See this whole passage discussed in the Monograph, "Are Souls Immortal?" III. Chap. V.

were created around him; that is, as Paul expresses it, "By him all things consist" (E. V. Col. i : 17). When, therefore, not as God, but as man, he was born into the world, he was "the first born of every creature" (Col. i : 15). How? Not temporally. The morning stars had sung together for millions of ages. Then how was he the first born? Why, logically : in that every thing else was begotten in the very first idea of him. The universe, as a whole, was decreed when Christ was decreed. "For by him ;" and, as far as this alludes to the human nature, we must take the copulative meaning of *dia*, as where John says, This is he that came by water and blood: therefore, making this change, and applying it to the man, let us begin again,—" For with him, or by means of him, as the unifying ideal, were all things created, that are in heaven, and that are in earth, visible and invisible, whether they be thrones or dominions or principalities or powers; all things were created with him and for him; and he is before all things; and in him all things stood together" (Col. i : 16, 17).

Now, using this apt context as a fine setting for the clause which is to be our second in the way of proof, let us bring in that clause at once. It is in the bosom of the next verse. It reads, " The first-born from the dead." Now, how is he the first born? John repeats the sentence—" The first begotten of the dead" (E. V., Rev. i : 5). The Greek is the same. Had not Lazarus been raised from the dead? How singularly we lose Scriptures by trivial interpretations! Who would look at these pregnant utterances, and say, they were thoroughly satisfied by the idea that, in the order of time, Christ was the first to break the bands of the grave? But if not, then where are our ideas carried? Precisely where Peter's were (1 Pet. 3: 18). Christ, before all time, was decreed in Adam. When time began he " fell with" Adam ; at least if that be a proper phrase in our " Confession" to apply to all mankind. Through the flight of ages, till he came, he lay with Adam ; and when he came, he was heir of Adam. As heir he would have been cursed in Adam, but for being redeemed. Though redeemed he *was* cursed in Adam, by being born infirm (Heb. v : 2). He was "begotten from the dead," just as you have been, or I have been, by the Holy Ghost. And he was the " first begotten"; not that he was regenerated before Job, or before Abel, or Abraham ; but that, as cause, he must be logically first ; that is, the new birth of Abel must be granted on account of the new birth of Christ ; and the new birth of Christ, though four thousand years after, must precede in court, that is in the plan and concession of the verdict, the new birth of Abel, because the new birth of Christ was necessary to that absolute obedience without which he could not have won the new birth of all his people.

We speak of new birth, but it must be with unspeakable distinctions. The new birth of Christ was not like yours or mine. It had no old birth behind it. He was never born at all, till he was born sinless. He never saw corruption. He was born infirm and tempted, but he resisted perfectly, as our new birth resists only partially. He was born Emmanuel ; and

## Christ and Death.   41

the presence of the Godhead curbed by main strength the forces of iniquity. It was done with human struggle, like ours or yours. But while we succeed partially in this prison-house of clay, he succeeded perfectly; though in terrible torment. And his birth into this fierce battle in which he lost never a field, was his begetting; and it was as " First Begotten," because it had to come first to him in the order of logic as the means and the purchase of the begetting of his people.

Of a piece with these views are many expressions in the prophets. He is called " elect" (Is. xlii: 1). Elect from among whom? He is called a " Branch" (Zech. iii : 8). A branch from whom? He is called an " abomination" (Is. xli: 24). An abomination why? And then, in broader terms, he is called " a rod out of the stem of Jesse" (Is. xi: 1) and " a root out of a dry ground" (Is liii: 2). He is said to " grow up from beneath" (Zech. vi: 12; see the Heb.) There is the command, " Write in it with a pen,—*Enosh* (that is, the sick, the mortal, the incurable one : it is the lowest name for man) shall hasten the spoil, and hurry the prey" (Is. viii: 1). He says himself, The Lord hath formed me from the womb (Is. xlix: 5): The Lord God hath opened mine ear (1: 5). We count this passage in Isaiah as throughout a testimony to our poor sin-visited Redeemer.

Of a like character is much in the Psalms of David. " I will praise thee, for thou hast heard me, and art become my salvation" (Ps. cxviii: 21). " The sorrows of death compassed me, and the pains of hell gat hold upon me: I found trouble and sorrow. Then called I upon the name of the Lord: O Lord, I beseech thee, deliver my soul" (Ps. cxvi: 3, 4). "Thou hast delivered my soul from death, mine eyes from tears, and my feet from falling" (ib. v. 8). "Thou hast delivered my soul from the lowest hell" (Ps. lxxxvi: 13). When it begins to speak of "iniquities" and "sins" and "transgressions," the translators shrink away at once: but when we remember that the Bible uses the word "sin" oftentimes for being treated as a sinner, we are driven from none of the Messianic passages. And yet we are not driven quite over to the idea of mere atoning guiltiness. Judah said, "If I bring him not unto thee, then I have sinned against thee forever" (Gen. xliii: 9; see also 1 Ki. i: 21). So that when David said, "Heal my soul, for I have sinned against thee" (Ps. xli: 4); or when he says, "Mine iniquities are gone over mine head; as an heavy burden they are too heavy for me" (Ps. xxxviii: 4); or when he says, "there is no soundness in my flesh, because of thine anger; neither is there any rest in my bones, because of my sin" (ib. v. 3),—we are not to be driven to dislocate the Psalms, and to separate Messianic and un-Messianic parts of the same brief poem; nor on the other hand are we to think of a mere vicarious guiltiness; but we are to think of the guilt, *i. e.*, in Oriental phrase, the sin, that lies closer than a mere assumption; the guilt that would have been inherited from Adam; the sin that lay menacing from the first moment of birth; the guilt that was of Christ himself, except as kept off by sacrifice; and the sin that lay natural to the heart, and was kept couching for its prey, and would have burst in upon Christ, were it not for the supernatural work of the directly purchased, because graciously imparted, agency, that had been promised, of the Holy Ghost.

Now we are going on to other chapters. But let it be here distinctly intimated,—All the other chapters will be proofs of this one. For example, we are to show in the next (Chap. IV.) that Christ was quickened, and that that quickening was often spoken of under the phrase, "resurrection from the dead"; in the next, that he was quickened by the Spirit (Chap. V.); in the next, that he was ransomed (Chap. VI.); then, that he was justified (Chap. VII.), adopted (Chap. VIII.), and sanctified (Chap. IX.); then, that he was the subject of humiliating ordinances, baptism and circumcision (Chap. X.); then, that he was glorified (Chap. XI.); then, *how* he was Jehovah (Chap. XII.); in all which chapters one truth will appear, viz., that he was lost in Adam; the influence of each being to cut off the possibility of mistake, and to show, in his justification and sanctification, *how* he was lost, and how the death of which I have been speaking, though it never occurred, was kept from occurring, simply as our perdition is, by a divine atonement.

CHAPTER IV.

CHRIST AND LIFE.

PAUL, in the second chapter of the Epistle to the Ephesians, tells those Ephesian Christians that they were "quickened together with Christ." There is no flinching from the expression. Let us quote it fully. "God, who is rich in mercy, for his great love wherewith he loved us, even when we were dead in sins, hath quickened us together with Christ (by grace ye are saved); and hath raised us up together" (Eph. ii : 4-6). The phrase is direct: "hath co-quickened us": and lest any one should say, "hath co-quickened us *by* Christ," Paul repeats the sentence in the Epistle to the Colossians, and there prevents such a use of the dative by the actual preposition (*sun*). Let me quote here that also,—" Buried with him in baptism ; wherein also ye are co-risen, through the faith of the operation of God, who hath raised him from the dead. And you, being dead in your sins, and the uncircumcision of your flesh, HATH HE QUICKENED TOGETHER WITH HIM, having forgiven you all trespasses" (Col. iii : 12, 13).

I beg you to notice how your mind, clinging to old thoughts, puts some gloss upon the passage, that will parry its more natural consequence. " Hath quickened us together with Christ." Of course our quickening, and Christ's quickening, must be, at various points, different ; because Christ's death, and our death, are different. Christ's death was never reached. He never died spiritually. But hence is best explained this quickening. He was quickened from the very womb. We are quickened not till we are converted. We are quickened only in part. We are quickened chiefly at the resurrection. We are born dead. But Christ was born fully into life ; and, therefore, we must mark a great difference there between him and his people. And yet he was born from the dead (*ek nekrôn*). And he was born in view of a ransom. And he was born of the Holy Spirit. He would have been dead by the flesh, but he was "quickened by the Spirit" (1 Pet. iii: 18). He was like his people, therefore, in many respects; but he differed in these two,—first, he was born perfect, and born without any interval of sin; and, second, he was saved by himself. We are quickened together with Christ, but we are quickened by a purchased Spirit; and the difference between that quickening and his, is that he bought for both of us. His glorious Deity was the foundation of a price which his hard-wrought obedience paid down " for himself and for the errors of the people."

Let us pursue this subject further. "God also hath highly exalted him, and given him a name which is above every name, that at the name of Jesus every knee should bow, of things in heaven and things in earth and things under the earth" (Phil. ii: 9, 10). And, yet, he delights to throw himself with his people. Nicodemus says to him, "We know that thou art a teacher come from God" (Jo. iii: 2). He immediately replies, " If ANY MAN be not begotten from above, he cannot see the kingdom of God" (v. 3). The forms of such teaching are endless. "The first born from the dead": that we have already noticed. And Paul repeats the idea; taking it away from the thought of the resurrection altogether, where he says, " That he might be the first born among many brethren" (Rom. viii: 29).

Moreover, in respect to the resurrection; are we not quite at fault in making that the mere resurrection of the body? Notice certain passages. "I am the resurrection and the life" (Jo. xi: 25). Does that mean the merely fleshly resurrection? Again, "And preached through Jesus the resurrection from the dead" (Acts iv: 2). This form of summing up occurs continually. " For which hope's sake, King Agrippa" (Acts xxvi: 7);—and when we come to understand the apostle's " hope," it is, " that there shall be a resurrection of the dead." " That I may know the power of his resurrection" (Phil. iii: 10). " Even baptism doth now save us, by the resurrection of Jesus Christ" (1 Pet. iii: 21). Again, "His Son whom he raised from the dead" (1 Thess. i: 10). Again, " Remember that Jesus Christ was raised from the dead according to my gospel" (2 Tim. ii: 8). Again. " Determined (*marg.*) to be the Son of God by the resurrection from the dead" (Rom. i: 4).

Now I say, Lazarus's resurrection, or Eutychus's, or Jairus's daughter's, or the Shunamite's son's, are no more the boundary of these resurrections which are the " hope" (Acts xxvi: 7) of the saints, than the grave is the boundary of the dominion of wickedness.

Yet if they are not, what do they refer to in Christ?

All men have noticed this; some with more wakefulness than others. And yet it has not dislodged the indolent impression, that Christ's resurrection was merely from the grave; yet every body agrees that there is a strange insisting upon this, considering the other events more central in his history.

Now, we believe that Christ's resurrection often

means his resurrection from his death in Adam. "If ye then be risen with Christ" (Col. iii : 1). Does that mean from the grave? Let us quote many passages. "God hath fulfilled the same, in that he hath raised up Jesus again" (Acts xiii : 33). Does that mean corporeally? No: for it immediately adds, "This day have I begotten thee." Some, therefore, have thought that the begetting of Emmanuel was at his resurrection (Sanctius, Camero., Cor. à Lapide; see also Poli Syn.). Why not rather that his resurrection was at his begetting? Our doctrine is, that Jesus was raised from the dead in the womb of the Virgin Mary. That is, that he descended to her lineally apostate, and that he was born of her, not wicked, because he was saved, and not guilty, because he was redeemed, and that that was his *anastasis*, and that all the other facts of it, viz., his bursting from the grave, and his *anastasis* into glory, are all a part of what, in many passages, are regarded as his rising from the dead (*ek nekrôn*).

And here let me say, that Christ's bursting from the grave is more than we usually make of it. He was born *enosh* (Is. viii : 1), that is, a mortal ; and that means more than a mere sick body : it means a sick mind. Sin belonged to him by certain tendencies of his nature ; and he was held up from sinning by the sheer power of the Holy Ghost. Hence his temptation. Hear his account in the Garden : " The Spirit truly is willing, but the flesh is weak" (Matt. xxvi : 41). When, therefore, he died upon the cross, he shut his eye to the great period of death, and finished it ; and did so in a great acme of tempted agony. That is the meaning, in my belief, of his cry, *Lama sabacthani?* God *did* leave him, till he was pushed nigh to sin. And this is the meaning of those strong words of revelation, "With strong crying and tears to him that was able to save him from death" (Heb. v : 7). Paul alludes to it, " Ye have not yet resisted unto blood, striving against sin" (Heb. xii : 4). And, therefore, the bursting of the grave was a new epoch. His soul came out to a relief. And, therefore, the resurrection often touches this part of the *anastasis ;* and even the mouldering of the body becomes a symbol of the apostacy that Christ escaped.

Hence it is that even the *grave*-deliverance is so much insisted on. " Thou wilt not leave my soul in hades ; neither wilt thou suffer thy holy one to see corruption." This is constantly repeated (Ps. xvi : 10, Acts ii : 27 ; xiii : 35). It is insisted on in cases where the theme is spiritual (Acts xiii : 34). It is illustrated by the case of David (Acts xiii : 36). And his silent sleeping, which Paul announces as still subsisting at Jerusalem, is made to glorify the difference of a perfected and ascended Emmanuel (v. 37).

Some of these passages we must husband. And yet we may be too fearful of a necessary and sufficiently important repetition. Why should we not quote often where there are different lights ? Notice this,—" Now the God of peace that brought again from the dead (*anagagôn ek nekrôn*) our Lord Jesus, THROUGH THE BLOOD OF THE EVERLASTING COVENANT" (Heb. xiii : 20),—our exact doctrine. Again, " Buried with him by baptism into death ; that, like

## Christ and Life.

as Christ was raised up from the dead (*ek nekrôn*) BY THE GLORY OF THE FATHER, even so we also should walk in newness of life" (Rom. vi : 4). " Raised from the dead"—How? Why, to " walk" differently from the way he would have walked if he had been given up to death. That is the very weight of the passage. Further ; " That I may know him, and the power of his resurrection." What power was there in his resurrection ? If he beat back *death*, I can see that his perfect obedience and his entire sanctification would have great power in it. But what power was there in Lazarus' walking out of the grave ? But notice further ;—" That I may know him, and the power of his resurrection, and the fellowship of his sufferings, being made conformable unto his death" ; and now, strongest of all, the *object* of this wonderful "power,"—" if by any means *I* might attain to the resurrection of the dead" (Phil. iii : 10, 11). Does that mean the mere resurrection of the body ? Why, all will have that. Now, notice again,—" That he should be the first to rise from the dead" (Acts xxvi : 23). " The eyes of your understanding being enlightened ; that ye may know what is the hope of his calling, and what the riches of the glory of his inheritance in the saints, and what is the exceeding greatness of his power to us-ward who believe, ACCORDING TO THE WORKING OF HIS MIGHTY POWER " (that is, not like it, but " according to" it), " which he wrought in Christ when " —What? when he revivified his dust ? Oh surely no ! " Which he wrought in Christ when he raised him from the dead" (Eph. i ; 18–20), that is " enlightened" his " understanding" and lifted his nature, and raised him, as, more slowly, he raises *us*, from the grave of sin, and from the ruin of a spiritual apostacy. Look further; "If we believe on him that raised up Jesus our Lord from the dead; who was delivered for our offences, and was raised again FOR OUR JUSTIFICATION" (Rom. iv: 24, 25).

Now, we do not deny that some raisings of Christ refer to the tomb (1 Cor. xv: 4); and that some are of a mixed character, strongly colored by the language of the sepulchre (1 Cor. vi: 14; Eph. i: 20). But we do deny that some refer to the tomb at all (Acts iii: 26; Rom. vi: 4; Eph. ii: 6); and we do aver that the main *anastasis* of Christ, which is the great hinge-point of all the Testament, is his *anastasis* from death, viz., that spiritual death, which he inherited, like you or me, from his first parents.

This will shock us less as we proceed in the investigation.

## CHAPTER V.

### CHRIST AND THE SPIRIT.

IF the *anastasis* of Christ mean often his entire quickening, then it is interesting to see who the agent is; for it brings him nearer to us, to find that the agent to save, is the same blessed Spirit that changes the heart of all his people.

We might suppose it would be his Deity. And so it is indeed. But we would suppose it would be expressed that way; that is, God being incarnate, we would suppose that He would enter into the man, and that we would hear no more of death or weakness. But how infinitely far it is from that! God enters Emmanuel with much of the same language with which he enters his people. Indeed, the very account of his begetting is all of that character. "The Holy Ghost shall come upon thee, and the power of the Highest shall overshadow thee; therefore also that holy thing which shall be born of thee shall be called the Son of God" (Lu. i: 35) We may throw, therefore, all the great processes in the life of our Saviour into one, and consider them together; first, his begetting; second, his anointing; third, his raising from the dead. And we may consider the agent the same. It was indeed his Deity. But the Bible delights to talk of it as the same agency that is in us; and, therefore, God, and the Father, and the Spirit, are all talked of as saving Christ; that is, as raising him from the dead.

1. In the first place, "God." Let me quote several passages. "We also are weak with him, but we shall live with him by the power of God" (2 Cor. xiii: 4). Listen in Jeremiah,—"Before I formed thee in the belly I knew thee; and before thou camest forth out of the womb I sanctified thee; and I ordained thee a prophet unto the nation" (Jer. i: 5). Isaiah; —" The Lord hath called me from the womb; from the bowels of my mother hath he made mention of my name" (Is. xlix: 1). He hath "formed me from the womb to be his servant" (v. 5). " In an acceptable time have I heard thee; and in a day of salvation have I helped thee" (v. 8). This is his beget-

ting (Rev. i: 5); his anointing (Is. lxi: 1); his rising from the dead (Rom. i: 4); his perfect sanctification (Heb. vii: 26). David uses all this language. "Thou art my son," God is represented as saying; "this day have I begotten thee" (Ps. ii: 7). "Mine ears hast thou bored," says another Psalm (Ps. xl: 6). One was just as much in the village of Nazareth as the other. And Isaiah repeats the language, "The Lord God hath opened my ear, and I was not rebellious" (Is. l: 5); the boring of the ear being just as much effectual calling, as the opening of *our* ears; and Christ seems to think it when he says, "Say ye of him whom the Father hath sanctified and sent into the world, thou blasphemest, because I said I am the son of God?" (Jo. x: 36).

And under the term, resurrection:—"Wherein also ye are risen with him, through the faith of the operation of God, who hath raised him from the dead" (Col. ii: 12). "Him that raised up Jesus" (Ro. iv: 24). "Believe in thine heart that God hath raised him from the dead" (Ro. x: 6). "He that raised up the Lord Jesus" (2 Cor. iv: 14). "Which he wrought in Christ when he raised him from the dead" (Eph. i: 20). This is soul-raising as of the regenerate sinner. For it is impossible to array these *anastasis* passages, and say, They mean the body. And if they transcend the body, then they mean the soul. And if they mean the soul, then they mean more than the soul at the last day. And if they mean more than at the last day, then they mean spiritual life. And if they refer to spiritual life, then it is a resurrection from spiritual death. And if it is so with man, then it is so with Christ. "We are quickened together with him" (Col. ii: 13). And if it is so with Christ, then the passages are complete which show that it is by the same agent. Christ, though Incarnate God, yet, as man, was "as good as dead" (1 Peter iii: 18), and the agent to save him was the same blessed God that quickens into life the grace of the meanest of his people.

2. Second, the "Father." There is no scruple that must always speak of "the Spirit." Christ says boldly, "I live by the Father" (Jo. vi: 57). Paul speaks of conversion as being *sealed*. "Who hath sealed us, and given the earnest of the Spirit" (2 Cor. i: 22). We are to have a *hegira* from one world to another, and the package is "sealed," so to speak, that our title may survive the journey. "Ye were sealed with that Holy Spirit of promise" (Eph. i: 13). "Grieve not the holy Spirit of God, whereby ye are sealed unto the day of redemption" (Eph. iv: 30). Neglecting to speak of the Spirit, and announcing the agent as his "Father," Christ not only speaks, by the Apostle, of "God the Father, who raised him from the dead" (Gal. i: 1); and not only says that the Father hath sanctified him, and sent him into the world (Jo. x: 36),—but he fixes upon this thought of *sealing*. He says we may count on him for eternal life, because he is to be "sealed," and sent across the ages:—"Labor not for the meat which perisheth, but for that meat which endureth unto everlasting life, which the Son of man shall give unto you; for him hath God the Father sealed" (Jo. vi: 27).

3. Thirdly, "the Holy Ghost." And, under the name of this agency, the Bible seems to delight to include Christ under the soteriology of his people. He is sanctified by the Spirit (Acts x: 38). He is quickened by the Spirit (Eph. ii: 5). He is raised again by the Spirit (Rom. viii: 11). He speaks by the Spirit; "for God giveth not the Spirit by measure unto him" (Jo. iii: 34). So, he lives by the Spirit (1 Pet. iii: 18); and is "justified in the Spirit" (1 Tim. iii: 16); and is "born of the Holy Ghost" (Lu. i: 35). There seems to be no point of mercy by the Spirit in which he does not claim a brother's share, though our Incarnate Redeemer.

And, therefore, we may multiply instances to almost any extent;—"The Spirit of the Lord God is upon me, because the Lord hath anointed me" (Is. lxi: 1). "I have put my Spirit upon him" (Is. xlii: 1). "The Spirit of the Lord shall rest upon him" (Is. xi: 2). And even the higher notions of Messiahship, and of being divinely begotten, and of spectacular adoption, as where the Spirit descends in the likeness of a dove, and abides upon him,—all this, the divine inspiration seems to take pains to associate with the history of his people.

Is he begotten? So are we: and he takes pains to tell an inquirer that, just at the first blush of his adoration. "We know that thou art a teacher come from God." Aye, but said the blessed Redeemer, If *any man*, verily I say unto you, is not begotten from above, he cannot see the Kingdom of God (Jo. iii: 3). And so Christ, or, in the Hebrew language, the Messiah, is not a name so separated from us that we do not borrow it. We also are *Christ*, *i. e.*, "anointed" (2 Cor. i : 21); and the very same word, kept from us as no ineffable speech, is applied to us again and again, and in the same sense of sanctifying (1 Jo. ii : 27), in both the Testaments (Ps. cv : 15). The scene at the baptism (Matt. iii : 16) is not to be made peculiar (Acts ii : 3); and though the Divine Son as God, is utterly out of our vision (1 Tim. i : 17); and though the Divine Son as man, because he is God, is lifted far above principality and power (Eph. i : 21); and though we are to worship him, and to trust our souls to him, and to recognize him as altogether above us, both now and at all times, yet as man distinctly in his own nature, born of Adam, and heiring from him eternal death, we never shall be simple till we get down to the literalness of his actual curse; "Anointed with the Holy Ghost" (Acts x : 38); enabled only by the Holy Spirit to offer himself without spot to God (Heb. ix: 14); his mother "with child of the Holy Ghost" (Matt. i: 18); his battle made possible by the Holy Spirit descending and resting upon him (Jo. i : 33); and the meaning of all this being, that without all this he would have been born a sinner; that as *Jesus* his Godhead was his helper\*; but that as *Christ* he had to be striven with like you or me; only with enough of the anointing to make his sinlessness complete, though desperately wrestled for under the agonies of inconceivable temptation.

\* "Jehovah, the Help."

## CHAPTER VI.

### CHRIST AND RANSOM.

IF Jesus Christ was guilty in such a sense as that, if born unransomed, he must, under the old covenant, have been heir of sin and death, we must expect to find passages that speak of his redemption. We have found passages that speak of him as *thanatoumenos* (Chap. III); and we have found passages that speak of him as quickened (Chap. IV); and the Bible delights to associate these things with man, and to make the deadness and the quickening just exactly that in his humanity that might be expected under the curse of Adam. Now, if to be born doomed and quickened, he must, in an important sense, not be born doomed, but be quickened *a parte ante:* and to be thus thoroughly saved, he must be redeemed like Job or Daniel; that is, as an anticipative result of a redemption not yet wrought out for himself and for his people. Now, announcements of this were that which first roused our attention to these unconsidered facts in the life of our Redeemer.

For example, Zechariah;—" Behold thy King cometh unto thee; he is just and having salvation" (Zech. ix: 9). We glanced at the margin, and there was the tell-tale rendering,—" He is just, and saving himself"; and we looked at the Hebrew, and there came out the plain passive, " A SAVED ONE." And even that was not all the intimation; for there is a pronoun introduced. Our version strives to give it by translating it,—" He is just and having salvation"; instead of simply saying,—" Thy king, just and having salvation." But every body knows that the expressed pronoun is emphatic. The sentence, therefore, is singularly ripe. " Thy King cometh, righteous, and himself a saved one"; marking as you see, with extreme exactness, first, that he was quickened, and, second, that he was redeemed,—a fact noteworthy enough to introduce the pronoun; for being a great lordly deliverer himself, it was the more remarkable that he should be "himself a saved one."

Now, where better bring in the testimony of Paul? We will bring it first from the Hebrews. Everybody knows that the high priest was a type of our Saviour. Three times Paul says that he offered for himself, and for the errors of the people. He actually applies it to Christ. He says, in the fifth chapter (vs. 1–3),—" For every high priest taken from among men is ordained for men in things pertaining to God, that he may offer both gifts and sacrifices for sins: who can have compassion on the ignorant, and on them that are out of the way, FOR THAT HE HIMSELF ALSO IS COMPASSED WITH INFIRMITY. And, by reason hereof, he ought, as for the people, so also for himself, to offer for sins." Listen again, " Who needeth not daily, as those high priests, to offer up sacrifice, first for his own sins, and then for the people's; for this he did once, when he offered up himself"\* (Heb. vii: 27). Again, " Into the second

---

\* Commentators have been unguarded enough to infer that he did " not need" to offer for himself; but a glance at the passage will show that the " not needing" refers to the offering more than " once."

went the high priest alone once every year, not without blood, which " he offered for himself, and for the errors of the people" (Heb. ix : 7). And, now, to this last instance, which, beyond all peradventure, shows that this expression " for himself" was painstakingly intended, is affixed another sentence explanatory of this last, and which, though tampered with like the passage in Zechariah,* is all the more on that account striking when uncovered of its translation. Let us go back. " But into the second went the high priest alone, once every year, not without blood, which he offered for himself and for the errors of the people. . . . But Christ being come, an high priest of good things to come by a greater and more perfect tabernacle, not made with hands, that is to say, not of this building; neither by the blood of goats and calves, but by his own blood, he entered in once into the holy place, having OBTAINED ETERNAL REDEMPTION (for us." E. V.†)

What are we to think of this addition?

Why, we are to think this about it. We have called it "tampering." We mean *quoad* the effect, not *quoad* the mind of the translator. The effect is sad. It shrouds the Spirit. But the mind of the translator was simply empty of the thought. The "*for us*" was added, as we say, to make sense. And the beautiful doctrine that Jesus Christ was a man, bone of our bone and flesh of our flesh, and, as a man, heired from Adam, as well as heired from the throne of heaven, had never entered their belief; and

* " Righteous, and himself a saved one" (Zech. ix : 9).
† No such Greek in the original.

therefore, that the Adam-side of their Saviour had to be redeemed, was not a thing in waiting, and did not rise to claim its texts, when sentences, plainly asserting it, were actually struggling in the translators' minds.

But let us proceed. I will not pause upon the Messianic passages. The words "save" (Ps. xxii : 21; xl: 2; lxxix: 1; Is. xlix: 8; Heb. v: 7), and "redeem" (Ps. xxxi : 5 ; lxix : 18 ; Heb. ix : 12), and "deliver" (Ps. xl: 13, 17; lxix: 14, 15), bear singular relations in respect to the Redeemer. I will not dwell upon the sentence, " Heal my soul, for I have sinned against thee" (Ps. xli : 4 ; see Chap. III. p. 42). I will not expound this passage,—" I will praise thee ; for thou hast heard me, and art become my salvation" (Ps. cxviii : 21) ; nor this, " Brought from the dead (*anagagón ek nekrón*) our Lord Jesus, through the blood of the everlasting covenant" (Heb. xiii : 20) ; for though this last sentence distinctly teaches Christ's quickening (Col. ii: 13) as having been purchased, yet perhaps mere quotation will be enough, and we may not load the propounding of a faith too much with lengthened comments.

Passing by all this ; and not noticing, either, "Jesus," *Jehovah His Helper* (Matt. i : 21), which is the sense casual commentators give the name, who have no thought of our doctrine,—I hurry on to the Prophet Zechariah, and to one scene in his book which wonderfully supports all that has been said.

It was the scene with Joshua.

Joshua was the reigning high priest. Joshua is distinctly announced as the type of the Messiah.

Not only has he His chosen name, but, when he

is exhibited on the stage, he is called a "sign" (Zech. iii : 8, see *marg.*), and he is distinctly told, when he is brought out in state with gold on his head " Behold the man whose name is the BRANCH" (Zech. vi : 12, also iii : 8).

Not only so, but the angel of the covenant is also present. It seems to be a passage where the Godhead and the manhood of Christ are both impersonated (see Jo. iii : 13) : and where the Godhead orders the relief (Zech. iii : 4), and the manhood receives it. Let me quote the sentences. "And he showed me Joshua the high priest standing before the angel of the Lord, and Satan standing at his right hand to resist him. And the Lord said unto Satan, The Lord rebuke thee, O Satan ; even the Lord that hath chosen Jerusalem, rebuke thee: is not this a brand plucked out of the fire? Now Joshua was clothed with filthy garments, and stood before the angel" (Zech. iii : 1–3).

Now examine the poetry thoroughly. Who is the angel ? All say, Christ the God. And who is Joshua the high priest ? By the evidence of the context (Zech. vi : 11, 12), Christ the man. And why is the prophet so negligent? Why does he speak sometimes of the angel (iii : 1, 6), and sometimes, as though it made no difference, of the Great Jehovah? Because it makes no difference. Sometimes the angel speaks (iii : 6), and sometimes Jehovah ; (iii : 2) and other passages are negligent in the same way (Gen. xviii : 2, 13, 14) ; and the meaning is that the angel *is* \* Jehovah ; that is, that the God-

---

\* I mean, significantly ; even though he be a common angel.

head part of Christ is God Almighty. And why is Joshua weak? and why does Satan stand at his right hand? and how can he resist him, *i. e.*, play Satan (Heb.) to him, and act the adversary (*marg.*)? Because he is *enosh;* that is, mortal, temptable. This is the reason for what immediately follows. He is not only called the Branch * (iii : 8); he is not only said to grow up from beneath (*mitahath*, vi : 12); he is not only said to be "a root out of a dry ground" (Is. liii : 2); but it is boldly said, " Is not this a brand plucked out of the fire?" (Zech. iii : 2). Moreover Joshua is said to be " clothed with filthy garments;" and the angel, that is, his Godhead, stands and sees the filthy garments taken away, and that he be clothed with a change of raiment (iii : 3–5).

Consider all this in the simplest style of exegesis, and in the light of other passages where he is called "an abomination" (Is. xli : 24); where he is called "dust" and "stubble"; where he is said to be "a saved one"; and where he is said to be kept from death (Heb. v : 7); and where he is said to obtain eternal redemption (Heb. ix : 12); and what can it mean but that, forensically, he was "plucked out of the fire"; and that, by right of blood, he was " filthy"; and that, by the hand of his Godhead, he was delivered; working out his own relief; setting " a fair mitre on his head"; and causing his iniquity (forensically meant, see Chap. III. p. 42) to pass from him ; and clothing him with other garments? (Zech. iii : 1–5.)

He is treated with terms, too, as though he were

* Equivalent to our word *sprout or sucker:* meaning a young tree out of an old root.

a mere probationer. "If thou wilt walk in my ways, and if thou wilt keep my keeping, then thou shalt also judge my house, and shalt also keep my courts: and I will give thee companions among them that stand by" (Zech. iii: 7).

And this leads me to speak more fully of these conditions. First, the need of them! We have shown passages that rate him dead (1 Pet. iii: 18), and we have shown passages that bespeak him quickened (Eph. ii: 5), and now we have presented some that call him ransomed. Of course there must have been a ransom; and it is time to speak of that, and show what was the substance of the price laid down for the delivery of the Emmanuel. Now, the Godhead part we have already noticed. He was raised from the dead by the glory of the Father" (Rom. vi: 4). That is, the dignity of the God gave price to the payments of the man; and thus the angel of the covenant caused the filthy garments to pass away.

But what were the payments of the man?

I think I will satisfy multitudes by saying, They were two things, suffering and obedience; and these things are more striking when we weave them together. Christ made his ransom out of two things, suffering and obedience, and these two may be woven into one. He made his ransom out of a suffering obedience, or an obedient suffering; an offering "without spot to God" (Heb. ix: 14), or an obedience even unto death (Phil. ii: 8). Most people will accept this as their own ransom; and we propound it as the same with the Redeemer.

Now, what obedience? Most people impair the

obedience of Christ by making it too easy. They make him God, and then, moreover, they make him not accursed man. They make him free of Adam. And therefore, if he suffer, I mean if he suffer in his obedience, they have to make it in some mysterious way. It is " the hidings of God's face." What does that mean ? Or it is temptation. But the ordinary account of temptation is strangely mystic. One would think Christ a child, and, with ample knowledge of why God hid his face, to be, so to speak, voluntarily deceived by it ; the whole being a house of cards which we dare hardly breathe upon, lest by any even child's question our blessed Saviour should seem even less sensible than the very thieves that suffered by his side. But Oh! if he was accursed ; that is, if he had a shattered nature inherited from Adam ; if it was fleshly (Rom. viii : 3) ; and would have fallen into sin, but for the sheer Spirit ; if his life, therefore, was by God, and his death would have been by the flesh ; then his obedience was a splendid triumph. We have but to imagine a supply of the Spirit barely sufficient sometimes to secure him victory (Matt. xxvii : 46), to understand what temptation meant ; what obedience in those fearful circumstances denoted ; what its merit was, and what its triumph was in fighting our battle ; and why the apostle should say with so much sturdy emphasis, " Humbled himself, and became obedient unto death, even the death of the cross. Wherefore," (surely not because he agreed to die as Peter did)—but " Wherefore," because of his most singular and hard-fought obedience, " God also hath highly exalted him, and given him a name" etc. (Phil. ii : 8, 9).

Now the suffering—what was that? We have spoken of the suffering obedience: what was the obedient suffering? And our answer promptly is, Temptation. We come at once to a full and satisfactory account.

Pain of body! Who ever dreams of that? Pain of mind! Yes, but what sort of pain of mind? Pain of guilt? How? and how administered? "Hiding" of Jehovah? In what way? Nay, with what possible result, if Jesus knew from the beginning that it was not a deserved frown, and was part of a splendid self-sacrifice? Why must we be so card-building in our systems? Rationally, what was it? Do you say it was a mystery? That is surely a better answer than the rest; but why make it? If Paul says, "Ye have not yet resisted unto blood, striving against sin" (Heb. xii : 4), and that points back to many a scene where we can fancy the "great drops of blood falling down to the ground :" if, in those very moments, He exclaims, " The Spirit truly is willing, but the flesh is weak" (Matt. xxvi : 41): if, in prophecy, he cries out, " In the day of my trouble I sought the Lord : my hand was stretched out through the night, and never ceased : my soul refused to be comforted. I remembered God and was troubled : I complained, and my spirit was overwhelmed" (Ps. lxxvii : 2, 3) : if he cries, just like a common person. " Will the Lord cast off forever? and will he be favorable no more? Is his mercy clean gone forever? does his promise fail forever more? Hath God for-

## Christ and Ransom. 65

gotten to be gracious? hath he in anger shut up his tender mercies?" (ib. vs. 7-9); if he break forth thus, and then Luke tells us he was tempted (Lu. iv: 2), and gives us to understand afterward that he was most horribly tempted (Lu. xxii: 40-43); and Paul discourses upon it thus, "Who in the days of his flesh, when he had offered up prayers and supplications with strong crying and tears unto him that was able to save him from death, and was heard in that he feared." (Heb. v: 7)—I say, when all this is absolutely volunteered in the word of God, why should we draw back? and I may say further,—Why should we draw back from a guilty Saviour, I mean, guilty in Adam? and from a fleshly Saviour, I mean inheriting from Adam? when he is said to be a tempted Saviour (Heb. iv: 15), and when he seems to have been a ransomed Saviour (Heb. ix: 12), when we are distinctly told he was a quickened Saviour (Eph. ii: 5); and why should we not think his temptation was his suffering, and his resistance was his obedience, and that the battle of it was his merit, and that the fierce throes of this battle was the substance of his expiation, and that his expiation, as Paul declares, was " for himself and for the errors of the people"? (Heb. ix: 7).

This really seems to be a consistent and not derogatory judgment of faith.

And it agrees with many incidental glimpses.

Jesus Christ was to trample Satan, but, in trampling, was to " bruise His heel" (Gen. iii: 15). It was to be a precarious, dangerous, and, to our poor Lord, a hesitating victory. And so Isaiah speaks of it; and shows how near he was to defeat; and honors the Combatant for persevering, and nursing the mere spark of hope, till he had received the victory. "A bruised reed shall he not break, and the smoking flax shall he not quench; he shall bring forth judgment unto victory" (Is. xlii : 3). He shall nurse his own graces. "He shall not fail nor be discouraged till he have set judgment in the earth: and the isles," lost without that "judgment," that is without that favorable verdict won by his expiation, may be looked upon as "waiting" while it hung in suspense (Is. xlii : 4), and shouting over the coming of deliverance (Is. xlii : 11).

Now, another incident. Our blessed Lord, all through his history, must have been the victim of a temptation so grinding as this,—that, through childhood and youth, he must have been waited upon by sin, and watched for as for a single trespass. Where had he a chance to grow, physically? Old views about that are probably all wrong. He was fiercely assaulted sometimes; and, in view of the fact perhaps that physical life could not have endured it oftener, he had his great trial seasons. One was in the Garden. We have already said that the worst seems to have been the very last (Matt. xxvii : 46); and that death came to his relief when he was pushed off to the very verge of his power to endure.* Now, how

---

* When he cried, Eli, Eli, lama sabacthani? (Matt. xxvii: 46). If, in that last moment, he had wavered and sinned, all would have been lost. You may say, He could not have sinned. Neither can the Christian, to the extent of final apostacy. But they can in a very intelligible sense. And it was only by "travail of soul" (Is. liii : 11)

could he grow under this pressure as a child? It has been, therefore, with extreme impression that we have watched the tokens in the Bible that our Saviour did not grow in strength and beauty. The Psalter says, " I may tell all my bones: they look and stare at me" (Ps. xxii: 17). Some of these old crucifixes, cut in ivory, would be the more authentic handling. " My days are consumed like smoke, and my bones are burned as an hearth. My heart is smitten like grass; so that I forget to eat my bread. By reason of the voice of my groaning, my bones cleave to my skin. I am like a pelican of the wilderness; I am like an owl of the desert. My days are like a shadow that declineth; and I am withered like grass" (Ps. cii: 3–6, 11). It may be said, This is all spiritual; and I confess it might be. Show me the Word all full of pictures of Christ in rosy youth, and of our Saviour in vigorous and glorious manhood, and I will give these texts up. For even if they were spiritual, like many other spiritual intimations they may have their *basis* in history and in fact. Show me any ground to think that Christ is to be painted in physical strength, and I will give up all my notion. But if it is the gloss of the painter; if glorious art encircles the Saviour with radiance; if he was a man of sorrow; if he was so haunted by sin that he had no time to grow, and so pressed by responsibility lest, as Solomon expresses it, he should destroy a race of Kings * (Prov. xxxi: 3); if flesh

that Christ was able to say, It is finished; and to reach the end, and safely give up the ghost.

* See Author's Commentary *in loco*.

and blood could not thrive under such a weight, except by miracle, and we have no testimony of such a miracle, and, indeed, all the oposite; if our Saviour, as a man, was a common man (Matt. xiii : 55 ; Prov. xxx : 2), and, as he seems to declare, "a less" man than John, whom he bears testimony to as the greatest born of women (Matt. xi : 11);\* and if there is positively not one Scripture that bears any testimony to Christ's physical strength and comeliness, then we may quietly finish our quotations, and quietly show, what has delighted us, and surprised us not a little, —that the earliest Fathers of the Church bear this very testimony to the stature and to the looks of Jesus.

Isaiah says "He hath no form nor comeliness; and when we shall see him, there is no beauty that we should desire him. He is despised and rejected of men" (Is. liii : 2, 3) : and I go so far as to say, that if he had the superb appearance that we think of, his villagers would have been more proud of him (Lu. iv : 29). " His visage was so marred more than any man, and his form more than the sons of men" (Is. lii : 14). And when they said to him at Jerusalem, " Thou art not yet fifty years old" (Jo. viii : 57), I believe there stood before them a man battered and worn, broken by the assaults of Satan, with the sweetness of grace breaking out upon his lips (Ps. xlv : 2), and upon his eye (Cant. v : 16), but with a

---

\* This I confess is a new comment, but *mikroteros* never means "*least*," and if it did, there is no meaning in the sentence. I know nothing to forbid the thought that Christ was lesser in mind and in natural talent and force than the child of a priest.

## Christ and Ransom. 69

feeble port, despised by the Roman soldiers * (Matt. xxvii; 27-29), laughed at in the palace of Herod (Lu. xxiii : 11), and looking, with his withered face (Is. liii : 2), as though he had borne the buffetings of near " fifty years" (Ps. xxii : 17).

Now, the Fathers! Let me *press the question*, Where did we get our notion of Christ as strong and beautiful?

" His beauty, says Clemens of Alexandria, was in his soul and in his actions ; but in appearance he was base. Justin Martyr declares him as being without beauty, without glory, without honor. His body, says Tertullian, had no human handsomeness, much less any celestial splendor. The heathen Celsus, as we learn from Origen, even argued from his traditional meanness and ugliness of aspect as a ground for rejecting his divine origin." †

Enough on this. We reject it as a regular proof, but suggest it as a beautiful illustration : that though God could have made Christ what he pleased, yet he did not make him physically beautiful; and that, if an heir of Adam, and having to fight from his earliest infancy sin and guilt, it would be natural for one daily haunted by temptation, to keep weak under it ; daily bringing heaven and all the saints into the risk, to wither under the sacrifice ; daily ruined if he sinned BUT ONCE ; and daily racked to commit some sin of thought or action, and daily deserted of God, so that he actually trembled on the verge of positive

---
\* He could not bear his own cross (Matt. xxvii : 32).

† Farrar's Life of Christ, Vol. I, p. 149. Farrar takes the opposite ground.

transgression,—to be just what the Bible paints him, a young old man, worn out in the intolerable fight; warning others that they were implicated in his temptation (Matt. xxvii : 41); telling them that the spirit was willing but the flesh was weak (ib.); and glad, if it were possible, to have, either from them or God, help (v. 38) or deliverance (Jo. xii : 27).

## CHAPTER VII.

### CHRIST AND JUSTIFICATION.

WE have spoken of death, life and ransom in connection with the Redeemer. Suppose we go further now, and speak of justification, adoption and sanctification.

"Justification is an act of God's free grace." Here we are perfectly at home. Christ is often spoken of in the Bible as an object of grace. If he was dead in Adam (1 Pet. iii : 18), and quickened into life by his birth of the Holy Ghost (Rom. i : 4); and if he purchased that quickening by suffering on the cross, and by his own God-inspired obedience,— then that help of the Godhead was a grace, and, on the side of man, it is so spoken of through all the Scripture. "The grace of God was upon him" (Lu. ii : 40). God pitied him; and he applied to Him for pity in a life of supplication (Lu. xxii : 44). Grace was poured into his lips (Ps. xlv : 2). "It pleased the Father that in him should all fulness dwell" (Col. i : 19). God gave "not the Spirit by measure unto him" (Jo. iii : 34).

Justification, therefore, if Christ was justified at all, might appropriate the language, " an act of God's free grace"; and we shall find that the Bible does appropriate the word " justified" (1 Tim. iii : 16) in respect to him, but makes modifications in the mode of speech commensurate with his necessity of being justified. " Justification is an act of God's free grace, wherein he pardoneth all our sins, and accepteth us as righteous in his sight." Now half of this is true of Christ, and half not true. Half is not true because he had no sins to pardon. Half is true, because by nature he was not righteous in God's sight. There were the sins of Adam. He needed justification, just as much as any of his people. And it must be a justification by Christ ; that is to say, Christ himself must win his own pardon. And it must be a pardon made efficacious just as with us ; that is by the dignity of the Godhead on the one hand, and by the obedience of the humanity on the other. Now, listen to the prophets :—" He hath covered me with a robe of righteousness" (Is. lxi : 10). " I the Lord have called thee by righteousness" (Is. xlii : 6). " Rejoice greatly, O daughter of Zion; behold thy King cometh unto thee, righteous and a saved one" (Zech. ix : 9). All of which will get us ready for one notable passage, which will define, in the most distinctive way, the actual difference. Christ wins his own ransom. That is to say, the Godhead puts upon him a robe of righteousness ; but he is himself God, and, therefore, he gives it to himself. Moreover he is an anointed man ; and this also is by the grace of his Godhead ; and this anointed man wins the righteousness for him, that is, works it out by his own bloody sweat. The Catechism, therefore, is not applicable to Christ. He is not "*accepted*" as righteous, remaining sinful. It is not "*imputed*" that he be righteous, that righteousness being derived from another. Here is a glorious difference. He works out his own righteousness. And yet there is grace in this,—that he does it by the Spirit. He would be as powerless as we, except for the Spirit. A glorious righteousness, sufficient for himself, sufficient for millions, and which actually does save himself and millions (Heb. ix: 7), was given to him. It had dignity from God, and it had possibility also from God; for without God he could not have achieved it. And yet it is not like ours: for ours is his righteousness received by faith; whereas his is his own righteousness, achieved by faith (Heb. xii: 2 *), and manufactured, every inch of it, by toil and risk under the influences of the Holy Spirit.

Now, the passage to which we allude, is that very distinctive one, "Justified in the Spirit" (1 Tim. iii: 16). It is aptly fashioned. It would apply also to any of us. But it is the only form of sentence that would apply to Christ as well. It may be said of any of us, "Ye are washed, ye are sanctified, ye are JUSTIFIED, in the name of the Lord Jesus, and BY † THE SPIRIT OF OUR GOD" (1 Cor. vi: 11). We are "justified in †

---

\* This passage interests me as referring to the personal faith of Christ. He is the only perfect example of it: and therefore we are to look to him "as the beginner and finisher of faith." "*Our* faith" shows its mistake by the Italics.

† The word is " in" in both passages.

the Spirit," therefore, as well as Christ; that is, it requires the Spirit to give us the faith by which we are justified. But it required the Spirit in him to be given "without measure." It required the Spirit to give him the ground as well as the condition. It required the Spirit without measure; and it was the Spirit without measure that achieved the righteousness that furnished the justification for him as well as for his people.

He had to be justified, however; and we mean, out of a native condemnation; but it had to be a justification " in the Spirit." " Mine own arm brought salvation to me" (Is. lxiii: 5). It had to be by the power of his divine nature ; and by the perfect obedience wrought by the Holy Ghost.

## CHAPTER VIII.

### CHRIST AND ADOPTION.

WHEN I adopt a child, he is not my child. But when God adopts, the case is figuratively different. He does not hesitate to mix figures.

" Adoption is an act of God's free grace whereby we are received as the sons of God."

The Bible does not hesitate, however, to speak of us as " begotten"of God. We are, therefore, his sons actually. Let me enumerate hastily some of the passages. " If any man be not begotten from above" (Jo. iii: 3). " Of his own will begat he us with the word of truth" (Jas. i: 18). " He that doeth righteousness is born of him" (1 Jo. ii: 29).

Now, so it is with Christ. It is with Christ exactly as it would be if he were born like us. He would have to be elected (Lu. xxiii : 35), called (Is. xlix : 1), appointed (Heb. i : 2 ; iii : 2), raised up (Acts xiii: 33), anointed (Acts x : 38), with every sort of other fact that betokened selection and redemption,—to be the man intended to be Emmanuel. And then, on the other hand, " begetting" would be just as emphatic.

Let me consider this grander side, first. Gabriel actually explains it to the Virgin. " The Holy Ghost shall come upon thee, and the power of the Highest shall overshadow thee ; therefore also that holy thing which shall be born of thee, shall be called the Son of God" (Lu i : 35). " The birth of Jesus Christ was on this wise : When as his mother Mary was espoused to Joseph, she was found with child of the Holy Ghost" (Matt. i : 18). " That which is conceived of her is of the Holy Ghost" (v. 20). Therefore now let us notice fully that he is called the " Son of God," and that the decree is four times repeated, " Thou art my Son ; this day have I begotten thee" (Ps. ii : 7 ; Acts xiii : 33 ; Heb. i: 5 ; v: 5).

And yet, on the other hand, if our theory is true that he was accursed, and would have been apostate, and had to be redeemed ; if we are to take it to be true that he was Incarnate God, but that he chose to be incarnated in apostate man, and that in order to be so incarnated he had to choose one, and to choose him from all eternity, and so beforehand to prepare for him as to send an angel to announce and to send the Spirit to beget him, so that in an accursed womb he might nevertheless be overshadowed with saving efficacy from the very first,—I say, if all this be so, " adoption" may well be talked of as well as generation ; for then the Incarnate Whole is God over all blessed forever, and, at the same time, a selected mortal, called into the family of the faith, and called to be the head of it, and called to be so deluged by the Spirit as to be made, through blood and agony, to obey to our redemption.

Now listen to such announcements:—" Mine elect : I have put my Spirit upon him" (Is. xlii : 1). " The Lord hath called me from the womb" (Is. xli : 2). " Out of Egypt have I called my Son" (Matt. ii : 15). " I will be to him a father, and he shall be to me a son" (Heb. i : 5). " No man taketh this honor upon him, but he that was called of God, as was Aaron" (Heb. v : 5). " Because he hath appointed a day in which he will judge the world in righteousness by that man whom he hath ordained" (Acts xvii : 31). " Born of the seed of David according to the flesh, and ordained * to be the Son of God in power, according to the Spirit of holiness, by the resurrection from the dead" (Ro. i : 3, 4). " Called the Son of the Highest" (Lu. i : 32). " Christ, the chosen of God" (Lu. xxiii : 35). " God hath made that same Jesus, whom ye have crucified, both Lord and Christ" (Acts ii : 36). "A prophet shall the Lord your God raise up unto you of your brethren like unto me"

---

* I translate " ordained" because the word is derived from fixing a boundary, and for the very consistent reason that the same word, on the same subject, in the text from Acts just quoted before it, is so translated.

(Acts iii : 22). " Therefore God thy God hath anointed thee with the oil of gladness above thy fellows" (Ps. xlv : 7).

We quote amply. Now look at these. Not severally. But look at them in their connection. It is possible that, one by one, they might be wrested, so as to appear to cover other ground. But, in their most child-like apparency, do they not seem to say that God, having to become incarnate, chose a mortal ; and that that mortal had to be redeemed ; and that that redemption had to be from birth ; and that that choice and that redeeming gives significance to these texts ; because that it was " being made perfect, [that] he became the author of eternal salvation to all them that obey him" (Heb. v : 9).

## CHAPTER IX.

### CHRIST AND SANCTIFICATION.

IT must be continually kept in mind that I am not theorizing upon Christ, but that I am noting passages of the Word of God that have been kept out of our theories, and that need to be explained as absolute averments of the Holy Ghost. I am not saying that Christ was doomed (Matt. ii : 15) ; or that he was raised out of an apostacy (1 Pet. iii : 18) ; or that he was ransomed (Zech. ix : 9); or that he was justified (1 Tim. iii : 16), and called (Heb. v : 10) ; and saying that I could see this from the very theory of such a being. I could not. I am only saying, Here are these texts. I am only pleading, They have waked me up. Come and explain them

## Christ and Sanctification. 77

with me. I am helped by them as stepping stones: that is, I step from one to the other, but the only theory I make is the link of their connection. I do say that they all agree in the idea that Christ was lost in his inheritance from Adam.

But, now, is it not time to pause? Christ was sanctified (Jo. x: 36). How possibly am I to give an account of that?

Sanctification is that change in the sinner by which, after his regeneration, he is weaned gradually from wickedness, and " enabled to die unto sin and live unto righteousness." Christ teaches that we " must be born again." Our doctrine, therefore, is, that we are "converted," or " called," or " regenerated," however you choose to entitle it, at the beginning of our religious history, but that, as that only imparts the germ of grace, we are dealt with afterward, and slowly resist our sins, and climb out of our corrupt condition.

Now what had Christ to do with any such slow change as this?

Our very theory is, that he was " begotten"; that the Holy Ghost came down, and that the power of the Highest overshadowed; and, therefore, that that " holy thing" had complete perfection. Christ positively never sinned; and, from the first dawn of his being, his renewal was so complete, that no touch of iniquity ever stained his mind.

But I think we can understand how a nature could be shattered so that by itself it would sin (Mar. xiv; 38; xv: 34), and yet be held up by the sheer power of Omnipotence (Heb. v: 7). I think we can understand humiliation and glorification. I think we can understand sin kept off by almost artificial assistances, and sin scoffed at by a better nature, where the Holy Ghost does not simply strive and rule, but where he lives and has become settled in the being.

These were the stages with Christ.

And, therefore, we are told positively, He was sanctified (Jo. xvii : 19). We are told of the means. Christ was not sanctified from sin (1 Pet. ii : 22); but he was sanctified in some way. For he was sanctified by the word (Jo. xvii : 19); and he was sanctified by suffering. He was made "perfect through suffering" (Heb. ii : 10). " Though he were a Son, yet learned he obedience by the things which he suffered" (Heb. v : 8). And we are told that, " being made perfect, he became the author of eternal life unto all them that obey him" (v. 9).

Is there not a shadow of how this may be in the history of man ? How are we sanctified ? We gain strength as well as purity. We are not only weaned from sin, but we gather life in our second nature by the battle we are called to wage. What is the consequence ? It is better for us to be in this world than to be moved immediately to heaven. Look at this, for a moment. If we are Christians, we are Kings. If we are kings, we are sovereigns over the universe. If we are sovereigns, all things are ours. If all things are ours, then we are on earth, simply because it is better than to be in heaven. If we were in heaven, we would be without sin. Then sanctification is not simply to make us without sin, but to lift high our moral nature ; and the old man, rugged with the storms of life, may be higher among the blessed, than the poor child snatched away into the everlasting Kingdom.

We see then how Christ may be sanctified, even though he never sinned. He may *learn* obedience: he may *settle* what is given him of grace: he may build-in of celestial stone what has been lent, so to speak, of moral scaffolding; and, instead of being racked by horrible temptation, he may win, at last, as we all do when we come to die, a second nature; that is, when we are glorified, something *pneumatical* instead of something *psychical* (1 Cor. xv : 44); a very body that responds to conscience (1 Cor. ix : 27); for which we are growing and prepared through the long fight of what we call our sanctification.

We are not responsible for what Christ means when he speaks of being sanctified (Jo. x : 36); but this is what we dream of it. He had to suffer (Heb. ix : 22), and he had to be obedient (Heb. vii : 26). His suffering was his temptation (Heb. xii : 4), and his obedience was his agony of resisting faithfulness. These were necessary in themselves. But, with all and beyond all, there was this other influence,— that they sanctified his spirit, and made the captain of our salvation perfect through suffering.

CHAPTER X.

CHRIST AND ORDINANCES.

THERE comes in finely, then, a complete solution of many of the riddles of the Scripture.

Christ was circumcised !

According to our account he might as well be, as any of the meanest of his people. He was born of the lineage of Adam; and if he had to be cut off from his stock, and, as Paul expresses it, "separated from sinners" (Heb. vii: 26), his parents could have made no mistake. And Providence was not trifling with the history, when it allowed a solemn share of the ceremonial rite to be provided for the Redeemer. Indeed Paul bases everything upon it. For, making our cleansing flow from His cleansing, and our circumcision, spiritually considered, rest on His,—he speaks of our "putting off the body of the sins of the flesh in the circumcision of Christ" (Col. ii: 11).

Now, further, he was baptized! And the true way to press our argument is, to insist upon a solution. Why was Mary purified? Why does there linger so in the manuscripts the reading, "after the days of THEIR purification" (Lu. ii: 22). Why was our Saviour circumcised? And now, much more strongly; for this was his own act, voluntarily resorted to,—Why did he go to John, and, against the distinct warning of his forerunner, insist upon receiving baptism? (Matt. iii: 15).

Neander * tells us it was official. But how foolish to talk so! Why should Christ mislead us by confusing what was intended for the people? Why should he snatch to another use a simple and easily darkened ceremonial? Neander says, It was his ordination. But why? We might give it a thousand meanings. Why did not Christ say so? Neander says, It could not mean his baptism. There is the

* *Gesch. Apos. Zeit.* p. 642, *note.*

very point. Our very doctrine shows it must and could. It becomes a gloss to the other texts, and shows, what all baptism shows, that Christ needed cleansing; that is, that he needed to be *Christ*;* that is, that he must be born from above : and though he was never cleansed as we are cleansed, I mean partially; and though he was never " born" as we are " born," namely, after we have sinned : though he was "born" redeemed, and "begotten" in the womb, and never saw corruption (Acts ii : 31),—yet it belonged to him so by Adam, that he might be baptized rightfully as we are, and baptized after his cleansing, just as we are, after we are born from above (Acts viii : 37).

Again, the priests! What did they wash for ? (2 Chr. iv : 6). The high priest! Why was he perpetually making lustration ? (Ex. xl : 31 ; Lev. viii : 12, 30).

And now, notice one thing about the Bible. Not only is Christ perpetually spoken of as tempted, and infirm, and compassed about with weakness, but, just like one of us fighting for his life, the whole is said to depend upon the High Priest keeping clean. The cases are everywhere. Christ must be obedient unto death ; or else there is no hope of any body's salvation.

" If thou wilt walk in my ways," Jehovah told him, " then I will give thee companions among them that walk with thee" (Zech. iii : 7). " He was heard, in that he feared," the apostle says (Heb. v : 7). " O God thou knowest as to † my foolishness (that

---

\* Anointed.   † See the preposition.

is, thou knowest that I have none); and my guiltiness" (just exactly of what sort it is) "is not hid from thee. Deliver me out of the mire, and let me not sink. Draw nigh unto my soul, and redeem it. The humble shall see and be glad; and your hearts shall live that seek God" (Ps. lxix: 5, 14, 18, 32).

I cannot repeat all the passages. The burden of all is, that Christ's power to save lay in his saving himself. "Who through the Eternal Spirit offered himself WITHOUT SPOT to God" (Heb. ix: 14). "For their sakes I sanctify myself, that they also may be sanctified through the truth" (Jo. xvii: 19). "Righteousness shall be the girdle of his loins" (Is. xi: 5). "Thou lovest righteousness, and hatest wickedness. THEREFORE God hath blessed thee forever" (Ps. xlv: 7). "The sceptre of thy kingdom is a right sceptre" (v. 6). "He became obedient unto death: WHEREFORE God hath highly exalted him" (Phil. ii: 8, 9). "And, being made perfect, he became the author of eternal salvation to all them that obey him" (Heb. v: 9).

Excuse the length of our list. He who said, "I have found David my servant," had only to add, "With my holy oil have I anointed him" (Ps. lxxxix: 20), to show how stoutly, and yet how humanly; how triumphantly in the end, and yet how agonizingly and hazardously through all the way, Jesus Christ, our incarnate God, fought the battle as a poor lost man saved by grace, but bearing all the way the miserable marks of an undone and terrible inheritance.

## CHAPTER XI.

### CHRIST AND GLORIFICATION.

THERE came a time when Christ ascended into heaven, and sat at the right hand of God. There are many mysterious things said about the change. He told his disciples, "If I go not away, the Comforter will not come unto you" (Jo. xvi : 7). He told Mary, "Touch me not," that is, not with high hopes of his highest gifts; for he could not bestow them yet. " I am not yet ascended unto my Father" (Jo. xx : 17). By our old notions this was rather meaningless. But if we take the idea that Christ was a heritor from Adam, then the Divine Man, like the common man, had a period of the " psychical body" of which Paul speaks. That is, being held up like you or me by the sheer power of grace from lapsing into sin, he had a carnal nature which reigned all through his earthly humiliation; which was subdued by "the things which he suffered" (Heb. v : 8); which was fought against and everywhere conquered; and which, though held in submission by the Spirit without measure given, yet evermore threatened, and evermore leaned over the gulf of positive and possible iniquity. But when Christ rose, he changed his nature. The "body psychical" gave place to one " pneumatical." When Paul says, " There is a psychical body, and there is a pneumatical body" (1 Cor. xv : 44), we do not understand an *ethereal* body at judgment. That may be as it may be. But we understand, a holy body; not one, as in the case of Christ, HELD IN HOLINESS by the supreme efficiency of the Spirit, but one naturally holy; no longer drilled and trained and striven with by a Visitor from abroad, but the home of that Visitor; incorporated with Him; now no longer His arena for a fight, but His throne to everlasting; the place of His abiding seat; glorious now in its strength, and quiet as a second nature.

Christ's glorification, therefore, was like man's glorification, with essential differences. Man's glorification was a release from sin. Christ never sinned. Man's glorification will take place hereafter (Col. iii: 4). Christ's glorification has already taken place. Man's glorification is lower. Christ's glorification is ineffable, as one with God. But, with these differences, there are similarities, which, with our view, become unspeakably more complete. Man's glorification is a rising to an untempted, unweakened condition of obedience. So is Christ's. His battle is over.

Now with this pneumatical life, where the Spirit reigns instead of battles, there are, as it might naturally be anticipated, changes of authority. Even the saint shall have his kingdom over the "five cities" (Lu. xix: 19). And though we do not understand entirely why "the Holy Ghost was not yet, because that Jesus was not yet glorified" (Jo. viii: 39), we do understand, in the first place, that this was only comparatively; as when Christ said, "They had not had sin" (Jo. xv: 22); or when Paul says, "Christ sent me not to baptize" (1 Cor. i: 17); and we do

## Christ and Glorification.

understand, in the second place, that it would not be in the least unnatural that Christ, with higher glory, should have higher reign; that Christ, escaped from Adam, should climb upon the throne; that Christ, with his case decided, should have its promises fulfilled; and that Christ, having actually paid the ransom, should have now higher power than those anticipative good things which a trust that he would conquer wrung out, in advance, from the law of the Almighty.

So we explain everything. And when Jesus, remembering the touch of the diseased woman (Mar. v : 30), says to Mary, " Touch me not," for the highest gifts, that I have often talked with thee about, cannot be responsive to thy touch till I am ascended to the Father, it throws a beautiful light on all our theory; which is, that he was of our fallen Adam; that he did not cease to be so till he rose to heaven; that he was staid from sin, or otherwise he never could have risen to redemption; but that he was not staid from moral weakness; that is, that he was not staid from a fleshliness (Heb. v : 2) that could be wrung by moral temptation; that he was accursed, therefore, all through his life; and that it was only when he rose to paradise, that the *psuchikon* put on the *pneumatikon*, and that an easy holiness reigned and became natural in a carnal heritor.

## CHAPTER XII

### CHRIST AND GOD.

IT becomes now intensely interesting to ask, how God could become one with such a man.

In the first place, God never could become one with man at all. This is the opinion of the most mediæval orthodoxy.

But then I must explain exactly what I mean by such an assertion ; for, thus nakedly standing, it will surprise many a reader, and awake an impetuous, No! against such an assault upon our creed.

But my meaning is simple. I mean that in the very simplest, and therefore the most important sense, God is not one with man, and could not be possibly.

The " Confession" says that Christ is " very man." Now if Christ is " very man," he has "a true body and a reasonable (reasoning) soul": and if he is a true man in these respects, he is finite ; and, moreover, he is a creature, and the creature must be distinct from the Creator. I shall cloud the thing if I pause. No mortal ever dreamed that the child of Mary was God in the most natural and simple sense.

But then he is God in certain senses, and that is why I think Paul chose *isa* instead of *ison* in his famous sentence (Phil. ii : 6). He is God (Rom. ix : 5), and ought to be worshipped (Heb. i : 6) ; and many a man will shrink from our view of his humanity, because it sinks him lower, and makes it harder to think of him as in truth the Son of God.

But let us look at all this, and let us make a list now of the *isa* (Phil. ii : 6), and show in what particulars Christ is God to the glory of God the Father.

1. And in the first place, to use a thought that will allow for every mystery, he is God just as far as the Omnipotent Jehovah *could* deify an elected and anointed intelligence. Making the universe, it would be strange if he could not elect a creature, and build everything around him. One might suspect he would ; for, being invisible, why should he not select a being, and become incarnate in him for his creatures? Because, " no being hath seen God at any time ; the only begotten Son, which is in the bosom of the Father, he hath declared him." This shall be our first answer then. Christ is God in every sense in which God by the use of his Omnipotence could unite himself with a creature.

2. And, therefore, secondly, he is God in the Spirit.

This is the celestial way of explaining his Godhead. " And the angel answered and said unto her, The Holy Ghost shall come upon thee, and the power of the Highest shall overshadow thee; therefore also that holy thing which shall be born of thee shall be called the Son of God" (Lu. i : 35). This makes *Christ* his great appellative—the Anointed One. And this Paul notices, " Ordained [*] to be the Son of God in power, according to the Spirit of holiness" (Romans i : 3). Christ is not particular to call Him Spirit, but

---

[*] Compare (E. V.) Acts xvii : 31.

says, "The Father that dwelleth in me, he doeth the works" (Jo. xiv: 10). He that hath seen me, hath seen the Father" (v. 9). And the prophets talk boldly of "God." They call him Emmanuel; and they address him (Ps. cx: 1). "Jehovah said unto my Lord, Sit thou at my right hand, until I make thine enemies thy footstool." In *substantial* ways, therefore, the Spirit is the incarnated Deity.

3. But in *authoritative* ways! There will be another aspect.

I will state at once three particulars (*isa*) in which Christ is God; first, *substantially*, in that he is the incarnated Spirit; second, *authoritatively*, in that "all power is given unto [him] in heaven and in earth" (Matt. xxviii: 18); and third, *forensically*, in that he stands for God. By eternal covenant his name is the Father's name; and by federal law, which has passed the inspection of eternity, his righteousness is God's righteousness, and they are so federally and substantially the same, that what Christ suffered in the fight is as though God endured it, under the pressure of intolerable iniquities.

*Authority*, therefore, to recur that way, is asserted everywhere. "Christ is head over all things to the church" (Eph. i: 22). He is able to say, "All power is given unto me in heaven and in earth." We are to know what is the exceeding greatness of God's power, " which he wrought in Christ when he set him far above all principality and power and might and dominion and every name that is named, not only in this world, but also in that which is to come" (Eph. i: 20, 21). *Authority* therefore, is to be one feature:

4. And now next comes the *forensic* claim.

He is "Jehovah our Righteousness" (Jer. xxiii : 6).

And we cannot exaggerate this. It is complete. "Through the Eternal Spirit he offered himself without spot to God" (Heb. ix : 14). He died as though God died. He obeyed as though God obeyed. And, therefore, no oracle shrinks. They say boldly, " Feed the church of God, which he hath purchased with his own blood" (Acts xx : 28).

(1) As *a mystery*, therefore, that is beyond what any body can fathom : (2) as *omnipotency*, therefore, making the man a God as far as the supreme Jehovah could make any of his creatures : (3) as *incarnation*, the holy substance being the Spirit born within : (4) as *kingship* awarded by authority: and (5) as *headship* by an eternal covenant,—the Deity is to be adored in Christ, and these are the points level to the worship of his people.

But then they do not forbid his having been lost.

We are always at a disadvantage as to our mode of speech.

How much more beautiful the expression, "Born from among the dead" (Col. i : 18).

Jesus Christ was never really lost.

But that he was doomed by lineage, does not in the least interfere with all these points of his divinity.

Once cumber him with guilt, and it may be federal guilt as well as that under the new dispensation. He was infirm (Heb. v : 2). The deeper and the deadlier, all the grander if he bore the triumph. He was tempted. That we have always known. If it shattered him, and snatched at his very life, all the more was he a man, and all the more, God, if he won the victory.

Take the peculiarities apart. (1) A mystery! It scarcely colors the mystery. (2) Omnipotence! If it could make Gabriel God, it could scarce be grander if it were a child of Adam. (3) The Spirit! It would befit his work. (4) Authority! A lost nature could be lifted to it as well as another. (5) Forensically he had guilt at any rate; and therefore there is nothing in these relations to God, that this brand plucked from the burning could not be fitted for as well as an un-Adamic Redeemer.

# III.

## CONCLUSION.

BUT it will be angrily uttered, Who dare thus change everything? The flush of anxiety will stand, as though at the very tomb of Christ, and say, 'They will take away my Lord, and I know not where they will lay him! Some schemings touch the outskirts of religion; but this ruins all of it. In the first place, it touches the very person of Christ; in the second place, it awakes the scandal of uncertainty; and in the third place it breeds this retort, How can you who are but a single reader of the word of God, and not very profound or discreet at that, set yourself in array against the tried doctrine of all mankind?'

There is something intimidating in this. And after the ripple of resentment, there follows a dead tide which is much more formidable still. Where is this change to end? And how can we anchor anywhere, if the faith *ubique et ab omnibus* is thus to be thrust aside by the speculations of a single mind?

Let us exhaust this sort of speech.

It will be said further,—Christ is simple. This was upheld, and was made a bright symptom of his excellence in the old conception of his person. (1) He was simple in his being,—Incarnate God, and perfect unincumbered man. To make him of the earthy earthy, and to debase him as an heir of ruin, is travelling a great way round, and reaching, in anticipative ways, the great trophies of his victories. (2) He was simple in his work. That is, the questions of life are much more easily met than by this new conception of redemption. " He that spared not his own Son, but freely gave him up for us all," was doing that which is much more easily understood if the child of Mary was aloof from Adam, than if we had to wade through all this retroactive thought, and reach our life through life first won back for our Emmanuel. (3) Again, he was simple in character. He knew no sin, neither was guile found in his mouth. It confuses everything, to imagine him attaint. It strains everything, to conceive of this attainder as lifted from him by his death. And though he never sinned under the curse, yet that he was tempted to it by heredity native in the flesh, bewilders all our faith, and spoils all our reverence for this great Omnipotent.

Now, let us answer everything. In the first place, the scandal! In olden time the unbroken faith was, that it was right to persecute. The Pagan persecuted the Christian. The Christian persecuted the Pagan. It was a settled doctrine. When Paul said, " Deliver such an one to Satan for the destruction of the flesh" (1 Cor. v: 5), the world leaped there at once. Hittites and Jebusites, under the old theocratic rule, personated *ab ictu* recusant believers; and the world's cup of faith filled itself up at once, and century after century did nothing to correct the evil.

## Conclusion.

Did that make it right?

Again, the power of Kings! Paul is again the teacher (Rom. xiii : 4; 1 Pet. ii : 17) ; and Christ (Matt. xxiii : 2). The world, we are to understand, when it sets a certain sense upon the sayings of Christ, seals it: that seems the argument ; and *ubique et ab omnibus* are to be infallible, like the work of the Spirit.

Now, I believe in infallibility : and here lies what is plausible in the intended argument. When Christ says, " On this rock I will build my church :" or when he says, " I am with you always ;" or when Paul *probably* says, that " the church" is " the pillar and ground of the truth" (1 Tim. iii : 15),—they do undoubtedly mean, that saving truth shall never fade from the earth. But what is saving truth? But yesterday all the Church believed in the " mystical presence." To-day, the most do. Then it is true? Can man or God warrant any such affirmation at our hands?

But if it be not true, who shall say so ? If the pent flood bore its way out through the burrow of a worm, is it audacious in the worm? Think of these things. The lion is crowded in a net. Then it is wicked in the mouse to gnaw it, and to cut him out?

Is not the true doctrine this ? that if the church lights her fires, the weakest may put them out? If the Jacobites rule, may not the peasant teach them better things ? And if *ubique* the wafer pronounces itself God, may not the poor, loneliest monk upset the understanding of the Word, and all the more proclaim that "the gates of hell shall never prevail against us?"

And now in regard to *simplicity!* (1) Where is the simplicity in Christ, if, like Gabriel, or like Lucifer, he comes from a foreign shore?

Deism is more simple than Christianity; that is, in form it seems to be: but does it explain more simply the great facts of our salvation? Christ is more simple, if created at a blow; but if a prophet the Lord our God has raised up to us of his brethren like unto us, may not the picture that has the fewer points be, like Deism, the least capacitated to explain the difficulties?

(2) So of ransom. "The lamb without blemish and without spot" might seem, if in the sense that has been prescriptive, to be more simple to explain the sacrifice; but if the sacrifice be suffering, and if the suffering be obedience, and if there be statements of the very fiercest temptation, and if, along with these temptations, there be statements of the very most dreadful risk, and, along with that, of a being rendered perfect by suffering, tell me,—which is simplest, that which gathers all these six in one, or that which leaves them at loose ends to be explained as mysteries?

Let me dwell upon this.

Our Saviour had a battle: what was it? It was a mystery. He was tempted. How? Being "holy, harmless, separate from sinners, and made higher than the heavens," how did temptation reach him? I mean under the old system? You have nothing to say but that it was a mystery. Again, he suffered

But so did the thief. Tell me what his sufferings consisted in. You venture a little way here, and say, It was anger. But what sort of anger? Did not his Father love him? Did Christ lose his mind by becoming a glorious Redeemer? You say, His Father hid himself. I have no doubt of it, but how? Could Christ put on a *guise* of terror; or could there be a hallucination of wrath, under which he could assume a torture? And then in respect to obedience (Heb. v: 8); why so difficult? And in respect to being " made perfect," How possibly can all these things be wrought in one? And why should that be thought simple that leaves all these useless for the teaching of the people?

But let me drop one magic word—Adam. Give me one text of Peter, " Made a dead man by the flesh"(1 Pet. iii: 18). Let me have one phrase out of the Vulgate, " *Primogenitus e mortuis*"; * and then one line from the Apostle, Being "quickened together with him" (Col. ii: 13),—and all these mysteries approach, and take off their masks by mutual assistance. These were the riddles of our faith. Now they can be built upon. Temptation ! It was incident to his lineage. Suffering ! It was the fruit of his temptation. Obedience! It was a most fearful battle. And perfecting himself! He did it like you or me. Only he was the God Incarnate. He had the Spirit without "measure" (Jo. iii: 34); or, as one codex has it, without " part" ; that is without just a part as we have it, leaving the rest to sin ; but nevertheless, not so without measure that his Deity

---

* " The first-born from the dead."

did not leave him, I mean the man Christ; did not stint him of his power as in the garden of Gethsemane; and did not leave him on the cross, to shrink with a scream of agony from the last passion of his life, viz., a fear of wreck, just as he was anchoring within the veil.

(3) Third, character; it brings me nearer to my Redeemer. Before, he was an alien, a something outside of me. Now, he is bone of my bones, and flesh of my flesh.

And this pleases me in three particulars : first, as an example. Before he was a mystery. I could not see how he was an example at all. He took things easily; *i. e.*, he had a good nature ; and though he was " compassed about with infirmity," I could not see how. There was a gravel stone in the socket of the cross. Now the cross sits straight in its morticed hold. I understand it perfectly: he was a poor tortured heritor. He was " tempted," blessed be God ! as well as " slain by the sword"; and now I understand that the latter was heaven in contrast with the former. And when the Apostle tells me to fight also my battle, " looking unto Jesus the author and finisher of *our* faith," I see why "*our*" was not put in the original; and why it should not appear at all. I see that it was Christ's faith of which Christ was the finisher; and that, under the hard torments under which he began and rendered it complete (Ps. xxii : 8, 19), he becomes a pattern for me, to fight and run my race of a new obedience.

Again, he can pity me. It seems Christ craved grace as well as I. He will not be arrogant over me.

## Conclusion.

He was a poor "worm;" for Isaiah is bold enough to say, "An abomination is he that chooseth you" (Is. xli : 24). And if any man says to me, "Who maketh thee to differ? and what hast thou that thou hast not received?" I Cor. iv : 7), Christ will not renounce my brotherhood, even there. As God, he is all my righteousness; as man, he is a child of the curse, lifted out of it by grace, and made to possess a splendid difference, by being one person with the Most High.

Once more; he gets strong hold of me because he is close by me, one of ourselves. Had he been an angel, his fingers would have been ice. Had he been from Saturn or from Uranus, some gallant fighter who had observed the law—had he been from the womb of Mary by some far off and alien power, I must have submitted, and bent that way the yearnings of my confidence: but as he is from *me*, that is from the sad stock to which I and my house belong, I grasp him better. It may not be so with others. I look at him as I look at Adam. And as I am quieted under the imputations of guilt, when I see it like the acorn from the oak dropping from the very fountains of my blood, so I can take hold more of Christ, when I sweep him under the thought,—"God has made of one blood all nations for to dwell on all the face of the earth" (Acts xvii : 26); and, when I look upon the millions of my kin, can look on One, crowned and blessed; and, gazing on Adam, whose guilt has settled on the rest, can gaze also on Christ, and see the finger of the King pointing to him in that glorious decree, "The Lord hath laid on him the iniquity of us all."

# III.
# IS GOD A TRINITY?

# PREFACE.

THE author of this book has no other occupation for the remainder of his life one-tenth part as interesting to him, as the undoing, as far as his feeble efforts can, prevalent superstitions of the church in respect to the justification of believers.

He finds piety in the Roman Catholic Church, but desperately marred by superstitious additions. So of the Baptist Church; so of the Methodist; so of the ritualistic Episcopalians: a great many good works, and a great many pious experiences, increasing in excellence and amount as the church becomes not Papist but Protestant, and not Protestant alone but down nearer the rock-bed of absolute Christianity.

But this he notices: Churches flourish numerically by force of their superstitions. I offer shares on Wall Street. I get the most bids if there be an element of gambling. If what I have to propose involves hard work, men bid slowly. If it have a speculative cast, men crowd upon me and buy. And so of the different denominations. There are pious people in every one of them. There are the most pious people in those that have most of Christ. But how obvious is it that the children of this world are wiser than the children of light ; and, therefore, that the way-making property of a church, or that by which it gathers numbers, is not the pious points in it, but the superstitions; or, in other words, the pious points give it character and favor with heaven, but its superstitions cut its way, and load on it its numerical strength, though they bring it at last to its ghostly dissolution.

Let me illustrate this. The Baptists are a pious sect, but who does not see that they make their way by immersion? The Jansenists were an excellent people : and who that has seen much of ritualism is narrow enough to deny, that there are singular instances of faith under the most direful idolatry? And, yet, it is the idolatry that fights the battle. It is the labor-saving principle. Or rather, it is that which does without purity of life. And, therefore, though good men get into such systems, they are flocked into by the bad; and the ritualism is the speculative cast that makes the sect attractive as in the Wall Street overtures.

Now take our Presbyterian communion. I have thought it the very soberest. It seems down at the hard-pan of actual revelation. What could be more plain? And, yet, watch its operations. Regard its scenes of present revival. What does it harp upon most? Precisely those things that are capable of superstition.

We have nothing to make a superstition of, ritualistically; nor in our forms; nor in our measures We have no idols that can be set up, and looked at, unless the eucharist and the sacramental baptism still have cleaving to them, specially in our symbols (Conf. C. 28, § 6; see also Sh. Cat. Qu. 92), a little of the rust of the middle age. We are shut up, like the culprit in a prison, with nothing to commit suicide with, except the bare walls, or the strips we can tear from our covering. And yet the Wall Street appetite is there. How do we gratify it? By seizing that which can be best exsiccated and made insignificant. Our Saviour says, " Repent." It is hard to get facility out of that. Isaiah says, " Wash you: make you clean" (Is. i : 16). Our Lord says, " If thou wilt enter into life, keep the commandments" (Matt. xix: 17). Ezekiel says, " Make you a new heart" (Ez. xviii : 31). The apostle speaks of repentance and conversion for the remission of sin (Acts iii : 19 ; Mar. i : 4). These are not easy instruments of superstition. And, therefore, faith, which is unspeakably more shadowy, attracts the eager instinct of our humanity as that through which can be made more facile the offerings of salvation.

Now, to a discerning eye, faith and repentance are co-essential: obedience and believing are the same *in nuce*: when our King says, Do well and be accepted (Gen. iv : 7), it is not necessary to have in eye the covenant of works, but repenting and converting. If any man says, We cannot obey perfectly, such a creed echoes, Nor believe perfectly. The true mind looks from Christ to James; and where Christ says, Do my sayings, and thou hast thy house upon a rock (Matt. vii : 24), it asks what those sayings are, and, finding them to teach truth (v : 33–37), and love (v : 44), and meekness (v : 5), and long suffering (v: 39), and honesty (vii: 12), and the commonest duties among men (vii: 1), it understands what the old nation ought to have understood when it was commanded, " Do this and thou shalt live" (Lev. xviii: 5; Lu. x: 28); and it reconciles Paul with James when Paul says, A man is justified by faith, and James, scouting an eviscerated faith, says, " Ye see, then, how that by works a man is justified, and not by faith only" (Jas. ii: 24).

Now, believing that hypocrites abound; and believing that there are profligates in the church; and believing that they come there under the hands of ministers; and hearing these ministers preach; and believing that they misapprehend the doctrine of salvation,—we would like to spend our life in earnest remonstrance. What the water is to one; and what the priest is to another; and what systematical conceits of order may be to the salvation of a third; that, I believe, mere trust, without a particle of moral trait, is to the everlasting salvation of many of our people.

Now, unfortunately to the outward eye, in this zeal for purity of life, this would-be reformation of my brethren, finds itself confronted with another faith, which, it is to be feared, will cast, oceans of distance from me, the purest of the people.

Why write about it?

This is the very point that is pressed by almost every friend.

There are men who deeply sympathize with these views of justification; men who are waked to thought; men who predict a large influence, even for humble means, to preaching in a consistent way justification by works (Jas. ii: 21). There might be a growing horror kindled, and a broken-hearted surprise, that we, who have been most bitter against the Pope, and most bewildered by the possibilities of a reviving ritualism, should find the monster in ourselves; and that we have made the very simplicities of faith a soul-destroying and church-corrupting instrument of superstition.

But publish this book, it will be said, and one man at least may leave the enterprise.

Nay, all that he has ever writ, and all that he may hope to write, will be a voice against it.

The advocate of a bare belief, who has cut off from it all elements of holiness, will take courage in the very fact, that the impulse to oppose him is so soon caught by other gusts, and is so soon showing its source by quarreling with other doctrines of evangelical Christianity.

What am I to do therefore? It would be such a pleasure to remain in shelter! Why not take one thing at a time? If Justification be the more important point, why not prefer that, and have something posthumous for the other?

This has been said to me.

But, unfortunately, we are all confessors. Each lives not a day but he avows the confession of his faith. There are honesties in this matter. And, though I might remain concealed, and not renew my avowals but upon some change of place; yet what for a defence is that? Do I not virtually avow, every day and hour, my original confession?

I will not meet my brethren, therefore, with anything concealed.

But, now ; a little on the other side.

When I finished my " Metaphysics," and found that I differed from the reigning school ; and when, under the light of an ethical belief, I criticised ten points in our prevalent dogmatic forms ; * and when, at a later date, I conceived the two monographs that will perhaps be bound up with this,—I began to take the alarm. My " Metaphysics" might be a matter of free lance. My " Fetich" had been confessed as true by a majority of Calvinistic chairs.† These monographs could not be mortally astray. But where was this thing to end ? I might, thus far, not be amenable to my church ; but where further ? I began to be anxious about the working of my mind. And, as a man must follow it wherever it will lead, I began to look eagerly ahead, and ask, where an erring intellect would carry me next, against the opinions of bodies of my brethren.

I did the only thing practicable. I plunged into my whole theology. Having returned from a lengthened route, made necessary by philosophical publication, I did what the old man does who taps the wheels after they come from a trip. I wished to see if I was sound. And, therefore, with as much prayer as I could offer, and with abundant purpose to be true, I studied the whole system of our faith ; and came out, as I was grateful to find, thoroughly and emphatically fixed on every point of our common soteriology.

So eminent was this, that I found myself utterly

* See " *Fetich in Theology.*"  † In America.

opposed to the usual changes that have been proposed for our Confession. Depravity; I found it philosophical. I found it of every faculty, and in every act. Why not call it "total"? I found there were but two commandments, and I kept neither; and, therefore, I had nothing to propose in the way of limit or qualification. Imputation; I found it forensic. Adam; I found him my ruin. He corrupted me naturally; but he corrupted me, also, federally. That is, a bad child cannot come from a father as an acorn does from an oak; but there must be justice in it. There must be some arrangement of law, to justify my corruption by my parents. Redemption; I believed it penal; conversion, immediate; regeneration, gracious; our call, effectual; our helplessness, entire; and our justification, adoption and sanctification all that they are ever made, and more, than by these mere trust believers. Moreover, I believed in Christ. I found him to be literally God: not God in the sense that he was not a man, or in a way that none of us entertain it, viz., that the true man was directly, and *qua* man, transmutedly the Almighty; but that he was God-man, having God incarnate in him ; and that he was all, and more than all, that the most who have been the purest in the church have glorified as the actual Almighty.

Moreover, I ennobled his redemption. Had he been a man, I could not trust him : or an angel ; or a God in the Arian sense; or divine after the Socinian pattern. To me, he was the Maker of the universe ; and more God in the actual sense, than he could be, under my old ideas.

Thus there emerged out of all my inquisition a remarkably rigid faith; and when I added that I was a *jure divino* churchman; and a far firmer believer of Scriptural Presbytery than the great majority of my brethren: and when I rechallenged all this, and found it seated in my thought, and impossible to be removed in any usual intellectual possibility at my time of life, I felt quieted from restless fever, and riveted in devoted affection to the communion in which I had been brought up.

Alas for me! that I should have any fear that I must be detruded out of it!

In the midst of all these studies, I found one great central object disappearing out of the firmament of my confession. It has been a singular history. Years ago I had a similar onsault. In reading the word of God, the Trinity suddenly deserted me. I said, It has been a fanciful conceit. I said, The divinity of kings, the right to persecute, the blood of Abraham, the grace of baptism, the sacrifice of the mass, have reigned unchallenged in the church. They are the "unsanctioned fables" of which Paul speaks (1 Tim. iv: 7). Now are we clear of such like? I was clear that we were not. And there broke upon me with dismay the panic-driven discovery that there was no Trinity; that it was all a figment; that it was, not odious to reason, but absent from the Word; and I searched and searched and searched, and the discovery almost was, that the Bible was colorless of such a dogma, and, by any reasonable mode, could not be made to teach those hypostatic differences.

But I rallied. I thought of this text; "The

## Preface. 11

glory that I had with thee" (Jo. xvii : 5); I thought of this, " Thou Lord in the beginning" (Heb. i : 10); I thought of this, " By whom were all things created" (Col. i : 16); I thought of this, " Of the Father, and of the Son, and of the Holy Ghost" (Matt. xxviii : 19) : I made a thorough reinspection of the proofs, and found myself restored to my old impressions.

I had almost forgotten it.

But now, a second time, at the same weak places, when I was inviting a thorough review, there came upon me the same assault ; and the texts that had stood by the doctrine, utterly failed me.

Stirred, as I naturally would be, where my very church was slipping away from me, I awoke to the full seriousness of the case. I gave up everything. For three months I did nothing but inspect the Trinity. A library happened to be near, uncommonly rich in all that literature, and I did the best I could. I scouted very soon all the criticisms of *reason*, except perhaps those that doubted whether there was any thought under the word " Person." I saw it was not a Bible word. But my investigations of *Scripture* led me to a verdict like this,—that if the Bible taught the Trinity, it taught the Mass more and better; that its teaching both was fancied by a mistake of figures ; that its teaching either was one of the vagaries of the human heart ; and that its teaching neither would long ago have been the faith, if the hypostatic distinctions of the Almighty disturbed our ransom in the same serious way as did the dishonored sacrament.

This, then, was the process of the study. Now

for the result. I do not believe in the Trinity. It may be said, You are a Sabellian. You believe that the Father is God, and the Son is God, and the Spirit is God. But you do not believe in the hypostatic difference that subsists between them. You believe in a modality. You believe that the Creator is God, and the Redeemer is God, and the Sanctifier is God; and that these are but modal differences that make up the triplicity of the Almighty.

I would have no objection to that. That is, I hold that these names are all different, for that these offices all exist. These divine appellatives have each a different sense. I would have no objection to the man who made these senses the divisions of a sermon; for undoubtedly God has all these features of versatile administration. But I will not so take that critical number, THREE, as to suppose that there is a norm in it; and that the infinite modalities of God are circumscribed by any Trinity. I will not admit any intended threeness. And after my three months' wrestle, I will speak in this way,—"They call him Indra, Mitra, Varuna, Agni; then he is the beautiful-winged heavenly Garutmat: that which is One, the wise call it in divers manners: they call it Agni, Yama, Mâterisvan" (*Rig-veda* I. 164, 46): " Wise poets make the beautiful-winged, though he is one, manifold by words" (*R–v.* x: 114, 5).

Now, to be a great deal more precise. All that Dr. Alexander and Francis Turretin would impute of Deity to Christ, I do, and perhaps more. That is I put the whole Godhead in him. I make the Father, as he himself seems to do (Jo. v: 19, 26, 36;

vi: 57; x: 29, 30, 36), his Godhead. My gospel, therefore, is safe: my redemption, perfect. Jehovah, among the old Jews, was Christ moving about without his incarnation; and, if you ask me what that means, I would say, It was God, under whatever name, administering in the name of Emmanuel: pardoning on the base of his obedience; creating on the faith of his advent; and intending, in the fullness of time, to unite himself with him as one person, and to be, as plenary God, what we have imagined as being the Eternally Begotten.

The difficulties of this will hereafter be relieved by Scripture.

I wish only to say, that God eternally, and before his Incarnation, is, to me, One Person; that God eternally, after his incarnation, is, as God, One Person; that, Spirit, Word, and Jehovah, he is but describing himself as the glorious Almighty; and that, when I pray for the Spirit; or reverence the Son; or worship the Father,—I am thinking of the One Personal God: and that it would have been infinitely better never to load the faith with the Platonic Trinity.

You may say, Explain all that.

And I do it eagerly.

"That the doctrine of the Trinity was indebted for its development to Christology, is universally acknowledged" (Dorner, I. A. p. 354). Undoubtedly the shock that this preface occasions, is due to our thought for the gospel. But suppose the gospel is in no sense implicated. Suppose the Arian affects our faith, and destroys our ransom; and suppose the

Socinian is just as dangerous. Suppose the Deity of Christ, and the helplessness of sin, and the preciousness of ransom, have all been denied, by previous impugners of the Trinity, till they have swollen themselves into monsters of unbelief. May not that now be just the difficulty? And suppose it all at last different. Suppose a new dissection. Suppose the gospel gloriously honored. Suppose the scheme carved deeper; and the strength of God's magisterial claim actually heightened. Suppose redemption made to stand apart like the works of a watch, and the metaphysics of the Deity separate like the case that holds them in; should anti-trinity thought be, any more, looked upon as fatal? And would it not be a preposterous stand; if I trust in Christ; and lean upon him as God : if I take his blood, and wash myself in it as the divine redemption : if I make him the whole Jehovah, and think he will reign so forever and forever: if I pray for his Spirit, but only think that "the Lord is that Spirit" (2 Cor. iii: 17), and that in praying for the Spirit I am praying for God,—to impugn me like mortal heretics?—praying for Christ, or praying for the Father, or, if you please, praying for grace in any guise in which it may be revealed most beautifully, to say, that, because I doubt a hypostatic difference, therefore, in what men are not sure they have an idea at all, I wreck my faith, and must be cast out of my communion?

And that brings me to the last point.

I have determined to be scrupulously exact with my brethren. I desire to be humble, too, and modest as to the belief that I am right. How unspeakably

## Preface. 15

absurd the attitude of one just in my place to arrogate the discovery of the light, when the very monarchs of the world's thought have been piously and earnestly against him!

But I must do something.

I had thought of an immediate interview with my Presbytery. But my friends entreat that I will test every position to the very last; and that if I find myself irreclaimably fixed, the result of all this industry and care may be, to offer my beliefs in the way most easily to be inspected by those above me.

That, then, is my plan.

But what will be the result? Would to God I exactly knew.

I am clear thus far. I had better not resign my position in the church. I doubt the legality of such a move. But if it were legal, why should I do it? I could but swim back thitherward as soon as I was able. Why should I not invite my Presbytery to keep me in?

And, now, as to the possibility of that.

Two things occur to me.

(1) In the first place, there are differences already. Turretin believes that Christ was generated by the Father. So does our Confession. A member of my Presbytery teaches that that is no where taught in Scripture. Our creed teaches a marked Eschatology, conspicuous in which is the advent of Christ, and a judgment at the last day. A member of my Presbytery teaches a premillenarian scheme; and traverses much in my Confession. So of an external church. My Confession accentuates it. My brethren make

light of it. The six days' creation : that is taught in our symbols. Who believes it? I myself would be, perhaps, one of the few men in my Presbytery to adhere prevailingly to the ancient thinking. Now, who will draw the line? A man publishes one year a *kenosis* of the Deity, and an actual suffering of God on the cross on Calvary. He is an excellent brother, and he is made the Moderator of the next Assembly. Undoubtedly, then, difference from the Confession will not cast a man out of the Church. The question is, How serious is it? And my course seems to be to defend my belief. If I can make it appear secondary; if I can show that I hold the vitals of the gospel ; if I can prove that I am not a Socinian ; if I can show that I approach my faith from another quarter; if I can show that Arminius and Pelagius and Arius have neither tampered with me ; but that I am a high Calvinist in all the realities of my creed, —then my Presbytery will have to determine whether one symptom of a Socinian's belief cannot become a feature in a far lesser disease, and whether a hypostatic difference in the Godhead is in such sense vital to the faith, that a minister must go out of his church, even if he puts the WHOLE GODHEAD in Christ, and builds on that scheme a perfect redemption.

The Presbytery must decide.

(2) But may I not say another thing ; How is a great church like ours to be corrected of any error? It may be answered, It has none. But is that certain? The time was when this very church persecuted. The time was when it was largely Jacobite. Across the sea it is still Erastian. In some cases at

least, it holds sacramental error. What is the relief? Must it be groomed with a foreign comb; or may it do something to its own recuperation?

Suppose the Trinity were a mistake; suppose it had bestrid the gospel in its earlier planting. Suppose it were a Platonic set, grafted by the Jews, and inarched from them into the faith of Christians. Suppose that John opposed it, and that his first strong text was meant to fence it out (Jo. i: 1),—how is the church to become satisfied of that? Why may there not be a little pause? And why must it be by bell and torch that the church must expel the truth, and that the light must go out from established fanes, and shine into some shieling church, that must become, in turn, the inveterate oppressor?

May God in his infinite mercy protect the truth! And if there be any who pity me, may they offer this prayer,—first, that I may be brought out of dangerous mistake; and, second, that I may behave humbly and well; so that when I have gained time enough to have my brethren thoroughly look into my case to see whether I am in dangerous error, or to see whether they themselves are certain of their faith, I may, if the Church is against me, do nothing to distract her; but step aside, with a modest doubt of myself, and with a heightened earnestness, to pray and find out, after such a verdict, what can really be known of the truth of the Almighty.

JNO. MILLER.

PRINCETON, Oct. 2d, 1876.

# CONTENTS.

## I.

THE TRINITY AND REASON.......................... 23

### CHAPTER I.
THE TRINITY NOT TO BE JUDGED BY REASON.............. 23

### CHAPTER II.
THE TRINITY TO GIVE SOME IDEA OF ITSELF TO REASON .. 26

### CHAPTER III.
THE TRINITY WITH NO IDEA: NO IDEA, EVER ATTEMPTED FOR A TRINITY, NOT PRONOUNCED NO IDEA AT ALL BY ACCEPTED TRINITARIANS............................ 27

### CHAPTER IV.
THE TRINITY WITH NO SHELTER IN INFALLIBILITY......... 30

### CHAPTER V.
THE TRINITY ACCOUNTED FOR BY HISTORY................ 33

*Contents.*

## II.

|  | PAGE |
|---|---|
| THE TRINITY AND SCRIPTURE | 39 |

### CHAPTER I.

METHOD OF TREATMENT ............................................. 39

### CHAPTER II.

GOD THE HOLY GHOST .............................................. 41

§ 1. *The Unity of God* ........................................... 41
§ 2. *The Unity of God's Person not Disturbed by Different Names* ................................................... 43
§ 3. *The Unity of God's Person not Disturbed by Emblems* . 44
§ 4. *The Unity of God's Person not Disturbed by His Holy Spirit* ..................................................... 45
§ 5. *The Unity of God's Person not to be Disturbed by Grammatic Differences—and first, not by Differences of Person* .................................................. 48
§ 6. *The Unity of God's Person not Disturbed by Differences of Gender* ............................................... 50
§ 7. *The Unity of God's Person not Disturbed by Difference of Number* ............................................... 54
§ 8. *The Unity of God's Person not Disturbed by Difference of Case* .................................................. 56
§ 9. *The Unity of God's Person not Disturbed by any other Differences* ............................................. 58
§ 10. *No Distinct Personality of the Spirit* ..................... 67

### CHAPTER III.

GOD THE SON ..................................................... 72

§ 1. *The Deity of the Son* ....................................... 72
§ 2. *The Humanity of the Son* .................................... 72
§ 3. *The Begetting of the Son* ................................... 73

§ 4. *The Son and the Spirit*.......................... 76
§ 5. *The Son and the Father*.......................... 78
§ 6. *The Son as Jehovah*............................. 80
§ 7. *The Son as Sent* ............................... 81
§ 8. *The Son as Wisdom*............................. 82
§ 9. *The Son and the Logos* ......................... 83
§10. *The Son and the Creation*....................... 90
§11. *The Son's Pre-existence*......................... 100
§12. *Angel of Jehovah*............................... 109
§13. *The Son as Father, Son and Holy Ghost*........... 112

## CHAPTER IV.

GOD THE FATHER....................................... 112

§ 1. *Meaning of the Name*........................... 112
§ 2. *No Name or Work Sacred to One Person*........... 115
§ 3. *The Father as Son* ............................. 117
§ 4. *The Father as Spirit*........................... 119
§ 5. *The Father as Jehovah* ......................... 121
§ 6. *The Father and His Glory*....................... 125
§ 7. *The Baptismal Formula*.......................... 127
§ 8. *The Apostolic Benediction*...................... 130
§ 9. *The Scene at Jordan*............................ 131

## CHAPTER V.

THE TRINITY NOTHING TO THE GOSPEL..................... 132

§ 1. *What are the Gospel Ideas?*..................... 132
§ 2. *The Incarnation* ............................... 134
§ 3. *Redemption* .................................... 134
§ 4. *Mediation* ..................................... 134
§ 5. *Intercession*................................... 137
§ 6. *Regeneration*................................... 141
§ 7. *Justification* ................................. 142
§ 8. *Adoption*....................................... 144
§ 9. *Judgment* ...................................... 145
§10. *Sanctification* ................................ 145
§11. *Glorification*.................................. 146

## III.

CONCLUSION... ............................... 148

### CHAPTER I.

THE SCANDAL OF THIS BOOK ....................... ... 148

### CHAPTER II.

THE BENEFIT OF THIS BOOK............................ 151

# I.

# THE TRINITY AND REASON.

## CHAPTER I.

### THE TRINITY NOT TO BE JUDGED BY REASON.

I WISH to set forward the statement, that I am moved to this book by Scripture. In order to do this, I hold the ground that the Trinity is not to be judged by reason. In order to do this, I follow that statement, and show that it is very peculiar. *Everything* is to be judged by reason. Until it be true that the eye is no judge of color, it will never be true that reason is no judge of anything ; for, in fact, there is no judge of anything but reason; and of all that our race can conceive, reason is the sole and universal arbiter.

What is meant, therefore, by reason being no judge of the Trinity? Let me explain by the instance of gravitation. Reaching far back to absolute sight, and to those most obstinate of all demonstrators of truth, mathematical figures, the mind has been forced into the faith that there is a gravitation. It is no judge of the phenomena, afterward. The man who is prolific of difficulties, and tells us that gravitation is impossible ; and who backs up his thought by saying that the sun is ninety-four millions of miles away, and that its grappling the earth over that distance is a sheer conceit, we laugh at. Let the sun get over his own difficulties. We have forever demonstrated the truth, that he does attract; and all inter-situated puzzles we neglect. Reason is a judge of everything; but, having made her judgment back at the original truth, we know what we mean by saying, that she is no judge of the doctrine afterward.

So of the Trinity. In a way that is universal and confessed, reason has made her judgment of the word of God. This is a broad field; and she has examined it thoroughly. This is the all-comprehensive fact; and she has established it by outward and inward evidence. She has come to the strongest faith (and no disciple of the Redeemer will lightly cavil at it), that the Bible is the voice of the Almighty; and this, not by mystic partialities, but by reasonable tests, which lift her ever afterward above the fear of what is contained in the recognized canon.

This is what is meant by reason being no judge of the Trinity.

The Papist has a kindred submissiveness. He does not deny the authority of reason; but he has spent all her power in examining into the authority of the Church. There has been his original question. He holds you to be right in testing him there. And, if you would witness patience, you have but to look at his books on the church. Where you are building up the authority of Scripture, he is laying the corner stone of Zion; and it is only after you have accepted the church, that he lays his hand upon your mouth, and tells you that you have no right of private judgment afterward.

And to show how sincere we are in all this, we say plainly, If the Mass were in the Bible, we would believe the Mass. The Papist believes it on the authority of the Church. We would believe it on the authority of Scripture. And, in either case, man's appeal is to his rational nature; for, in the one case, it has led him to accept the Church, and in the other, Scripture; and it is only on the lower ground, that he denies, in such things as the Trinity and the Mass, any right to the judgments of the mind.

But it may be said, What if a doctrine seems flat against reason? Even then I would not disown it. We have seen the reasonableness of this in the instance of gravitation. If Paul tells me to persecute the heretic, I will do so, as the voice of the Almighty; if he pronounces boldly upon the truth of Jacobitism, I am a Jacobite; if he tells me that Christ is in the wafer, I believe it: and my principle is here:—I am under a great hardship, and my conscience revolts at the texts, but I am the devotee of a great process. I have gone through all labored proofs. My conscience, and everything besides, pronounces for the Bible; and, when that great huge fact comes athwart that lesser one, a belief in transubstantiation, I yield. Bring me any miserable faith that does not positively deny the grace of the Almighty, and, if you can deceive me so far as to make it Scriptural, I will accept it; and on the sheer base that I have accepted the word of God as "the only infallible rule of faith and practice."

CHAPTER II.

THE TRINITY TO GIVE SOME IDEA OF ITSELF TO REASON.

BUT, though we admit that the Trinity is not to be judged by reason; and though the fact of transubstantiation, if you will prove that it is taught in the word of God, I will compound for as made possible by some mysterious miracle; though I will become an Inquisitor, in spite of all its contradiction of conscience, and will get over this difficulty by remembering that heretics are the property of God; though I will believe in the right of kings, to the extent of enduring a bad king even though I could unseat him, if you will convince me that God ordains it; and I will hold He is the Lord of Providence, and can adjust the consequences of all His commands,— yet there is one right that reason retains, and that is, to know distinctly what it is that it believes. To say, I believe in the Mass, and to be left with nothing but the four letters; or to say, I am a Jacobite, or, if you please, I am an Inquisitor, and leave me no idea under the formula professed,—is of course the most awful solecism. And, therefore, coming now to the case of the Trinity, if when you come to propound the doctrine, you give me positively no conception of it, it is preposterous beyond the need of a discussion. I wish to draw a distinction between understanding a doctrine, and having a conception of it. I understand no doctrine under the sun. I have a conception of every doctrine. That is to say, No doctrine can possibly be embraced, that remains wrapt up in an expression, so that positively no thought comes out from what is spoken. I wish to insist upon this, upon the very outset of our teaching. What is the Trinity? It may be said, It is the doctrine of the Three in One. Of course our first landing place is upon the reserve that God is Three in a different sense from his being One. But when we come to remember, this is a mere speech, this is a mere exsiccated shell; this is no form of thought, till we say what the sense is. And there, now, precisely is our position. Reason is no judge of that sense after it is once announced. But the Trinity is no doctrine at all, and, therefore, in the court of intellect must be held by hypocrites; or else some conception must be given, in what sense God can be Three, and yet the most simple of all possible existence.

Think of excommunicating a man from the Church for failing to believe that of which you can give him no idea!

### CHAPTER III.

THE TRINITY WITH NO IDEA: NO IDEA, EVER ATTEMPTED FOR A TRINITY, NOT PRONOUNCED NO IDEA AT ALL BY ACCEPTED TRINITARIANS.

AND I am the more confirmed in this careful preliminary, because every idea of Trinitarianism that has ever been held, has been declared to be no idea at all by accepted Trinitarians. I confess that this is no positive argument. In the first place, it is impossible to declare who are accepted Trinitarians In the second place, the argument would not be positive, if we could. There might be ten men that held a particular doctrine ; and each nine might denounce the tenth, in turn, as holding it in a form that is perfectly unmeaning. This would not amount to refutation. All the classes of nine might be wrong, and yet, if one reflects a moment, one man of the ten might survive as right.

Let me illustrate. (1) Our Confession speaks of the " Eternally Begotten." The idea there contained is, that the Second Person of the Trinity is eternally derived. Hosts of thinkers pronounce that unmeaning. And one of our most distinguished divines disagrees with Turrettin; would conceive derivation unthinkable ; and boldly declares that it is not taught in the word of God (Hodge, Theol. V. i : p. 486). It will be noticed, therefore, that a man who denies the Trinity altogether, is but denying that which, in one form or other, has been denounced as senseless by the most pious of the orthodox.

Again :—

(2) The Trinity has been held to be the One conscious Divinity. Sherlock objected to this ; and denied, in that case, the possibility of threeness. He found in the Bible separate wills ; and proclaimed, as his notion of all that could be thought of as Three, separate consciousnesses. John Howe partially defended him. The Church broke out against him. And, yet, he never lost his See: and, though his belief was unvarnished Polytheism, yet it was distinctly enforced, on the principle we mentioned,—

that the opposite was unmeaning; that a belief requires something to be conceived; and that, if God is Three Persons, it is like saying he is a gnoot, or Abracadabra, unless it is a tri-personal Three, in the sense of separate intelligence.

(3) Andover has furnished another theory. Schleiermacher, explaining Sabellius, has rather adopted his thought, that the Trinity became a Trinity in time: that God did not eternally create; and that he did not eternally redeem: that, therefore, he became each of these in time: that the Trinity is the Creator and Redeemer and Sanctifier; and that, therefore, God grew to be these; and that this is the meaning of the inspired Trinity.

Moses Stuart modified this into a scheme. He said; and this was the foundation of his system; that what God lived to become in time, he was fitted to become from all eternity. And, therefore, his fitness to become this or that, was his trine relation. Accordingly, without pursuing this account, it will still farther illustrate our understood position. This learned man's appeal was to the *uselessness of the unmeaning;* and, seeming to forget that God was fit for a multiplicity of things from all eternity; that he came to paint black, and to paint yellow; that he came to make stars, and to make flowers; and that it was impossible to distinguish between what might be called Trinitarian fitnesses, and fitnesses for less hypostatic things,—he nevertheless continued in the church, unchallenged; and yet managed to add another whole theory to the faith, which lived only by denouncing everything else as vague and notionless.

## CHAPTER IV.

### The Trinity with no Shelter in Infallibility.

THUS the doctrine is like Maelzell's Chess-Player. We open each door in turn, and there is nothing in it. Yes, some one will say, there was a man in the Chess-Player, after all. I grant it; but on terms that no avowed Trinitarian will be willing to admit. There was a man in the Chess-Player, because, before each opening, he altered his position. A man proposes a Trinity: another man exposes it. He offers his in turn, and some third man shows there is nothing in it. He asseverates another, and a fourth man opens that door, and finds it empty. Now, a notion can be supported in this way; but it is, as a missile is, by flying through the air. I do not make a point of all this; and I discard reason as an intermediary. But this I do say, that reason ought not to be suborned *against* us.

Try any company.

Go among twenty ministers, and say,—Our fellow presbyter has denied the doctrine of the Trinity. The very first bubbling up of censure will be from that form of reason which is embalmed in the vote of the vast body of believers. The arrogance of the presbyter!—is the first thing that will strike every body. But how long should this outcry last? Always, if the Church is infallible; and, past doubt, the Church *is* infallible in vital matters. Let us consider this. There has always been a church. There cannot be a church without a gospel. There cannot be a gospel if there be damning error. Immunity from damning error is of the very faith of the gospel. And, therefore, when Papists claim infallibility, they are groping after some truth. And he is not hastily advised, who, convinced of the piety of his Zion, claims that Christ keeps it (Matt. xvi: 18 ; xxviii: 20), and holds that, let the Trinity be among the vitals of the scheme of grace, it is among the infallibilities of true believers.

But now, definitely, there is covered up the very question.

The ritualist holds that baptism is of necessity to grace. If so, it is vital. And if so, some church will possess it.

The orthodox hold, that Christ is necessary to pardon. If so, that is vital. And if so, the church will never lose that doctrine.

It is this true figure of infallibility that moves darkly in the background, and gives rancor to religious hate ; for when a man has been sufficiently ridiculed for pitting himself against the profound and pious, then this that is ghostly comes in, and he is made to tremble for his pride in arraying himself against the church of the Redeemer.

How, then, may we meet infallibility ? By rejoicing and trusting in it ; and by singing psalms to God that we are invulnerable through our infallible Redeemer: but not in any way that is prescriptive. Paul gives the rule :—" Prove all things. Hold fast that which is good." Doctrine must be vital first; infallible afterward. Otherwise Luther was apostate.

Here is a fellow presbyter. He comes to us in the fairest way. He invites us to the closest scrutiny. He says, Here is my system of Christ. I believe that the Trinity, like the Old Man of the Sea, has jumped npon the back of Sinbad, and made Christianity coarse and heavy through all its journey. I believe it is a robbery of the heathen. I believe it awakened Mohammed. I believe it has worn out missionaries. I believe it has kept back Pagans, who were obliged to perish in their sins, while their nation waited to learn an " unsanctioned fable" (1 Tim. iv : 7). I believe the great God in heaven was born himself into Jesus, "and so was and continueth to be, God and man, in two distinct natures, and one person, forever" (Sh. Catechism, Qu. 21). I believe just this is sufficient; and that ransom, and grace, and divine power, and all that was needed of sacrifice, and that all that there will ever be of glory, is sufficiently secured in this One Person, Jehovah.

And if a Christian says to me, Avaunt as a heretic, and never examines my faith, and never says, Is this discriminateness sufficient? if he never says, Is not the Trinity with this man a minor doctrine? and, even if he be in error, does he not hold the chief truths? and has he not a well knit system ; and does he not seem to say all for Christ except that there is a hypostatic difference between him and the Father? —if he has never done any thing for me like that, I'll tell you what he is like ; he is like the man that threw the first stone at Stephen, because he proclaimed the Galilean; he is like the court that imprisoned Ken because he refused the Declaration ; he is like the priests that burned Huss on the plea that he decried the sacrament. And there is a family likeness which I wish particularly to press; which claims a just infallibility, but which sins only in this, —that it brings within the reach of that blessing of God minor things, under the claim that these are of the essentials of salvation.

Men are not to choose how able shall be the man who discovers error. The mouse is not to be weighed who eats the lion out of the net. Galileans bearded Jewry. A miner's son shook St. Peter's. Poor peasant women sickened the world of martyrdoms. And if the humblest minister can put the Trinity alongside of the consecrated wafer, and make both seem figments of the sense, the Church has nothing to do but to examine it, and, laying all prerogative apart, give thanks for her infallible life, when she has thoroughly understood and thoroughly made good that it is fatal.*

CHAPTER V.

THE TRINITY ACCOUNTED FOR BY HISTORY.

ANY of us would say, before study, that the Trinity is revealed in the Old Testament. Any of us would at least declare, that it was revealed in the

* Is there not something that proves the Trinity a superstition in the very Creed of Athanasius, and in the fact that the church has not awoke her thunders against that long ago. Let us quote a part of it. "Whosoever will be saved must hold the Catholic faith. The Catholic faith is this,—that we worship one God in Trinity, and Trinity in Unity, neither confounding the persons nor dividing the substance. For there are three persons, but one Godhead. The Father is neither

Bible. Any of us would suppose, that it was taught in the first age of the church.

Now, to cut off all wandering, and to confine ourselves to the testimony of Scripture, I would say that all these things have been doubted, and doubted too by Trinitarians themselves. Athanasius holds that the Jews knew nothing of a Trinity. I mention other names in the margin.* Bellarmin holds that it is no where taught in Scripture. He builds it on tradition. Petavius holds that it was not caught by tradition. That is, he quotes from the fathers, and shows that it was not known in the first age of the

made, created, nor begotten. The Son is of the Father alone, not made, nor created, but begotten. The Holy Ghost is of the Father and the Son, neither made, nor created, nor begotten, but proceeding; and in this Trinity none is afore or after another; none is greater or less than another. This is the Catholic faith, WHICH EXCEPT A MAN BELIEVE FAITHFULLY, HE CANNOT BE SAVED." That this spurious creed, fraudulently palmed upon the church, and which, whatever Athanasius might have thought of it, never saw Athanasius, and was written centuries after he was dead,—should survive with vigor, and be treated with general respect, is itself an invitation, I think, to a reinvestigation of the whole subject; and to a strong suspicion of a faith that speaks so definitely of inconceivable things; and wields so insolently the anathemas of heaven for that of which the good people of an earlier world must certainly have had no idea.

* " The Papists deny that the doctrine of the Trinity is to be found in Scripture. See this plainly taught and urged by Card. Hosius, *de Auth. S. Scrip.* L. III : p. 33 : Gordonius Hunlaeus, *Cont. Tim. Comb. de Verbo Dei*, c. 19 ; Gretserus and Zanerus, *in Colloquio Ratisbon ;* Vega, Possevin, Wickius. . . These learned men, especially Bellarmin, and Wickius after him, have urged all the Scriptures they could, with the utmost industry, find out in this cause, and yet, after all, they acknowledge their insufficiency and obscurity."—*Locke's Commonplace Book. King's Life of Locke*, Vol. II. p. 104.

church.* Now what does that prove? Why, that tradition is very colorless; and that reason can do very little, on that tack, to relieve the faith.

Now, another matter.

History accounts for things.

If I am waked up by Scripture, and utter a cry, Why, where is the Trinity? and suddenly search, and find myself deserted of the idea, I naturally ask, How did it arise? and not in a way that we can pronounce decisive, and yet in quite a sufficient way, we find how it could have arisen.

Plato invented a Trinity: some think, by himself; some think, out of a spark of tradition. It is not in a form that Christians love; and many deny that it had any common origin with ours. While Plato was working in the schools, Rabbis were working in the Law, and making changes in it; that is, they were writing Targums, that is to say, paraphrases of the text. These were read in the Synagogues. One of the changes that the paraphrases made was, to put " Word of Jehovah" for " Jehovah." They found it once or twice (Ps. xxxiii: 6; cv: 19), and it fell in with reigning thought, and they took out the word "Jehovah," and they put in "Word of Jehovah" two hundred times. The Jewish ear, accordingly, was accustomed to it; and, when Alexandria was built, and the Septuagint was written, and the Alexandria Jews became the repositories of law, Philo and the men that preceded him worked upon these Targums, and brought in Platonic aid; and the writings remain which actually cast the Scrip-

* *Pet. de Trin.* I. 5, 7: 8, 2.

tures into Platonic moulds. Now, what was the result? Confessedly a species of Arianism. These men deified the Word: not as I do, by making it a name of God; but contrariwise, by making it an emanation. They did not all agree: and Philo himself was better than others of the school; but the tendency was this,—to say, The Word was an emanation. It was not God: and it was not man; but it was between them. It was not God; and it was not a creature; but it was an emanation. It was not eternal; and it was not yet to arise; but it was intermediate and in time. The distinct teaching was, that the Word was an emanation from God; subordinate; intermediate; and the origin of all the creatures.

Thence bring it to account that this teaching was in all the schools; and that John came upon the stage when pious thought was helplessly saturated with all these ideas.

What was he to do with them? Reply? Why, they were chameleon-like; and had no fixed expression. Not reply? Why, that would be to be waterlogged with hopeless prevarications. What could he do? Precisely what he did do. "In the beginning was the Word;" thus shearing away all thought of an emanation in time: " And the Word was with God" (E. V). Let me alter that at once. The preposition never means *with*.\* We have the

---

\* Perhaps I had better temper this by saying, that the few exceptions that might be imagined (as Mar. vi: 3 ; Matt. xiii: 56), are not absolute exceptions; and perhaps I had better refer, for the facts about this preposition, to Gesenius. He is a fair party to quote, be-

expression, " things pertaining to God" (E. V.: Heb. ii : 17 ; v : 1). The preposition means "*towards*," or "*pertaining to.*" Let us read it so. " In the beginning was the Word, and the Word pertained to God." That is, it did not emanate and go out and become subordinate and intermediate, but it was simply God's word. It was like God's arm, or God's power. It was just God expressing himself, and God revealing himself, as though he had said, like Paul, " Whom therefore ye ignorantly worship, him declare I unto you" (Acts xvii: 23).

But, to cut off all mistake, he gives another and most trenchant expression. " In the beginning was the Word, and the Word pertained to God, and God was the Word." Alford admits that, if it be translated this way, it denies the Trinity ! and old Middleton has, for decades, stood like a tower, to say that the Greek must be reversed. It is a judgment upon the Greek article (Gram. iii. s. 4, § 1) ; but the finest scholars have now reversed that opinion (Winer, Glassius, *etc.*). The old Vulgate never obeyed it. And the article has another way to account for itself, viz., that it is the specific mark that it is "*the*" Word in the great reigning sense,—which, John would teach, was nothing but the Almighty.

But we are anticipating. We are not among Scriptures yet. We quote this in the way of historic elucidation.

We verily believe much could be made of his-

cause his very principles are, to the very utmost bent, to supply the force of " *with*" in this very passage. And yet the strict reader will see, for all that, which way his authority inclines. See, also, Winer.

tory; and that we could trace the Trinity like the fossils in a rock. Indeed, we think that it is impossible that it was an apostolic dogma, if for no other reason than that it is thought vital, and that it is laid down so infinitely not so in their books. But let all this pass. We are now finishing our account of reason; and all we wish to do is, to bind it hand and foot, now that we have got out of it a decision for the canon, while we ask, simply, what that canon says. Let us *suppose* an idea. Let us *imagine* that we apprehend it. Let it be, with more or less sense, *triplicity in unity;* and while with reverent appeal we beg to be enlightened in the word, let reason, on the other side, not treat us in any way we do not deserve, after our appeal, like Paul's, has gone to a higher tribunal.

# II.

# THE TRINITY AND SCRIPTURE.

### CHAPTER I.

#### METHOD OF TREATMENT.

THE best way to prove a doctrine is to state it clearly, and then show, text by text, that it is supported in the word of God. This is the method of expert scientists, when they discard a theory like emission, and establish a doctrine like undulation, as the true theory of light. It is eminently the natural way. They state their theory clearly, and, then, open the book of nature; and their highest exultation is, when fact after fact weaves beautifully in, and when such a phenomenon as two light rays fitting wave into wave and producing darkness, demonstrates the undulation of the ether, rather than its direct emission.

Should I take this most natural plan, therefore, I should, first, state my express doctrine of God. I should say, God is one person. I should say, God is incarnate in Christ. I should say, No hypostatic difference separates off the Father from the Son; but the one God is Emmanuel. God with us. I would say, God furnishes a Mediator, the Man Christ Jesus; and the suitedness of that Mediator is, first, that he is a man, to stand between God and us, and, second, that he is God, to bring the whole being of the Godhead in to give value to his atonement, and to furnish the regenerating power; the idea being that, on the side of God, the Father and the Son are one; and that it is only on the side of man that the Son stands off from the Father, and can be looked upon, with the higher truth in the emblem, as a glorious Mediator (1 Tim. ii: 5).

Then my part would be, to trace this in the Word: to show, wherever I read, that my doctrine is the one advanced, and not the doctrine of the Trinity; to show that one agrees, and the other does not agree, with the main tenor of the book; and to show, as I confidently might, that where the Trinitarian has spun a tenuous thread of apparent connection for his scheme, the Bible itself breaks it; that is, that a discrepance in God, shadowily made out by a discrepance in facts or titles, is carefully obliterated; some wave of simple denial coming up from the Word, to wash out the lines of distinction that might seem to have been implied in other passages.

This plan we should have preferred. This plan would be noble, for example, in blotting out from the dream of the church baptismal regeneration.

But now, simply to meet a prejudice, I take another. Theology is an intricate scheme; and men have gotten to believe that anything can be tortured out of the Bible. If I state my theory, and then go on to find it, men will say, and say truly, that my glow of enthusiasm is just that which infidels have, when they are picking up the ingots of truth, as they regard them, in physical nature.

My plan, therefore, will be worse, but more conciliating. I will not take theism bereft of hypostases, and then prove it; but I will take my adversary's ground, and follow it along as long as it will bear me; and when I come to the spot where Scripture forsakes it, I will put the staff into my neighbor's hands. I will not frame a doctrine, and then support it; for the mass will say, I am expounding to suit myself. But I am going to take my neighbor's doctrine, and follow it along as far as we agree. And where we differ, I am going to make my neighbor expound. In other words, I am going to take the doctrine of the Trinity, and strip it of all in which we all agree; and then I am going to take the dry husk that remains, bereft of all that I can see established, and ask my neighbor to establish it; in other words take the HYPOSTATIC DIFFERENCES, which are the only points which this book rejects, and simply stand on my watch, and refuse anything baseless that may be supposed to cover them.

## CHAPTER II.

### GOD THE HOLY GHOST.

### § 1. *The Unity of God.*

ACTING on this method,—My neighbor and I agree in the unity of Jehovah. I would not be satisfied with meekly counting this as an agreement, if my neighbor did not insist that his merely dividing Jehovah into Persons did not interfere with His essential unity. If this were a new controversy, the whole would be abhorrent. I would quote at once, and insist upon the great zeal of the Bible to cut off everything *like* division. " Hear, O Israel; the Lord our God is one Jehovah" (Deut. vi : 4). But when, in the long controversy of ages, my neighbor tells me that all this has been considered ; when he takes the passage, " I and my Father are one" (Jo. x : 30), and calls my attention to the fact that "*one*" is neuter, and, therefore, merely means one substance, one essence ; and when he takes the opposite text, " Now a mediator is not a mediator of one, but God is one" (Gal. iii : 20), and says, True enough, the "*one*" is masculine, but it means one Person as Jehovah, referring to a different personality from that of the Trinity,—I decline debate; I take the man's theory as he holds it. I think it too long a path to weary him down on these isolated texts: but I take his theory : his theory is, There are three persons : he tells me it is consistent : I mean by that, that he professes to see a consistency between the absolute unity of God and three Persons : * and, therefore, I follow the plan that I have stated. I take the unity of God, and consider it a ground on which we both unite. And then I ask him to go further. And when he expounds to me that the Spirit of God is of one essence with the Father, I say, Beyond doubt,

* Though the Bible says, " There shall be one Jehovah, and his name one" (Zech. xiv : 9).

God the Holy Ghost. 43

but beg him to leave this ground in which we both agree, and lead me to the ground in which I can Scripturally see the disturbance into different Persons.

## § 2. *The Unity of God's Person not Disturbed by Different Names.*

Of course he cannot do that on the basis of different names. If he quote the words, The Father and the Son and the Holy Ghost, no matter where it can be found, whether in gospel form (Matt. xxviii : 19), or priestly benediction (2 Cor. xiii : 14), it proves not a single thing. The exuberance of the East multiplies appellations. That their sense is different, affords no evidence at all. And a confirmation of this is, that nobody dreams so. The Mighty God, the Holy One of Israel, the King in Zion, and any unnumbered list, Jehovah, Redeemer, the Lord our Righteousness,—on any account of their number,—or on any account of their diversity of sense,—are no proof of a Trinity. There must be more special reasoning. For, thus far, all parties must agree; that the Holy Ghost, for example, as an appellation, is not to be set down as not an appellation for the Almighty, or to be set off to some distinguishable Person, except for special reasons different from the fact that it is a different name, or that it means differently from other words for the Most High.

Again we are in agreement, therefore. No man would take the words, Jehovah, and, the Lord Almighty, and, simply because they mean differently, conceive a hypostatic difference. We still have, therefore, the evidence unfurnished. If the Trinity is true, we are driving in all imaginary outposts, and taking the very wisest plan to shut it in its citadel, and make it tell its actual clue for its discovery in the Word of God.

### § 3. *The Unity of God's Person not disturbed by Emblems.*

It cannot prove itself by emblems—I mean by the mere fact of emblems.

If I read of the " arm of God," there is no reason that I should discuss it. There is no demand in the English, and none especially in the richness of the East, that I should even stop to notice it. The " hand of God," the " eye of God," the " foot of God," and a perfect wilderness of such expressions, require not a word of comment. I should only vex people by stopping to explain. If I should ask, Is the " arm of God"(Is. li : 9) the same as God, people would laugh at me; not that the question might not be answered, Yes, and No, but that when it was answered both ways, with every possible distinction, the very best mind would be less clear than it was at the beginning. All men understand such expressions. Trinitarians could make a list of them by hundreds ; and they would never dream that they had reference to a Trinity. And if I were to read, " The word of God," they would agree with me—I am sure a fair Trinitarian would,—that the "*prima facie*" impression should be, that it is a mere emblem. He would admit that he must bring contrary evidence from otherwheres ; and that the " finger of

God the Holy Ghost. 45

God" is no less evidence of a divine Person, than "the word of God" (Ps. cvii: 20), if it is to be anything in the emblem itself that is to reveal to us the mighty difference.

§ 4. *The Unity of God's Person not Disturbed by His Holy Spirit.*

Here, then, we are confronted, in a way easy for the estimate of proof, by the mention of the Holy Spirit.

Let us proceed cautiously.

Imagine our reading of "*the Spirit*" for the first time.

To a Hebrew eye the word would be "*breath.*" We read it as "*spirit.*" We read it by a word that has strayed away from its sense. But the Hebrew had only partly done so. It was like a bird with the shell still partly upon its back. Therefore, when the Jew read about the " spirit," he was really reading about " breath" ; and the word remained sufficiently often in its sense of "*wind*" (Gen. viii : 1), or in its sense of "*breath*" (Is. xxx : 28), to make him the exegete each time the word occurred. And, therefore, when he read of the Breath of God (Ps. xviii : 15), the most candid arguers must confess, that, even if it appeared to him as Spirit, and even if he had grown familiar with what is meant by the spirit of man, he would not be led, in the multiplicity of Bible emblems, to keep it out generically from the class of God's finger, or God's eye, or God's power, which are to be taken as they stand, without any reference at all to any Trinity.

When any violence is done to this, I mean to the simple stand that no doctrine of the Trinity is to be learned from emblems, see what a desperate work is made. The whole emblematic skies break into hypostatic differences. Listen to Cyprian. He says, "That Christ is the hand and arm of God." He finds it in Isaiah; "Is God's hand not strong to save? or has he made his ear heavy?" (Is. lix: 1). The singular thing is, that such men drop the "ear," and take the "arm," without the least logical remorse: just as modern Trinitarians drop the "finger" (Lu. xi: 20), and take the spirit (Matt. xii: 28), without the least halting at their implied equivalency. "Also in the same place, 'Lord who hath believed our report? and to whom is the arm of God revealed?' (Is. liii: 1): also in the same, 'All these things hath mine hand made' (Is. lxvi: 2): also in the same, 'O Lord God, thine arm is high, and they knew it not' (Is. xxvi: 1): also in the same, 'The Lord has revealed his arm, that holy arm, in the sight of all nations' (Is. lii: 10): also in the same place, 'The hand of the Lord hath done these things, and the Holy One of Israel hath shown them': Is xli: 20." (Cyprian, Vol. II. p. 101, Clark's Ed). This, of course, as a *reductio ad absurdum*, carries the war directly into the Trinity. The Valentinians furnished the like. They said that "*Arche**\* was a divine Hypostasis, distinct from the Father and the *Logos*" (Irenaeus, Haer. I: viii: 5). The Patristic view made it the "Divine Sophia" (Origen). Cyril made it the "Everlasting Father" (see Meyer on John i: 59). All which most distinctly

\* "The beginning" (Jo. i: 1).

## God the Holy Ghost. 47

teaches; that there has been a tendency in the theologic world to do just what our fathers did with the wafer, that is, to exalt it into a mystery, and to make the simple utterance, " This is my body," imply a divine sense, utterly beyond the meaning of the emblem.

" Wisdom" is scarce so ripe an instance; for the majority of commentators cling to it yet. It is instructive in that respect. It is a myth in the transition stage between a superstition and more sound intelligence. The church, giving up the " *Arche*," and the church giving up the "Arm," and the " Hand," and, now, the church slowly giving up the hypostatic " Wisdom," and, let me add, giving up the wafer, and giving up the mystic baptism, may be a type of the church giving up the Trinity; and, therefore, this transition link, viz., the Divine *Sophia*,\* may be looked upon with more concern, as showing how fast or how slow the church will change her theories in other Scriptures.

Look well, indeed, at this instance of wisdom. It is loaded with hypostatic appearances. " The Lord by wisdom hath founded the earth" (Prov. iii: 19). I hardly know how personification could have been carried further. " I love them that love me, and those that seek me early shall find me" (viii: 17). The *Sophia* leaps upon the throne of the universe. " I will pour out my spirit unto you; I will make known my words unto you"(i: 23). There is emptied upon it an exuberance of Eastern *prosopopœia*. And so, if we hypostasize anywhere, why not

\* " Wisdom."

in this moving and speaking reality? And yet all the time, close under the eye of the church, and still unlistened to, are the most ample texts (Job xxviii: 28; Ps. cxxxvi: 5; Prov. iv: 5, 7), to show that wisdom is mere piety; that the Lord by wisdom has founded the heavens, just as he is righteous in all his ways; that " by me kings rule," just as justice and judgment are the habitation of a throne; and that, categorically, Wisdom *is* righteousness (Prov. i: 2, 3); a statement made just where it should be, at the opening of the Proverbs; but singularly overlooked in a false and ungrammatical translation.*

Emblems, therefore, are no evidence of a Trinity. And the abuse of emblems, made hypostatic and then universally recalled, will bring the church to this mind,—first, that there is a proclivity to typical mistake, and, second, that there should be the most inexorable care, to sift the evidence before we divide the Deity.

§ 5. *The Unity of God's Person not to be Disturbed by Grammatic Differences—and First, not by Differences of Person.*

Verging on to points where more special evidence is imagined, I think we may still maintain agreement with Trinitarians in saying, that differences of person, in a grammatic sense, are not to establish the Trinity. I know it has been imagined differently. I know that advocates of Trinitarian belief have said, that the Thou and the I and the He in the mouths of the Father, Son and Holy

* See Author's Commentary, Prov. i: 1, 2.

Ghost, in speaking of each other, betokened hypostatic distinction. I know that they have brought this into the forefront, and given it a place as though it were an irrefragable appeal. But did they really mean that this did anything more than merely match the facts? Did they mean that it established them? They can hardly have meant the latter; for the expression " Awake, O Sword, against my Shepherd" (Zech. xiii : 7), would then mean that the Sword was a separate hypostasis. Or the expression, " His arm shall rule for him" (Is. xl : 10) : or the expression, " Awake, O Arm of the Lord" (Is. li : 9). I do not deny that if there *be* Persons in the Trinity, then I, Thou and He would agree with the facts. But that is not the question. As there is man and God in Christ, I, Thou and He agree with the speaking of Christ, and communing in his human nature directly and perpetually with the Divinity that was within him. Such were not the points at issue. The points at issue are, whether God, outside of Christ, is so distinguishable into three hypostatic personages, as that the grammatic persons *prove* the hypostases, or that the I, Thou and He are actual evidence that there are three Persons in the Godhead.

And that they are not, take these texts, " Bless the Lord, O my soul" (Ps. ciii : 1). Does that prove that the soul and I are, in any sense, different ? Take this text, " And then will I say to my soul, Soul, take thine ease ; eat, drink and be merry" (Lu. xii : 19). Or take this, " My heart said unto me, Thy grace, Lord, will I seek" (Ps. xxvii : 8). " My soul, wait thou only upon the Lord, for my expectation is from him" (Ps. lxii : 5). See the force of my reasoning. It is, that if the Trinity were established, there are moulds of Scripture into which it would run, just as there are grammatic differences that agree with the idea, that a man was united with the Almighty. There are modes of speech that will fall easily into place, if it were found that a man and his soul could commune and hold intercourse together. But the proof of the original fact must be outside the grammar. I think we have swept our horizon on, and not as yet discovered a distinct article of proof, which, even an honest promoter of the Trinity would be likely to declare, could build, in its own strength, the smallest demonstration.

§ 6. *The Unity of God's Person not Disturbed by Differences of Gender.*

Now as to gender.

The argument here is twofold. First, it may be said, The Holy Ghost is neuter, and, therefore, so bold a severance proclaims something very distinct hypostatically. And, second, the Holy Ghost, though neuter, has the masculine pronoun, as though the divine text would take pains to intimate, that this Spirit, first hewn off by being neuter, should, nevertheless, be redacted into a Person, by force of the grammatic proof to be gathered from the pronoun.

Now this is somebody's proof; and there ought to be somebody willing to stand for it. And when somebody is willing to stand for it, he ought really to stand. Theology, among all possible schemes, ought to retrench its arguments, till it gets down to those which it can possibly vouch: and when it has arrived at them, it ought to stand by them. It ought to be willing that they should stand distinct; and, when they distinctly and by their own merits fail, it ought to give them up; and not carry into the war crippled and everywhere defeated evidence.

For, look now at these genders. In the first place, the Holy Ghost is found to be neuter, because, in many a text, it is really neuter; that is, it verges gradually from meaning God, through all possible shades of thought, till it means a creature. This was the secret of the Arian mistake. There were so many passages inapplicable to the Almighty, that they seemed forced into some other scheme; and, therefore, conceived of the Highest of the Creatures, instead of that Holy Ghost which, in most of the texts, was nothing but the Almighty. Why can we not resort to a simpler exegesis? The arm of the Lord, or the power of the Lord, or the voice of the Lord, are nothing, *qua essentia*, but God Himself. They might, or might not, be neuter, just as it might happen. They might, or might not, in rhetoric, be convertible with the name of the Almighty. But who would require that some nurse should go with him, like a Duenna with a child, to pencil the shades of meaning? and who would not be pestered, if, instead of being left to his own quick conceptions as he reads, he were followed by somebody, incessantly to explain how much the hand or the foot or the breath of Jehovah was convertible with Himself, or how far it was to be considered distinct, and was subjective or resultant in its character?

So, now, in the instance of the Spirit. Sometimes it is plainly God; as where it says, "Now the Lord is that Spirit"(2 Cor. iii : 17). Sometimes it is plainly man; as where it says, "Every spirit that confesseth" (1 Jo. iv: 2). And between these there are all grades. It is a mere question of rhetoric, how quenching the Spirit (1 Thess. v: 19), or sowing to the spirit (Gal. vi: 8), or "your love in the Spirit" (Col. i: 8), or lusting against the spirit (Gal. v: 17), or joining to the Lord in one Spirit (1 Cor. vi: 17), or standing fast in one Spirit (Phil. i: 27), or worshipping God in the spirit (Phil. iii; 3), or the ornament of a meek and quiet spirit (Jas. iii: 4), may, or may not, refer to God, or to God subjective in the soul; that is, to the soul itself imbued with the grace of the Most High.

Undoubtedly the whole emblem, God's Holy Spirit, ought to keep near, for its exegesis, to the idea of a breath. When we say, God is a Spirit, we wander a little. God is not a breath. God is the most solid of all subsistencies. When we say, God's Spirit is himself, we talk more rationally. It is like saying, God's power is himself; or God's arm, or God's word is but himself acting or uttering his voice. But when we say, God is a Spirit, it is like saying, God is an arm or a shoulder. It is not a natural expression; and, therefore, let me say just here, It is no where found in the word of God. Christ says to the woman of Samaria, "The true worshipper shall worship the Father in spirit and in truth" (Jo. iv: 23).

And then he adds, "spirit is God" (v. 24). This passage has been wonderfully perverted. Middleton has helped the delusion by saying that the article betokens the subject (Chap. iii: s. 4, § 1). I will not dwell upon this. Winer has amply refuted it * (Gram. § 18, 7). Suffice it to say, The order is given in the Greek. And it is not, " God is a spirit," which would be an unprecedented sentence ; but, " spirit is God ;" that is, the worshipping seat in man is conscience, which is the voice of the Almighty, that is to say, the spirit which is bred within him of God. " Spirit is God ;" and, therefore, " they that worship him, must worship him" in the God-part ; that is " they that worship him, must worship him in spirit and in truth" (v. 24).

Returning to this passage at another stage of our inquiry, I say, There is plenty of reason why Spirit should be neuter; first, and very prominently, because it happens to be neuter, *i. e.*, the word, and, second, because it is used in so many subjective ways, the disseverances of which are to be made by the simple reader.

So much for the first argument.

Now, for the second.

We meet the second by an immediate denial.

The first argument was, that Spirit, being neuter,

* I do not mean that Winer, either here or in Jo. i: 1, translates as we do ; but I mean that he refutes Middleton's rule. So do Glassius and Rambach. See also Röhricht in Jo. i: 1. See, moreover, Middleton himself; who does not make the rule absolute ; but states, with great reasonableness, why the subject should *usually* have the article ; reasons which throw their strength the other way in the instances with which we are at present concerned.

it was very different from the Father; a very good Arian argument; but not very good for the orthodox. The second argument was, that, though neuter, it drew to itself the masculine pronoun; an argument that I heard the other day in a sermon; an argument not conclusive, if it were correct; but an argument singularly unhappy, inasmuch as it is King James that puts-in the masculine (e. g. Jo. xiv: 17 xv: 26). With an uniformity that would be hard to equal, the Greek *pneuma* is every where followed by neuters (Mar. i: 10; Jo. vi: 63; xiv: 17; Gal. iv: 6); and almost the only places where it varies, is where the emblem has been kindled into a higher glow by the use of the word Comforter, which *is* a masculine, and which once or twice (Jo. xv: 26; xvi: 13, 14) draws the Spirit into its gender, and creates the cases, which are the sole warrant for any such thought of change.

The change of the neuter, therefore, in the common noun *pneuma*, is anything but an argument; in the first place, because it would be but a higher instance of personification, and, in the second place, because it does not occur, at all in the measure, or at all under the circumstances, which, as an argument it would lead us to suppose.

§ 7. *The Unity of God's Person not Disturbed by Difference of Number.*

Number possesses advantages over person and over gender if anything could be made out of these grammatic differences. Number stands out in actual letters. For example, God (Elohim) is in the plural.

There is no blinking the fact of this unnatural name; and no resisting the conclusion that it must have some peculiar explanation. If it were but once, or if it were but of one name!—but sometimes Maker (Ec. v : 7 ; xii : 1), sometimes the Most High (Dan. vii : 18), oftener Lord (*passim*), are presented in the plural. And, then, there are whole sentences ; " Let us make man" (Gen. i : 26) : " Let us go down" (xi : 7) : " Let us confound their languages" (ib.) ; " Let us make man in our image, after our likeness" (i : 26) : " Behold, the man is become as one of us" (iii : 22) : sentences that have been eyed curiously for hundreds of years ; and that were looked at very closely by the schoolmen, as betokening a Trinity.

But now, as of all other rights that can be pled, certainly it may be pleaded that orthodox men shall choose whether these do, or do not, support what has been imagined.

Strange to say, here has been a difference.

Men have found it so easy to explain these plurals. Some have said, they were regal plurals, as when a king, or high officer of State, said "we" or "us." Some said they were plurals of honor (Gesenius, *Lex* :), a form quite familiar in other passages of Scripture (Gen. xxxix : 2, Prov. i : 20 ; xxiv : 7). Some said, they were the remains of polytheism, and habits bred upon speech by a plurality of Deities (Naegelsbach, *Heb. Gram.*). Some said they were comprehensive terms, intended to associate the angels (Philo) ; or intended to gather in all traits, like *shamayim* for heaven, or like *mayim* or *hayim* for water or life (Ewald, Dietrich). This last is probably the best solution. But our object is altogether in the way of argument. What it means, or what it does not mean, does not concern us, unless it is insisted that it means the Trinity. So that we have a right to ask, Is this the case? Great numbers have utterly abandoned it. So has Hengstenberg. So have the great mass of the learned. So have nearly all who are not, in a conglomerate way, going back to all traditional arguments. I merely ask, Am I to answer it? If I am not, I shall leave nothing posted in my rear. If I am, I simply resort to this:—I say, The most devoted Trinitarians admit that it can prove nothing by itself; and I explain, Not simply because it can mean so many things; but because it would mean too much; for if God hypostatically differs, because he is spoken of in the plural, then the Spirit hypostatically differs, and wisdom hypostatically differs; that is to say, the Spirit must be in seven persons, because he is spoken of as "the seven Spirits of God" (Rev. iii : 1), and " wisdom" must be divided similarly, because it is stamped with the same mark ; that is, it has the same plurality of name, and that by no unfortunate accident of manuscript revelation (Prov. i: 20).

Number, therefore, can do nothing for a Trinity. Nor can case.

§ 8. *The Unity of God's Person not Disturbed by Difference of Case.*

Jehovah is often in the nominative where some other name of God appears in the accusative, and where action and reaction are insisted upon as show-

## God the Holy Ghost.

ing that the Actor and the Acted-on must be in a distinct hypostatical condition.

But now, boldly,—God sent his truth (Ps. xliii: 3; lvii: 3). Does that legitimately mean that God, and the truth that he sent, are different agencies? God sent down his power (Acts x: 38). Does that mean what the argument would imply? I know that, if there be a Trinity, there is no contradiction at all in such expressions; and, therefore, two things must be kept in mind,—what a sentence will tally with, and what it will prove. It will tally with the Trinity to say, God sent forth his word (Ps. cvii: 20). But to take two texts, and say, Send down thy power, and, Send down thy Spirit; and say, One proves a Trinity, and the other does not; or to say, Send out thy word (Ps. cxlvii: 18), and " Send thine hand" (Ps cxliv: 7), and insist, One is hypostatic in its very self, and the other not hypostatic in the least, but visibly and *in se* not so, is trifling with human thought. "Went not mine heart with thee?" says the prophet (2 Ki. v: 26). A book thronged with the exuberance of the East, that is said to have a clue, in its figures, by which they separate themselves in instances like these, is made to injure itself with the wise. Let us have the real proof for what we are to believe. For I beg an eager scrutiny thus far, that I may not leave upon the field anything valid, but may keep within the narrowing line everything that can be gravely introduced to support the Trinity.

## § 9. *The Unity of God's Person not Disturbed by Any Other Differences.*

I suppose many a grave man, if he did me the honor to read what I have written, would settle back upon his creed, and say, This is trifling, after all. All this may be honest; but yet it has the effect of a trick.

The scheme is one for matching Scriptures. Scriptures being found that uphold the Trinity, they are counterfeited; that is, like ones are put forward as meaning the same; and as neutralizing all the others. There is a ghastly cousinhood to those feats in Egypt. Aaron came forward, in the majesty of truth, and, the magicians, they also did likewise with their enchantments; for they also cast down their rods, and they also became serpents. I feel uneasy, myself, in every word I set forth. And when I hear Paul casting this old account into a form of general apostacy, and hear him say, "As Jannes and Jambres withstood Moses, so do these resist the truth," I wince under the picture. For this is indeed my very method. My challenge is, Bring on your sentences, and I will match them. And this springs from a persuasion that it can be done. All my study of the texts leads me to believe, that there is not one that usually supports the Trinity, that cannot be matched by another; and that the Father and the Son and the Holy Ghost cannot be presented in any form in the Bible, that cannot be matched by some other form: the form, seeming to imply a Trinity, having the implication taken out of it thus,—that

## God the Holy Ghost. 59

(always reserving the peculiarities of the Son) the Father, the Word and the Holy Spirit can always be expounded by the light of other passages, where the conjunction is similar, but where the Lord of hosts and the Mighty One and the Holy One of Israel, or like groups, cannot be considered in any triune relation.

There is nothing, therefore, but to advance.

Grammatic case, grammatic gender, grammatic person, grammatic number, and all grammatic differences, have been appealed to. Now let us have everything else. What are the special forms of proof on which the ages could have built so great a doctrine?

1. It may be said, The Holy Ghost stands out so as an agent! Personification may answer in poetic writing : but in the most lengthened prose, and in so many and such varied portions of revelation, the Holy Ghost is talked of as so strictly a person, that the style of the thing, rather than any distinctive case, betokens the cause of the belief of Christendom.

But be careful! Who is denying that the Holy Ghost is a person? That may be a good argument against the Arian, and against similar mistake. Our very claim is, that the Holy Ghost is a Person ; and that he is only One Person. Our doctrine is, that the Spirit is God. When, therefore, it is said, that the Holy Ghost spake (Acts xiii : 2), or that the Holy Ghost came on them (Acts xix : 6), or that the Holy Ghost did any act or work (Acts x : 44 ; xvi : 6; xx : 28 ; Rom. v : 5), we do not object, in the least. What does it prove? It proves that the Holy Ghost is a person. We *claim* that the Holy Ghost is a person; and we aver, that not one of these passages shows that he is any separate person from the Word or the Father.

2. The same is our conclusion from his being an object of worship (Is. vi: 3, 9; cf. Acts xxviii: 25). We are right in riveting the proof. If any man has it, let him produce it. We are reasonable in tracing the evidence along. And if we say, This is not evidence; and this is not evidence; nor this,—we are, in method, right. Nay, we are doing a favor to the truth, if we cut off meaningless appeals, and bind the Trinity down to its actual demonstrations.

3. But it may be said, Whole passages are demonstrative of what we are seeking. It may not do to quote, "The Holy Ghost spake" (Acts xxviii: 25), and then say, that, by the force of that one expression, there is some other Person than the Father; or that, because that Person is worshipped (Jo. iv: 24), and prayed to (Ez. xxxvii: 9),—that therefore he is a distinct hypostatic divinity; but when a whole narrative occurs; as, for example, like this, " If I go not away, the Comforter will not come unto you; but, if I depart, I will send him unto you : and when he is come he will reprove the world of sin and of righteousness and of judgment:" or, when we read, "And whosoever speaketh a word against the Son of Man, it shall be forgiven him; but whosoever speaketh against the Holy Ghost, it shall not be forgiven him" (Matt. xii: 32): or, when we read, that certain worshippers did not so much as know that

there was a Holy Ghost (Acts xix: 2), there is a cast about this that should operate differently from any isolated text, and a persistence of using a name, that seems to imply a more than mere rhetoric for the Almighty.

But why?

Let me press the point just there.

Solomon breaks out in the most remarkable personification of wisdom. He follows it, chapter after chapter. He harps upon it; till we should suppose he had worn out the figure, if persistence is any sign that that could be done. The Spirit is nothing, in elaborate drapery, to the personification of wisdom. I beg a close inspection of the comparison involved. Wisdom; which has not an advantage like the Spirit; because it is not really a personal Deity,—nevertheless builds houses, and shelters guests (Prov. ix: 1). It actually builds for the Almighty (Prov. viii: 27, 30); and props kings upon their thrones (v. 16). And if any one says, Yes, because it is a Person, I hail that as confirming my demonstration. Wise persons believe that it is not a person; and if the *prosopopœia* is piled so high that it seems so, it is all the better argument. If Paul talks so of Sin (Rom. vii: 13), that she seems like Milton's Goblin, scaly and venomous before us, I think, with the superior advantage that the Comforter is really a Person, we can be spared from admitting, from the text, that it need be a Person separate and distinct from the Father.

But it may be said, That strange expression,— They did not so much as know that there was a Holy Ghost! (Acts xix: 2). Well; let us look at that.

Will the Trinitarian really admit that they did not know that there was such a Person? If he does, then the world-wide doctrine, such as he believes the Trinity to be, was not known to the Jews of Ephesus. That is unreasonable enough. But then, another consequence. There could not have been a Holy Ghost. There could not have been one, because there was none in the days of our Saviour: and an eternal Spirit must have existed always. And there was none in the days of our Saviour, because we are distinctly told, that " there was no Holy Spirit yet,[*] because that Christ was not yet glorified" (Jo. vii: 39). We have got, therefore, to retrace our steps; for this, of course, no man will endure.

What then is the meaning?

We have already explained, that Spirit is often subjective. Indeed, we have shown that it is more and more subjective; until it settles, at last, to be no more than conscience. When, therefore, John said, that there was not yet any Spirit (Jo. vii: 39), he meant, undoubtedly, the great promised work of the Spirit. And when the Ephesians said, that they did not so much as know that there was a Spirit, they meant his promised work (Acts xix: 2). They, no doubt, had fruit of the Spirit; but they were speaking comparatively, just as when Paul said, Christ sent me not to baptize (1 Cor. i: 17). So that the whole meaning was, that the great Pentecostal blessing had not dawned upon their minds.

But here now a very strong argument! Why use

---

[*] "Given" (E. V.), as will be seen, is in Italics. The Greek, as to the point involved, is, in each case, precisely similar.

such language? If there was a Holy Ghost separate and distinct from the Father, and such a hypostatic Personage was a great reality of the gospel, John would have been very shy of using such language. Such slight considerations have often the force of demonstration. If God were not in Persons, but were simple; if he were not hypostasized literally, but were Spirit or Word rhetorically, or as the case may be, the pen would not hesitate to write, "There was as yet no Holy Ghost": but if the Trinity is true, it would seem unreasonable and wrong, and, in fact, rhetorically impossible, to write in one of our theologies, for example, that there was at any given time no Holy Ghost.

In respect to the unpardonable sin—what is it? If the Son of Man appear as an outward revelation; and if the Holy Ghost be felt as an inward influence, —I can understand the sentence at once. If any one speak a word against the Son of man, he merely denies a doctrine, or is found denouncing God as outwardly revealed. But if any man speak a word against the Holy Ghost, the implication is, that he is resisting inwardly; that is, that he is doing violence to conscience; that is, that he is trampling the Spirit of grace, which is God at work upon his mind.

The passage, therefore, is adverse to the doctrine of the Trinity. If God be in three persons, the speaking a word against Father, Son or Holy Ghost would seem equally offensive. Indeed, a speaking against the Father would seem to be the most bold. Each would have its point of heinousness. The Father, as the great King and Judge; the Son, as having tabernacled in clay, and as having been the price-affording strength of the obedience and the ransom; or the Holy Ghost, as our Sanctifier, would be each most reverend and great; and that would be a useless mystery that would seem to erect the one over the other. But explain the whole as I have said, and mystery vanishes. Jesus Christ can be looked at in his humanity. Jesus Christ, in his humanity, was an outward thing, and could be looked at like the Bible. Jesus Christ, like the Bible, could be rejected by a profound mistake. But Jesus Christ, in the Spirit; or, as we could then expound it, the Father in the Spirit; or, to speak still less figuratively, the Great God operating as a holy breath,—is a Monitor inside the heart. It is a monition that has gained access to the spirit. It is a conviction that has passed out of the category of mistake, and become inwrought in the soul. Then to quench it, is insolent wrong. And hence the intimation, that, whereas the susceptibilities of life can be so worn away, that, according to the rules of grace, a man is past feeling (Eph. iv: 19), so this process may be hastened, and a violence to the inward light sovereignly poured down, may grieve the Almighty to depart, and may finish, at a stroke, the possibilities of salvation.

Glance, therefore, at the argument. We are not denying the personality of the Spirit; nor his divinity; nor a meaning in the name. We pray for the Holy Ghost. We depend upon the Holy Ghost. And without this blessed Monitor, we are lost forever. His work is a work of the new birth, sanctification and calling into life. All this we delight in.

We only say, It is God thus beautifully described. When he descended in cloven tongues, of course nobody believes that God was a fire. When he dwelt as a Shekinah, he was not the luminiferous ether. When he descended on Christ, he was only in the *form* of a dove. And, so, I carry what is spectacular to a still higher degree. I hold the Holy Breath to be only God (2 Cor. iii : 17). When I pray that it be poured out, I pray for God. When waiting for its coming, I wait for the Almighty: and for all-abounding reason; for, as we have carefully seen, gender and number and case have all been appealed to, and every opportunity has been given for each imaginable trace, and no footstep has been seen of a divided Deity.

4. One thing yet remains, and that is the testimony of believers. I value this. In vital matters the testimony of believers is unquestionably infallible. But that is the very question. Is this a vital matter?

" The people of God have always regarded the Holy Spirit as a person. They have looked to him for instruction, sanctification, direction and comfort. This is part of their religion. Christianity (subjectively considered) would not be what it is without this sense of dependence on the Spirit, and this love and reverence for his person. All the liturgies, prayers and praises of the Church are filled with appeals and addresses to the Holy Ghost. This is a fact which admits of no rational solution, if the Scriptures do not really teach that the Spirit is a distinct person. The rule, *Quod semper, quod ubique, quod ab omnibus*, is held by Protestants as well as by Romanists. It is not to the authority of general consent as an evidence of truth that Protestants object, but to the application made of it by the Papal Church, and to the principle on which that authority is made to rest. All Protestants admit that true believers in every age and country have one faith, as well as one Lord and God" (Dr. Hodge's Sys. Theol. I. p. 526).

Notice the errors. First, faith in a Trinity has not been positively universal. Dr. Hodge would hardly deny the quality of faith to all Monarchians, or even to *all* Arian professors. Second, universal belief does not prove the truth of a doctrine; but it only proves it in case it is vital. Third, universal belief does not prove a faith vital. Witness the doctrine of the Mass, which has been universal in some ages, and is preponderant in this. The belief that it is vital does not make it vital, any more than it makes Jacobitism vital, or the right to persecute. And, therefore, fourth, the great flaw in this argument is, that it does not settle whether the doctrine is vital. If it is, I grant the Church has it; for if the doctrine is vital, it is only tantamount to owning that there is always a living church. But that it is vital because the church has it, I utterly deny; for the church has had masses, and auto-da-fés, and all sorts of barnacles, that have grown upon it as a penalty of iniquity.

There is no proof, therefore, thus far, that God exists hypostatically separated.

But, now, there is proof very positively the other way.

## § 10. *No Distinct Personality of the Spirit.*

Of course, theologians will not expect me to find expressions declaring, polemically, that there is no Holy Ghost. And the reason why not, will be altogether understood, when I declare, that there was no such doctrine. The East had no such polemic. The nearest we come to it is in the first texts of John, which, as we have already shown, were against the errors of the Platonists (Irenæus iii : 11). And, perhaps, prophetically, Christ had some inkling of the kind, when, after more than usual hypostatic expressions about the Spirit, he says, " The time will come, when I will no more speak unto you in Proverbs, BUT WILL SHOW YOU PLAINLY OF THE FATHER." In the main, therefore, we cannot hunt up positive denials ; because our plea is, that the Bible is colorless of the Trinity; and, therefore, we cannot array it either for it or against it.

But, *incidentally*, there are singular proofs.

1. In the first place, there is no care at all about the names of the Almighty. If there were a Trinity, there would be some precision that exegetes had reached. Jehovists would have gained the day, or *Malachists*, sifters-out of the meaning of the " Angel." The scene in Isaiah (Chap. 6) is applied to Father (v. 1), Son (Jo. xii : 41), and Spirit (Acts xxviii : 25), with no possible order. We appeal to every principle of frankness, whether the scheme that makes these names rhetorical,* and makes them all descrip-

---

* Excepting always the Son.

tive, does not apply to the confusion of their use, more happily than to distinct hypostases.

2. Second, the confusion of powers! God is said to create (Gen. i: 1); and Christ is said to create (Heb. i: 10); and so the Spirit (Ps. civ: 30). They all garnish the heavens, and work the works of the Great Builder, promiscuously together (Jo. v: 17). And this has been urged to prove that they are but "One Substance." But does it not go further, and hint that they are but One Person? Are they not, like the mason's tie, binding the wall, and bringing back these garnishings of speech to what our Saviour calls, a telling plainly of the Father?

3. Then we have the confusion of the Persons. We have the direct declaration, "Spirit is God" (Jo. iv: 24). Paul declares to us, "Now the Lord is that Spirit" (2 Cor. iii: 17).* In Matthew we are told, I cast out devils by the Spirit of God (Matt. xii: 28), and, in Luke, I cast out devils by his finger (Lu. xi: 20). We hear "of the Spirit and of power" (1 Cor. ii: 4). We hear, "The Holy Ghost shall come upon thee, and the power of the Highest shall overshadow thee" (Lu. i: 35). "Whither shall I go from thy

* We ask special examination for two texts, one in John, and the other in the Epistle to the Philippians. The one in John is translated, "For God giveth not the spirit by measure" (Jo. iii: 34, E. V.). Why not translate it, "For God, the Spirit, giveth not by measure"? The other passage reads, "Which worship God in the spirit" (Phil. iii: 3, E. V.). Why not translate that, "Which worship the Spirit God"? or, as the Greek is contested, and the reading, *theou*, is believed to be correct, why not discard Meyer's rendering, "Who worship in the Spirit of God," and fix on the more natural translation, "Who worship the Spirit of God"? The whole pneumatology of the Bible is worth a careful revision.

Spirit? or whither shall I flee from thy presence"? and Clement goes on with this passage, " If I ascend into heaven, thou art there ; if I go away even to the uttermost parts of the earth, there is thy right hand ; if I make my bed in the abyss, there is thy Spirit" (Chap. 28). The very Fathers seem not to have traced a Trinity. We hear them say, " The Word is the Spirit."* Hermas says, " I wish to explain to you what the Holy Spirit, that spake with you in the form of the church, showed you ; for that Spirit is the Son of God" (*Pastor of Hermas* ; Clark's Ed. p. 404). The Targumist renders Zach. vii : 12, " by his Word," instead of, " by his Spirit." And Hermas takes up the emblems at will, " No one shall enter into the kingdom of God, unless he receive his holy name . . . Whosoever shall not receive his lips, shall not enter into the kingdom of God" (p. 416). We can multiply into any multitude these ignoring revelations. " In the Scriptures themselves the same work is often ascribed to God and to the Spirit of God, which led some, at times, to assume that these terms expressed one and the same thing ; as the spirit of a man is the man himself. In the Scriptures, also, the terms Word and Breath (or Spirit) are often interchanged ; and what in one place is said to be done by the Word, in another is said to be done by the Spirit. The *Logos* is represented as the life of the world, and the source of all knowledge ; and, yet, the same is said of the Spirit. Paul declares, in one place (Gal. i : 12), that

* No one can examine Lightfoot, Vol. II. p. 520, without seeing that those attributes that are ascribed by the Targumists to the Word, are precisely those specifically belonging to the Holy Spirit.

he received the doctrines which he taught by the revelation of Jesus Christ; in another (1 Cor. ii : 10), that he was taught by the Spirit. Misled by such interpretations" [as Dr. Hodge thinks], "some of the Fathers identified the Son and the Spirit. Even Tertullian, in one place, says, ' *Spiritus substantia est Sermonis, et Sermo operatio Spiritus, et duo unum sunt*' "* (Hodge, Theol. I. p. 533).

Let us quote other Scriptures. Job says, " By his Spirit he hath garnished the heavens; his hand hath formed the crooked serpent" (Job xxvi: 13). The Psalmist says, " By the word of the Lord were the heavens made, and all the host of them by the Spirit (breath, E.V.) of his mouth"(Ps. xxxiii: 6). We are told of miracles by his finger (Lu. xi : 20), by his Spirit (Matt. xii : 28), and then, traversing both, of " miracles and wonders which God did by him," that is, by Christ (Acts ii : 22). We hear of the Spirit of God as tantamount to, and illustrated by, the spirit of man (1 Cor. ii : 11). We are wearying the reader. Our argument will be understood. It is not that the Trinity is guarded against in Scripture : the fact that it is in no way mentioned, is our most important proof: but now,—with this subsidiary consideration, that, if the Trinity had been intended to be revealed, it would never be traversed and cut to pieces by incongruous appellations.

4. Fourthly ; the offices of the Persons are confused. The Father would seem preëminently the

---

* *Adversus Praxeam*, 15, *Works*, edit. Basle, 1562, p. 426 [" The Spirit is the substance of the Word, and the Word the operation of the Spirit ; and the two are one thing"].

Person who elects us into life ; and yet the Son says, " Ye have not chosen me, but I have chosen you" (Jo. xv : 16). Kindred things are said of the Spirit (Eph. i : 13 ; iv : 30). The great work of redemption is by Christ ; and yet the Father, in actual prophecies of the Son, calls himself the " Redeemer ;" and the Holy Ghost, preëminently the Sanctifier, does not monopolize that title in the least, but shares it, whenever it is rhetorically fit, with the Father, and with the God Incarnate (Jude 1, Eph. v : 26). We shall recur to this indifferency of title under another head (1 Chap. iii: § 13 *et al*). But, in the meanwhile, like the lines of the spectroscope, the evidence may seem slight, but it is determinate. It is impossible for one moment to suppose that God was eternally three, and that that threeness was so original and of course as to have penetrated into human consciousness : it is impossible that, as Dr. Hodge declares, " it underlies the whole plan of salvation, and determines the character of the religion (in the subjective sense of that word) of all true Christians : " that "it is the unconscious (*sic*) or unformed faith even of those of God's people who are unable to understand the term by which it is expressed :" that they " believe in God the Creator and Preserver, . . . and, therefore, of necessity, in a divine Redeemer, and a divine Sanctifier ;" and that they should " have the factors of the doctrine of the Trinity in their religious convictions"\* : (Dr.

---

\* " It is not too much to say with Meyer (*Lehre von der Trinität*, i. p 42), that ' the Trinity is the point in which all Christian ideas and interests unite ; at once the beginning and the end of all insight into Christianity '" (Hodge, Theol. i : p. 443).

Hodge's Theol. I: p. 443): I say it is utterly impossible to dream of such a thing,—if the Word of God, which I suppose Dr. Hodge, in spite of our "consciousness," will still admit must be the source of the doctrine, is so utterly careless to keep the great terms of the doctrine, Creator, Redeemer, and Sanctifier, at all apart, and that in the most critical revelations.

CHAPTER III.

GOD THE SON.

§ 1. *The Deity of the Son.*

BEGINNING on the plan that we have laid down, we seize first, as a fact in which we are all agreed, upon the Deity of our Redeemer. Nobody doubts it. The Trinitarian believes that the whole substance of God is present in Christ; and we believe, precisely in the same language. Nobody, at all engaged in this polemic, is concerned about the Deity of Christ; for that is settled. The question is, Is the Deity in Christ the Second Person of the Trinity, or the One Personal Jehovah; the degree and measure of his divinity, if there could be any conceivable difference, being rather against the Trinitarian: for the Trinitarian believes in but one of three Persons as in Christ, whereas we believe in the Sole Person of the Almighty as present in our Great Redeemer.

§ 2. *The Humanity of the Son.*

So of the humanity. The Trinitarian believes that there is one body and one soul, and that these in nature are distinct from the Godhead. He believes in a finite body and in a finite reason ; and, though there is a great deal of crude thinking about Emmanuel, yet, when put to his proofs, he believes that this finiteness remains, and that, this moment in heaven, there is a soul, one with the Deity, which is ignorant, —that is to say, unspeakably wise in comparison with what it was on earth (Phil. ii : 9), but still a soul ; for the Trinitarian believes that Christ is " very man" as well as "very God": and, therefore, that the man should become God transmutedly, so that the faculties of the man should become the faculties of the Almighty, our brethren would be just as averse from as we are, and from the same articulate reasoning.

The humanity, therefore, is at rest between us.

### § 3. *The Begetting of the Son.*

The begetting of the Son is more agreed in than we would at first imagine.

It is true that we are coming, here, to the most violent differences.

But the begetting of the Son, in one distinct form of it, we would describe alike.

If I were to quote the passage, " Thou art my Son ; this day have I begotten thee" (Ps. ii : 7), there are very few people that would say, with some, " Thou art my Son ; this day art thou my Son" (Hodge, Theol. Vol. I. p. 475), as though it were a mere asseverance that thou art my Son at any and every period. Nor are there many that would say with others, Thou art my Son ; I am he that have begotten thee.

(J. A. Alexander, Acts xiii: 33). These strained overcomings of the meaning are offensive to the most. But most exegetes, in good Saxon way, will admit that it refers to a temporal begetting; and will resort to the suggestion of Dr. Hodge, that there may be two begettings (Theol. Vol. I. p. 474). This, as will be seen, will analyze our subject. We will take the second begetting as a thing in which we are all agreed, and get that fixed first. And then we will go to the first, and, having stripped away all the passages that belong to the second, we will press the argument, that there are no such passages to substantiate the first as are worthy of the least consideration.

And, in regard to the second, Gabriel gives the best account of it. " The Holy Ghost shall come upon thee, and the power of the Highest shall overshadow thee; therefore, also, that holy thing which shall be begotten, shall be called the Son of God" (Lu. i: 35). This testimony might seem to be confused in the Acts of the Apostles (xiii: 32, 33), where this begetting is spoken of in connection with Christ's being "raised up again" (E. V.); but Dr. Hodge agrees that "again" is an interpolation (p. 475). The Greek means that Jesus was "raised up." We believe that that means more than a mere birth.* But Dr. Hodge's interpretation is enough for our present argument. He concedes that the birth may be alluded to in the expression, " this day." And, now, as the expression occurs four times in the Bible (Ps. ii: 7; Acts xiii: 33; Heb. i: 5; v: 5), we have that much attained at least: Trinitarians confess that,

\* See the Treatise, " *Was Christ in Adam*" ?

## God the Son.

"This day I have begotten thee," may refer to the birth of the Redeemer.

But they say, There was another birth, also; and that eternally of God. Now we desire the passages. It speaks of the first begotten of the Father. But, of course, that we hold ourselves. That was the child begotten of Mary's womb. There was no son like that Son. All other sons were shadows; and therefore the expression, "The only begotten Son of God."

Moreover, "in (by, E. V.) him were all things created" (Col. i : 16). We are to come to that hereafter (§ 11). When he was born, all things were born. That is, the shape of the universe so hung upon him, that not only did the Divinity that was in him make the universe, but it was made " in reference to him" (*eis*, Col. i : 16), as well as "by him." And, therefore, we are told that "in him all things stood together" (v. 17). Christ was not born as soon as the universe was born "in" him : that is, the whole plan of it took color from his advent. All the pardons of it were built upon him. All the government of it was to be laid upon him. The central kingdom of it was to be man's commonwealth (Heb. ii ; 8). And, therefore, it was eminently true, that "in him were all things created," and that he was "the first born of every creature."

Under this head of "begetting," let the Trinitarian produce his arguments.

If he says, He was the "first begotten of the dead" (Rev. i : 5), that of course is in our favor, for an eternal begetting did not, of course, bring him out of a charnel-house; and that, therefore, helps our view; for it obtrudes another passage, confessedly applied to time; fixing this word "begotten" in connection with our Redeemer.

### § 4. *The Son and the Spirit.*

And while we are on the subject of the "begetting," let us trace the connection with it of the Spirit.

Listen to Gabriel: "The Holy Ghost shall come upon thee" (Lu. i: 35).

Christians are said to be begotten of the Spirit (Jo iii: 5).

Now, this lowering of the description to the case of man, does not make the Trinitarian averse to applying it to the Messiah.

He will confess that the "*Theanthropos*" was begotten of the Spirit.

See, now, what then he must embrace: first, that there was a true body; second, that there was a reasoning soul; third, that there was a Holy Ghost settling upon the Virgin Mary, and entering the child at his conception, as the great inspirer of his human life; fourth, a Second Person of the Trinity; and, fifth, a plenary God, that is, both Son and Spirit, possessing the plenary Deity, because being "the same in substance equal in power and glory."

Now, where is the proof of all this? The angel Gabriel seemed to say quite the opposite; for he stated the simple fact, "The Holy Ghost shall come upon thee." Why did he not speak of the Logos? Why is there no *soupçon* of a Second Person? Why

## God the Son. 77

did he exclude the Great Mystery? It may be said, He was not giving all the facts. Then why did he profess to? He said in the most oracular way, " The Holy Ghost shall come upon thee;" and then, fixing the doctrine for all time, he says, "Therefore—" and we can hardly suppose that he would tell a part of the reality—" Therefore," you a poor Israelite, and he a child in a cradle ; you simply overshadowed by the Spirit, and he with a body and a mere rational humanity—" Therefore,"—as though, on a brief visit from the heavens, and on the brink of the most important of created histories, he would tell, at least, the most illustrious reality of the case,—" Therefore, that holy thing that shall be begotten, shall be called the Son of God."

I think, therefore, we may press two things, and urge a friendly answer; first, why was he to be "called the Son of God," at all, for any event in time, and not rather from his eternity's begetting? and, second, why was he "called the Son" for the overshadowing of the Holy Ghost, and not rather for the entrance of the SON, there being by that earlier name a Second Person in the Divinity, whose actual entrance into the man would be, as the Trinitarian would declare, the cause for his being the Son of the Almighty?

It will be noticed that a recoil of the question, and a demand how *we* get over the difficulty, would give us the most favorable chance for explaining the simplicity of our system. The five discordant things give us no confusion. We fold them up like a telescope. The (1) soul and the (2) body; they are the man. The Trinitarians will agree with us there. The (3) Spirit and the (4) Word and the (5) Deity: they are the God. When Gabriel said, " The Holy Ghost shall come upon thee," he was expounding the nature of Emmanuel. Did I believe that the Holy Ghost was one Person, and the Word another, and a Godhead comprehensive of both, I would be all at sea; but believing that Gabriel chose for his rhetoric the image of a Breath, and brought with him the title of a Spirit out of the vocabulary of heaven, I am at no loss at all. He simply meant, God shall come upon thee; and he confirms that by the synonym, " the power of the Highest :" and we have no room for confusion; for, in this way, he was announcing at once, God as tabernacling with clay.

§ 5. *The Son and the Father.*

It will be noticed that our blessed Redeemer never speaks of a Son as tabernacling with him. He never speaks of a Second Person. And, if that is considered as taking advantage of a something which is in modern speech, he never speaks of anything answering to that. He enters into long metaphysics in respect to his person (Jo. Chaps. v—xvii); but he never dreams of a hypostatic subtilty. He always speaks of " God,"or " his Father." This, we insist, is an enormous evidence.

Think of it.

ʃ He often speaks as a man,—" I thirst" (Jo. xix: 28), or, I hunger (Lu. vi: 3), and he often speaks in ways which can only be understood if we suppose him as separating his divinity from his humanity (Jo.

## God the Son. 79

v: 19, 30; viii: 28). In these views he speaks of his Father; but he never speaks of—what shall I say? There is no *Person* that can afford us a name outside of the One Divinity. All this is inexpressibly unlikely. Thirteen chapters in the heart of the Evangelist (v—xvii) discuss the Redeemer in the most unexpected ways. He says, "I and my Father are one" (Jo. x: 30). He says, "He that hath seen me, hath seen the Father" (Jo. xiv: 9). He says, "As the living Father hath sent me, and I live by the Father" (Jo. vi: 57). He says, The Father dwelleth in me, and I in him (Jo. xiv: 10; xvii: 21).

Now, Trinitarians agree here. They cannot change this language. They are reverent people, and would not desire to. And they have a meaning for it; and would cheerfully agree that it expressed a relation with the Father. But will they go further, according to our plan of discussion, and we, having ventured where we agree, will they venture where we differ, and explain how Christ should refer everything to the Father, and that in critical passages where he is discussing everything that belongs to his subsistence?

"The Son can do nothing of himself, but what he seeth the Father do" (Jo. v: 19). "As the Father hath life in himself; so hath he given to the Son to have life in himself" (Jo. v: 26). "I can of mine own self do nothing" (v. 30).

Now, our distinct argument is, not, that Jesus Christ is not God; for we hold that he is, in common with the Trinitarians; not, that he can do nothing of himself: for we hold that he can, when he speaks as the Most High: but that, when he is speaking in human weakness, and that when he is saying those things that account for his subordination in the Deity, such chapters about himself declare three things, first, that there is no ante-Marian Son, or he would sometime speak of him; second, that there is no ante-Marian *hypostasis* of any sort, or it would be brought into the philosophy of his case; and third, that there is no Father: that is to say, that there is no hypostatically separated parent, different from the One Almighty (Jo. xiv : 9).

§ 6. *The Son as Jehovah.*

Hence he is called Jehovah. Isaiah says, I have "seen Jehovah" (Is. vi : 5); and John says, "These things said Esaias, when he saw his [Christ's] glory, and spake of him" (Jo. xii: 41).

But when, under the enthusiasm of such a discovery, we hunt up the texts that will make it more complete, we may, for a time, sail in very tranquil seas, Paul confessing "that the Lord is Jesus Christ"* (Phil. ii: 11), and the writer to the Hebrews quoting a strong Jehovistic passage (Heb. i : 10, Ps. cii): but hardly have we settled our theory, before it is chopped into by all sorts of cross waves. For, in the first place, the Holy Ghost claims the name. "Well spake the Holy Ghost by Esaias" (Acts xxviii : 25); and when we trace the speaking, it is that spoken by Jehovah (Is. vi), and that which John claims for Christ (Jo. xii : 41), and that which, in this way, becomes a link bind-

* The English translation has it "that Jesus Christ is Lord."

## God the Son.

ing the imagined Persons into One, rather than an authority giving an hypostasis to any one of them.

Matters grow worse as we read more generally. The Jehovist can make no stand at all. The confusion becomes complete, as we study more deeply. And, not only is Jehovah one of the universal names for Heaven's Majesty: but more than that: it defies hypostatical treatment: and, for this sharp reason; —that there are passages, where the term Jehovah is employed, where it is applied to One who is speaking at the very time of his Son, our Redeemer.

I think I am making myself understood. I say that Jehovah cannot be a name of Christ, except as Christ is our One God and Creator, because Jehovah is a name for One who actually speaks of Christ ; as, for example, in Isaiah,—" Jehovah said, In an acceptable time have I heard thee" (Is. xlix : 8) : or again, in the Psalms, " Jehovah said to my Lord" (Ps. cx : 1 ; see also Ps. ii : 7). That cannot be an hypostatic name which is applied to the Father as well as to the Son. And as it is applied also to the Holy Ghost (Acts xxviii : 25), it becomes a mason's tie to bind together the structures of rhetoric which the antiquarian, man, treats with hypostatical separation.

### § 7. *The Son as Sent.*

Passing on to more difficult details, it may be asked now, why is the Son spoken of as sent? If he was born of the Virgin Mary, and if his separate subsistence from God was only as a man, then all those expressions which speak of him as " coming" (Eph. iv : 10), and, above all, those which speak of him as

82    *The Trinity and Scripture.*

on a mission (Mal. iii : 1-4), or as being "sent" (Jo. x: 36), would seem rhetorically unmanageable.

This has been an argument much insisted on. But why should the rhetoric be significant when the very same is applied to John? Jesus Christ himself says, "Scripture cannot go for nothing" (Jo. x: 35). We insist, therefore, upon a meaning. " There was a man sent from God whose name was John" (Jo. i : 6). Prophets were "sent" (Jer. vii: 25). In fact, where a man's whole message came from heaven, it was not unnatural to speak as though the whole person of the ambassador descended also. In Christ's instance, all that gave him life came down from heaven. But without going into the intricacies of his person, it is enough to remark, that, if he could say of his disciples, "As thou hast sent me into the world, even so have I sent them into the world" (Jo. xvii: 18), it cannot be much of an argument that makes the expression, "sent," or the corresponding rhetoric for his advent, stand as a token of hypostases in the Almighty.

### § 8. *The Son as Wisdom.*

Christ, as "Wisdom," we have already dealt with (Chap. II. § 4). And yet I think we ought to go further. The fact that the Redeemer was ever dreamed of: nay, what is far more than that, the fact that, among modern commentators, nine-tenths, without a shadow of a relenting, take the old view ; that Solomon should be directed to state, Wisdom is righteousness (Prov. i: 2, 3), and yet commentators declare, No ; it is the Redeemer ; that he should say, " Wisdom is the principal thing : therefore get wisdom : and with all thy gettings get understanding" (Prov. iv : 7), and yet trusted scholars declare, Wisdom is a Divine Hypostasis (Glassius, Calovius, Bp. Hall, Bridges, Scott, *et al.*), is like Cyril saying that *Arche*\* was the Father ; or like Philo saying that it was the *Logos ;* or like the Valentinians saying, it was a new hypostasis (see Irenæus, Hær. i : 8 : 5). We should not be content simply to deride it ; but we should go further. We should say, Is not this a proof that the soul tends to an abuse of figures? that it tends, for example, to make Divinity of a wafer ? and ought not these confessed hallucinations to make us very wary of our work, when we are turning " Word" or " Spirit" into hypostatic Deities.

§ 9. *The Son and the Logos.*

This query comes directly into place when we take up, as we intend next to do, the doctrine of the Logos.

The doctrine of the Logos, we are frank to admit, is one of the strong points of the Trinity.

Would it not be fair, first of all, to ask, whether there is any argument for it in the Old Testament Scriptures ?

The hypostasis of " Wisdom," we have seen, is well nigh universal. And " Wisdom," under the hand of a master, affords a most tempting chance for it. This figure stands out upon the canvas with most marvellous life. She speaks like a Deity. " I love them that love me." And, when she says, " I

---

\* " The beginning " (Jo. i : 1).

also will laugh at your calamity," and when she says, "I have called, and ye refused;" or when she says, "I will pour out my spirit upon you: I will make known my words unto you,"—it would seem easy, if the New Testament encouraged the idea, to make "Wisdom" Christ, and sweep all this beautiful speech into the volume of the gospel.

But when we are shown, by proof, that Solomon is meaning piety, I think we should allow more than all this drapery to fall, and should carry our sobered view *a fortiori* into the Logos.

For listen, now, to the theologians. One of the most distinguished boldly plants himself on this position. "In the Hebrew Scriptures the manifested Jehovah is called the Word of God, and to him individual subsistence and divine perfections are ascribed" (Dr. Hodge, Syst. Theol. Vol. i: p. 505). This, if it were launched at random, would be less to our purpose: but the texts are picked out (Ps. xxxiii: 6; cxix: 89; Is. xl: 8; Ps. cvii: 20; cxlvii: 18). Dr. Hodge has selected five of the Old Testament expressions. And I beg the reader to notice them closely; for these are picked texts. "Wisdom" has passed, in all the splendor of her dramatic realness. And, now, these are to go by. I do not doubt that Logos has the more formidable claim. But where does it get it? We are mustering everything in turn; and, just now, are to be busy with the Old Testament revelation.

And, now, the first of Dr. Hodge's five texts is this; "By the word of the Lord were the heavens made" (Ps. xxxiii: 6). The question is, whether that

## God the Son. 85

would teach a hypostasis any more than the "voice" of God, or the "name" of God. "By the word of the Lord were the heavens made, and all the host of them by the breath of his mouth." The question is, why one should be treated hypostatically, and not the other : and the question lies further, why translate the other word, "breath"? Why not translate it, "Spirit"? And if it be translated "Spirit," why give the same hypostatic work indiscriminately to both hypostases? and why, in fact, imagine hypostatic condition of either ; I mean, in deference to the proof that can be extracted from this foremost one of the five selected passages?

The second is this, "Forever, O Lord, thy word is settled in heaven" (Ps. cxix : 89).

The third is this, "The word of our God shall stand forever" (Is. xl : 8).

The fourth is this, "He sent his word, and healed them" (Ps. cvii : 20).

The fifth is this, "He sendeth out his word, and melteth them" (Ps. cxlvii : 18).

These are the five texts.

I beg everyone to read them. And then I beg a verdict : whether "in the Hebrew Scriptures [these being the ones selected] the manifested Jehovah is called the Word of God, and to him individual subsistence and divine perfections are ascribed." And I ask this further verdict : whether, if this question be answered in the negative, the fact that these texts were ever thought of to teach a Trinity, is not an argument against it ; and whether we do not start, in the consideration of the Logos, with some store of grounded motive to watch well the proof, before we think the Word of God is the base of any hypostatical relation?

If any antagonist declare, that the Jews looked very narrowly at these same passages, we shall begin there a series of remarks, which we shall depend upon entirely, to introduce us, in an intelligible way, into the New Testament testimonies. Beyond a doubt the Old Testament doctors of the law did deal with the Logos, and that in very extraordinary ways. Would it be unfair to ask, what was the propriety of what they did? As they resorted to very notorious expedients, the question has long ago offered itself, Were they right? or were they wrong?

And the world has answered.

They prepared important Targums; that is to say, they paraphrased the Old Testament revelation. These paraphrases were universally accepted; and, when Christ came upon the earth, they were in many synagogues, and the reading of the Targums was a thing familiar to Israelitish worshippers.

I beg you, pause at this. What the Targums taught, the Bible taught; so thought the Jews: and by that superstitious bent, notorious among the Rabbis, the Jews knew no difference; and what was surreptitiously brought into the faith, stood as well with vast herds of the people, if it was writ in the Targums, as if it was originally fixed as part of the word of the Almighty.

Now, one of the things superstitiously tampered with was "The Word of Jehovah." The Targums had multiplied it. Instead of the few cases inciden-

## God the Son.

tal to an easy rhetoric, where the term, if it had been left, would have been easily understood, they made it memorable by writing it all the time. They cast out the word "Jehovah" two hundred times, and put in "the Word of Jehovah," with no other warrant than some growing and unquestioned superstition. This came down to New Testament times. Of course we have a right to be aware of it, and to watch it very narrowly. John, Irenæus tells us, wrote his gospel to oppose certain errors which he goes on to describe (Irenæus, III. 11). These Targums came into Africa. They were the treasures of the Ptolemaic time. They were coincident with the Septuagint. They mingled with the Greek literature. And, as the result, we have an understood form of faith. That is, it is a matter of history, that the Platonic Trinity, which is the first we read of as in the possession of Israel, wove itself upon this Targum frame; and now, as a thing actually confessed, produced a " WORD" which orthodox and errorists alike, confess was miserable superstition.

Irenæus describes it: "Monogenes* was the Arche,† but Logos was the true son of Monogenes. This creation, to which we belong, was not made by the primary God, but by some power lying far below him; and that [power was] off from communion with things invisible and ineffable" (Iren. B. iii : C. 11).

The Apocrypha, we ought long ago to have said, hypostasizing the "Word," and hypostasizing also "Wisdom," came out, on these superstitious grounds,

\* " The Only Begotten."   † " The Beginning."

in the strongest manner; and climbed up, partly by the help of such outspokenness, into unquestioned rivalry with the better canon. Philo came upon the scene. " Logos" became the *bête noir* of all Judaico-Ptolemaic thought. Philo ripened it into a system. Philo rooted it in the East. Though, the remark applied to him by Newman applies better perhaps to others his disciples, that, " associating it (the doctrine of the Logos) with Platonic notions as well as words, [he] developed its lineaments with so rude and hasty a hand, as to separate the idea of the Divine Word from that of the Eternal God, and so, perhaps, to prepare the way for Arianism" (Newman's Arians, p. 95).

Now John came. But before we seek light upon him, let us ask, What was this system, after all? It is impossible to say. Philo was full and explicit. But Philo was quickly departed from. There was no one system. But yet the tendency was this, to teach what was called a " Second God." The Logos was an emanation. It was not eternal; nor was it equal to the Father. Yet it was not a creature. It was intermediate, and subordinate; not brought into being by an act, but begotten; and yet not born from eternity, but, to express all in a single sentence, intermediate, and an emanation in time.

Undoubtedly this paved the way for Arianism; and John, when he came into the church, had to choose, whether he would ignore it, or refute it, or by a few strong words trample upon it; and this last, by the testimony of Irenæus, and as we tried to show in another part of our book, he took up his pen emphatically to do.

"In the beginning was the Word" (Jo. i: 1).

Let us now look at this somewhat more carefully. The Philonists taught that the "Logos" was an emanation in time. John denies this. He says, "In the beginning was the Word:" and, whatever he means by the "Logos," he sweeps, at one blow, all its intermediate nature. Then he goes further. He says, "The Word was *pros ton Theon;*" and, in Paul, *pros ton Theon*" twice means, "pertaining to" the Almighty (Heb. ii: 17; v: 1). It never means "with;"* I beg to insist upon this. The Greek "with" is entirely a different preposition. Then,— The Word was in the beginning, and it pertained to God. That is, whatever the Word might be found to be, it was always: it was not an emanation. Moreover it referred to God, like his " hand," or his " arm." And then, to put aside all doubt, " God was it;" just as we would speak of his " voice" or his " finger," if men began with them as a superstition. "In the beginning was the Word, and the Word had reference to God, and God was the Word:" and we have already shown how Meyer objects to this last, saying that *it would subvert the Trinity!* (see also Alford, *et al.*); and how Middleton has reigned for generations under the false syntactical pretence (see Gram. Chap. iii: s. 4, § 1) that the article before the " Logos" must necessarily reverse the Greek.†

---

\* See note, I. Chap. V.

† On the contrary, the article is or is not before a word, simply for a purpose. It is not before it usually in the predicate, because the

To sum up; John does not discard the "Word." On the contrary; he uses it. It was used in the legitimate Scriptures. It had grown in the use of the people. It had been wonderfully abused. But it still means *God uttering himself:* and that he did in the Redeemer. And, believing that it was a graceful type, and believing that he must wrest it from its heresies, and uttering those sharp expressions in its case, he launches it again upon the page, alas! to be yet more misconceived, and to be made, like sentences of Christ (Jo. iii: 5; vi: 53; Matt. xvi: 18; Jo. xx: 23), the base of perpetuated superstition.

### § 10. *The Son and the Creation.*

Turning from the "Logos," which I ought to have said John returns to in its most ordinary signification* (Jo. xii: 48; xiv: 24; 1 Jo. ii: 14; Rev. xx: 4), I come next to that class of passages which speak of Christ as the Creator of the universe. Let me quote some of them. "By him were all things created" (Col. i: 16, 17). "By whom also he made the worlds" (Heb. i: 2). "Thou Lord, in the beginning,

predicate is usually generic, and not specific. But, in this case, it happens to be specific, and actually demands the article. We put it in the English. To get at our meaning we do not say, The God was Word, as we would say, " The knife was steel" ; but we say, " God was the Word," just as in another case we say, " Spirit was God" (Jo. iv: 24; see the Greek); a case equally perverted and lost in the sense that was designed.

\* Would there not have been more care about this, if John had really thought it was a Person of the Trinity? Would he not have been more saving of the term, and tried to keep it apart, just as we have said of Jehovah, if it had so rare a meaning?

## God the Son. 91

hast laid the foundation of the Earth" (Heb. viii : 10). If Christ came to be, as a distinct actor upon the scene, only when he was born in Bethlehem, how possibly can we carve our way through these remarkable attestations?

And I ask, in the first place, How can anybody? We believe that Jehovah was incarnate. That which was incarnate, therefore, made the world. We believe that Christ was born as a man. Christ as a man, never made anything. That, all will concede. We believe that Christ was of one substance with the Father. So do all of us. We believe that one substance made the world. So do all. We believe that the Three Persons made the world, if there are Three Persons in the Trinity. So do all (Eph. iii : 9; Heb. i: 10; Job xxvi: 13). We believe that there are not Three Persons in the Trinity, but that the One Person made the world. This is our sole point of difference.

Now if we thought as most persons think, we would take our stand upon this line, and say, Jesus Christ created the world, because he was incarnate Jehovah.

Why not say that?

It may be answered, because " by " or " through " Jehovah would not seem a significant revelation. Why not? as that very word is employed? (1 Cor. i : 9; Heb. ii : 10). At least, it may be said, God creating " by " God, or Jehovah " by " Jesus Christ, would not be a significant revelation, if Jehovah's One Eternal Person was all that was engaged in the creative act. Again I say, Wherein does the Trinitarian complain? for One Person creating "by" another Person, and One Person equal to that other Person, and that Person the same in substance, and all the Persons equally engaged in the work of creation, does not leave the Trinitarian much better, on a basis of grammatic sense, if *we* believe in the incarnation of our original Creator.

We are weak, however, in any such polemic, because we are fighting against our thought. We do not believe that it is referring to the original Jehovah. And when the apostle speaks of creating " all things by Jesus Christ" (Eph. iii : 9), I do not think the Trinitarian himself can exclude the Humanity from this assertion.

Let me explain.

If it were left peremptorily to decide whether God necessarily were a Trinity, because he created by Jesus Christ, I would say that One Person creating by Another Person, when both were one, and all shared in the creation, were a much more confused account than God creating "by" himself (Gen. xxii : 16; Heb. i : 3) : but as I believe that neither is the true solution, and both are alien from what is meant, I feel it far better to pay little attention to either, and go at once to that light which can be gathered from a more general survey of the sacred text.

I said, in treating of the Spirit, that it is in all degrees of subjectivity. When it says, The Holy Ghost spake (Acts xxviii : 25), it is hardly subjective at all. When it speaks of "a meek and quiet spirit" (James iii : 4), it is hardly Divine at all. Between the passages where it is so barely God as to retain

## God the Son. 93

little emblem of a "Breath," and those passages where it is so barely man as to retain little of the attitude of the Almighty, there are all degrees that intervene; and it has been a failure to keep up with the rhetoric, that has squared men down to Arian views of some intermediate Almighty.

Now, it is the same with Christ and the creation. Between the extreme of creation "by" Jehovah, and the extreme of creation "by" our fellow Man, there are all degrees of difference; and I wish to mention three, that almost stand by themselves with little other shading.

(1) For example, first, there is a passage in the Hebrews in which the Son is mentioned, and in which we read, "by whom also he made the worlds" (Heb. i: 2); and in which this Scripture is quoted in attestation: "Thou Lord in the beginning hast laid the foundation of the earth; and the heavens are the works of thine hands" (Ps. cii: 25). We turn to the Psalm, and it is throughout Jehovah. There is no sign of any discrepance of Person; and it is perhaps, beyond the majority of the Psalter, free of the Messiah. We bow our heads, therefore, to the fact, that the Jews referred it to the Messiah, or, at any rate, to the proof, that Paul, speaking by divine revelation, quoted it that way, and, therefore, that God's making all things by Christ is illustrated, in this particular case, by the fact, that Jehovah, who was incarnate in the Redeemer, originally and by himself made the worlds. This is the extreme in one direction; viz., the particle, "by," enfolding direct causation, as we know by all the Lexicons that it does in other parts

of the word of God (Rom. xi : 36 ; 1 Cor. i : 9). Then comes an intermediate case, where " by" is used for the norm or the rule. For example, in the instance of " Wisdom :" " The Lord by wisdom hath founded the earth ; by understanding hath he established the heavens" (Prov. iii : 19). To get rid of prejudice, let us take the second clause. " By understanding" cannot mean causally or efficiently ; it must mean modally ; and, therefore, we are given the warrant for God's doing " by" things that which he does causally and in himself; and that of which the " wisdom" and the " understanding" express the mere normal relation.

Now, carry that to the instance of the " Word." "All things were made by him" (Jo. i : 3). Here the case is a little different. Here it is not mere " Wisdom." Here the rhetoric has been carried further ; and God has positively been announced to be the " Word." Still, I do not think *mere* causality is intended. If the Scriptures had said, " God is Love ;" and then gone on to say, God by Love made the heavens,—I would not think that it merely meant that God created them. I would think that there was more in the rhetoric. I would not think that it separated Love hypostatically from God, but that it was mere spoken common-sense ; mere Oriental effective speaking. I would not conceive that it implied a separate Person, but that God by the norm of his Love created all things under that modal inspiration.

So, now, of the " Word." I believe it is more rhetorical than " Love," because it is more the person.

## God the Son.                               95

It is more God actually uttering himself; and yet, for all that, when it says, "All things were made by him," I think it means more than that God made all things himself; and calls up the idea of a word, or universal decree, uttered from the beginning of time, "by" which, as the norm and also utterance of power, everything was made that was made.

(2) We mark this down, therefore, as the second shading of the representation.

(3) But there is a third. God from all eternity was not complete for the work of creation. He was complete in power. Give him the name of "The Word," and imagine that Word to be himself, uttered out in all his endless purposes: give him credit for all he is to be, and means to do, and then he is complete. But cut off from him future plans and the long-subsequent incarnation, and he can create nothing. I mean by that, he determined to build everything upon Jesus Christ. We see this in every part of the revelation. Christ was to be "head over all things to the church" (Eph. i: 22). And when we remember that God forgave for four thousand years, and ruled the world for four thousand years, and laid his plans before the creation of the stars and all upon Christ, I think we can begin to see what he means by creating "all things by Jesus Christ" (Eph. iii: 9). Moreover, considering that Christ was a man; considering that Jesus Christ was preëminently the Incarnate God; considering that he had no name like Jesus, before he was incarnate; and considering that Trinitarians themselves must believe that God out of Christ was a consuming fire; and that it was the suffering

and obedience of the man which it was necessary to build the world upon, as to the whole scheme of its creation,—I should think that even the Trinitarian would agree that there is a certain sort of sense in which God created the world by the man Christ Jesus.

Now, if there is any such sense at all, it is sufficient to be the whole sense. That is the argument we press. (1) " Thou Lord in the beginning" : that is Jehovah ; and means that Christ created all things, because he was Jehovah. (2) " All things were made by it" (Jo. i : 3). That is Jehovah too ; but Jehovah as the manifested Word ; and means that God created all things by one consistent self-uttering manifestation. But (3) " By him were all things created" (Col. i : 16); that is a much more complete idea; and means that God, without Christ, is imperfect ; that is, that God, without Christ, is impossible ; that life, without Christ, cannot be ; that the world, without life, is a waste ; that the universe, without Christ, is a failure ; and therefore, that the Babe of Bethlehem, though a trifle (Is. xli : 24) ; though in himself a worm of the dust (Is. xli : 14) ; though an easy outbirth of God's omnipotence ; and, therefore, sure to be ;—nevertheless *had* to be ; that is, that God was doing oceans of work without him, which depended upon him ; that he was forgiving millions of souls ; and that the whole shape of the creation was given by the man (who, nevertheless, was eternally God), who was born in a manger in the town of Bethlehem.

Now, that this was the meaning of the passages, we can tell by looking at them. Listen to the Apostle

## God the Son.

Paul, " And to make all men see what is the fellowship of the mystery:" what mystery, except these unbased and unexplicated pardons?—but he goes on to explain: " which from the beginning of the world hath been hid in God :" now he is going to utter our very idea : " which from the beginning of the world hath been hid in God, who created all things by Jesus Christ" (Eph. iii : 9). These ideas are everywhere repeated. Paul says, " Who hath saved us according to grace, which was given us in Christ Jesus before the world began" (2 Tim. i : 9). Christ says, " Come ye blessed of my Father, inherit the Kingdom prepared for you from the foundation of the world" (Matt. xxv : 34). And Paul absolutely lays bare the whole rhetoric ; for he speaks of such a case in Abraham, where God talks to an old shepherd, and calls a thing done, before there is even a gleam of it ; and then says, " before him whom he believed, even God, who quickeneth the dead, and calleth those things which be not as though they were" (Rom. iv : 17).

Our doctrine, therefore, is, that Christ created all things. We agree with the Trinitarian that he is God, and, as God, built the universe. But as we do not think this exhausts the passages, we would not, even if we were a Trinitarian, explain them of the Almighty. We believe that the MAN gave shape to the universe ; and, though we believe that God gave everything to the Man ; yet we believe he needed this Man, to complete his works ; and, therefore, that, when he says, " All things are created by him and for him " (*i. e.* in reference to him) ; and when he says, " He is before all things ;" and when he says, " In him all things stood together" (Col. i : 16, 17),— he means, that he is the husband (house-band) of the universe ; that " without him was not anything made that was made" (Jo. i: 3) ; that God had " chosen us in him before the foundation of the world" (Eph. i: 4) ; that our life was hid with him in God (Col. iii : 3) ; and that it was on the man alone that the promise could stand complete of eternal life " before the world began" (Titus i: 1, 2).

Possibly we should stop here : but let us take another glance ; and then we will finish. There is another meaning to "*dia.*" Not only does it mean *causally ;* as, for example, where God says, " I will answer him by myself" (Ezek. xiv: 17); not only does it mean *normally ;* as, for example, " The Lord by wisdom hath founded the earth" (Prov. iii : 19) ; not only does it mean *instrumentally*, in such a sense that the new Christ was necessary to the old creation ; or, in other words, that God, in an age of pardons, and in an eternity of divine decrees, was really building upon Christ, and could not advance a step, except on the faith of what he was yet to be : but, once more ; it means *accompanyingly ;* nay more ; *pregnantly.* That is ; when Christ was created, all things were created. This was a bold rhetoric utterance ; because Christ was created long after the heavens. But the idea, meant to be conveyed, is, for all that, apparent. " Without him was not anything made that was made." Logically, he was the precursor of the universe. That *dia* has such a meaning, we see often. " Praying often by all prayer"

## God the Son. 99

(Eph. vi: 18). "Neither by the blood of goats and calves, but by his own blood." (Heb. ix: 12). "Who by the eternal Spirit offered himself" (Heb. ix: 14). "This is he who came by water and blood" (1 Jo. v: 6). The shades are very different; just as the word "Spirit," we saw, had different shades of subjectivity: but all the uses show that *dia* has singular versatility of meaning. It means, first, " by," *causal*. It means, second, " by," *normal*. It means, third, " by," *instrumental*, and instrumental in a very peculiar sense, viz., not actual, but logical, the inexistent Man being the *sine qua non* of the world's creation. And it means dia, *inclusive*.

These four all blend. The *dia* causal includes of course all that is in the Cause, viz., the wisdom and the word by which he operates. The *dia* normal refers more to the decree or plan which the unspeakable Word or self-manifesting Jehovah had before all time. The *dia* instrumental involves the instruments which that self-manifesting Word must ordain, and in the end call into being. And the *dia* inclusive is just a further thought, viz.,—when Christ was decreed, all things were decreed; and that not merely accompanyingly, as in your case or mine, but *pregnantly*. When Christ was laid down in the plan, all things were laid down. " In him all things stood together" (Col. i: 17). By him; that is, as an efflux from him,—logically all things followed. And though he was long after in time, yet John struck the key when he said, " He was before me" (Jo. i: 15); that is to say (I of course now mean the Man) was to be " head over all things to the Church (Eph. i: 22);

was to be above all "principality and power" (Eph. i: 21); was to have "all authority (power, E. V.) in heaven and in earth" (Matt. xxviii: 18); was to have "all things made with him and in reference to him" (Col. i: 16); and was, therefore, even though as a man, the first born of all things; or, as Paul expresses it, the "first born of the whole creation" (Col. i: 15).

§ 11. *The Son's Preëxistence.*

There are three ways in which the Son may be regarded; either, first, as Jehovah; or, second, as Jehovah and man; or, third, as man, apart from the Deity; that is to say, as man, aside from the other nature, but still inseparable from it, and carrying about the glories that belong to the man as the only begotten Son of the Father. Now, in all these three ways the Scriptures speak of Christ.

When, therefore, we are told, "Before Abraham was I am" (Jo. viii: 58), we have an easy course; because in that text we need only think of Jehovah. If Jesus Christ was God, we may expect him to speak of being before all time. And, therefore, when he says "I am Alpha and Omega" (Rev. i: 8), we have nothing to remember but that agreed-upon fact, "that Jesus Christ is Lord, to the glory of God the Father" (Phil. ii: 11).

But, now, by the light of what we have learned in dealing with the creation, let us remember that God was not enough to be our Maker. Forgive the irreverence. God was the Father of the Son; that is, everything that was in the Son came from the

Almighty. Therefore the Father *was* enough; for all that the Son needed God gave him. He was not only the God himself that dwelt in the Redeemer, but he made the humanity. So that all the Christ came from him; so that we cannot say, in any disparaging way, at all, that God was not sufficient for his works, and that he was not sure to execute all that he had decreed.

But we do say, that he could not execute it without Christ. God could not save without the man born in Bethlehem; and, therefore, Christ was more, in an intelligible sense, than the Almighty; for he was God in the plenitude of his substance, and he was also Man; and that Man was necessary, as a great essential of our sacrifice.

Why then should it be thought unnatural that Christ should loom up from eternity? that he should be talked of from eternity? that he should be built upon from eternity? that is to say, that nothing should be done that did not look at him; and that nothing should be planned that did not make him the central figure; so that, not yet born, he became the most familiar thought in the decree, and the most familiar object in the wide creation.

Now, immediately we can parcel out all the texts that seem to speak of a preëxistence.

1. In the first place, He did preëxist. Jesus Christ was literally God; and, therefore, he preëxisted nakedly, and in the most disentangled way (Jo. viii: 58; Heb. i: 10).

2. But, secondly, he was God and man; and there are passages that speak of him as coming down

from heaven (Jo. vi : 38); there are passages that speak of him as ascending up where he was before (Jo. iii : 13) ; there are passages that speak of him as emptying himself, and taking upon him the form of a servant, and becoming obedient unto death (Phil. ii : 7); and hypostatic theories seize upon this, and say, Here is no one original Jehovah without Trinity and mutuality of being, but here is a Second Person ; and they conceive of these as the very strongest texts to argue an eternal Logos.

But why ?

If we needed to divert our thinking, we could show that the theory of a Second Person untied these knots no more completely than the theory of One. But the reality is, that neither unties them. These beautiful sentences need more than either. The form that rises to explain them is the Theanthropos ; and the second range of passages are those, which, realizing a God-man, and realizing that the man is the slenderest component of the Redeemer, talk, even when contemplating both, of the majesty of the One ; and make the Great God our Saviour preëxist of course; because, though he did not pick up his humanity till the fulness of time, yet he used it, and acted upon it, from all eternity.

3. Now, there are a third class of passages, that are more rhetorical still.

Let it be remembered that the first talk nakedly of God, because God is incarnate in the Redeemer: let it be remembered that the second talk also of the Man, because God and Man are one, and yet God, being the great Fountain of the whole preëxistence, is the attribute of the nobler and constituent part of our Deliverer. But, lastly, the Man talks as though he had had immortality. That is the great phenomenon! He talks of it in a way that no Trinity could explain. He talks of it in a way not hypostatical and divine, but incarnate and human. And the question is, How could Christ, being a man, utter things before the eye of the Almighty, that seemed to imply that he, the carpenter's son, was from everlasting?

Now, it was rhetorical.

Jesus Christ, the great King of Heaven, was necessary to the universe. He did not live, till he was born; but he reigned, and was uppermost in creation, through myriads of years. "All things were made by him"; and not by him as Jehovah; and not by him as Theanthropos; but, also, by him as Man. He was before all things. Not a stone could be laid in the creation but in his name. And so familiar did he become in all time, that the whole Scripture is colored by his presence, even though he were yet to be.

Now take some of this rhetoric: "Glorify thou me with thine own self" (Jo. xvii : 5). Of course that is perfectly understandable, because Christ has just explained it: "Glorify thy Son, that thy Son also may glorify thee" (v. 1). But "glorify thou me with thine own self, with the glory that I had with thee before the world was" (v 5). The Trinitarian says, This is the Second Person; and builds at once all the mutuality of the Trinity. But let him take another text, a "Lamb slain from the foundation of the world." It is obvious that these are rhetorical liberties of the Bible: and that the Father *had* a glory; a glory that had existed from eternity; a glory in an administration based upon a Man; a glory of which that Man was an element before he was created; and a glory which, being but a Man, and being but a breath of the Almighty, and being easily commanded and summoned up, whenever his time should come, he could be imagined as having been possessed of from everlasting, and as having had actually discounted before the foundation of the world.

" When therefore," says Augustine, " he saw that the time of his predestined glorification had fully come, that that should now happen in fact which had already happened in predestiny, he prayed saying: ' And now, O Father, glorify me, with thine own self, with the glory which I had with thee before the world was:' as though he had said, The glory which I had with thee in thy decree, it is now time that I should have with thee actually, living at thy right hand" (Augustine, Com., Jo. xvii: Tract 105, § 8).

This argument is negative. It is mightily confirmed by the testimony of such a man as Austin: but before abandoning this subject of the preëxistence, we would like to glance at something more positive. We would like to turn away from showing that certain texts do not prove the Trinity, and quote others that reject it. And I will do so in this manner. I will quote a certain text, and then ask the Trinitarian to explain it: and my object will be to show, that a downright positive sense will drift the sentence away from the preëxistence of Emmanuel.

## God the Son.

For example, this sentence, "The first born of every creature" (Col. i: 15). If it be said, This is the eternal Logos ; and if we give in to eternal generation ; and if we say, This Word was derived in the beginning; and if we then seek a settled meaning by saying, This Word, being derived from eternity, preceded all creatures, and, therefore, was first derived among them all : dispensing with the hint that this is rather a gross idea, we immediately encounter other texts, which the slenderest fidelity to truth must recognize as having the same intention. Paul speaks of "the first born from the dead" (Col. i : 18). John repeats the idea (Rev. i : 5). Now, I defy any one to read from the Apostle Paul, " The first-born from the dead" (Col. i: 18), and move his finger three sentences back, and read, " The first-born of every creature" (v. 15), and say, The " first-born" in the fifteenth verse, and the " first-born" in the eighteenth verse, are heaven wide in their interpretation. The thing is impossible. And, yet, if they are not, the " first-born" in the fifteenth verse must mean the birth in Bethlehem, or else the " first born" in the eighteenth verse must mean an eternal begetting, and how, then, could that eternal begetting be a begetting from the dead ?

If it be answered, They do mean differently, and it is a chance that they are thrown together: and such combinations do occur, as for example, "Answer a fool according to his folly" (Prov. xxvi: 5), and " Answer not a fool according to his folly" (v. 4), Solomon actually choosing next door positions for these utterly discrepant ideas,—I say, No exegete will be hardy enough to say so. No fair scholarship will attempt to maintain it. For, not only would one instance of just such a nature forbid, but there are other instances : not only the instance in Revelation, and not only the expression in the Psalm, fixing a time, " This day have I begotten thee" (Ps. ii : 7), but this in the Epistle to the Romans,—" For whom he did foreknow, he also did predestinate, to be conformed to the image of his Son, that he might be the first-born among many brethren" (Rom. viii : 29).

Again, I will quote another case—a text already pointed out, " The Lamb slain from the foundation of the world" (Rev. xiii : 8). Does that mean some fact that was from eternity? Did anybody ever pretend it? And if not, will the Trinitarian show what it means? And, in showing it, will he tell by what law of hermeneutic light he can read this speech of things happening in time, and save the hermeneutic strength of passages of a kindred rhetoric.

Would it be wrong to claim some positive answer to these appeals?

And, thirdly, the " Son" of the Almighty. Where did we get that word?

We have a fancy that, of all Bible names, it is the most legitimate. What a wonderful thing is theological training! The student who should be suddenly asked, Why do you say the Son of God? would answer, Because all men in all ages have used that title: or, cooling down a little, All men in Scriptural ages. And, yet, let him examine the Bible, and he will find that it is no where used except of the birth at Bethlehem.

## God the Son.

Let me make one exception. Nebuchadnezzar says, "The form of the fourth is like the Son of God" (Dan. iii: 25). We turn eagerly to examine; and the first glance knocks off the article. This is positively the only passage. We have "trees of the Lord" (Ps. civ: 16); and "rivers of God" (Ps. lxv: 9); and here we have "a son of God." What can we prove by it? The monarch, in his Persian speech, says, "The form of the fourth is like a son of God." There might be bodings of a son of Abraham (Gen. iv: 1; xxii: 18; Ps. ii: 12), which might fill the world with such a speech, but how slender any influence whatever! The Psalmist says, "Kiss the Son" (Ps. ii: 12); and he says again, "Thou art my Son" (v. 7); but, of course, these are prophecies. He says, in that oft quoted announcement, "Thou art my Son: this day have I begotten thee" (v. 7), but, by the last fragment of the sentence, fixes and defines what precedes. The word "Son," like the word "Bishop," (Acts xx: 28), or like the word "Person" (Heb. i: 3), must either be borrowed, with a confession that that is not its use, (Lu. i: 35; Jo. x: 36), or this very serious adverse argument must be met— that it was no name for a preëxistent Deity.*

---

* Why should not this argument have overwhelming weight? If the filiation of the Son be eternal, and he be a Person, by that Sonship made distinct, and having subsistence in a Trinity, why is not that accented? Why is the main emphasis on what Gabriel announced? Why does not God say, and why does not he say, that he was generated before time? And why does not the birth of the Holy Ghost (Lu. i: 35) stand aside as a mere sequence in the case, and the word Son dot all the earlier annals, as chiefly belonging to a being begotten in the heavens.

Lastly, that wonderful passage in Philippians, "Who, being in the form of God, thought it not robbery to be equal with God" (Phil. ii: 6). Here I wish to ask a very different question. Here I wish to ask, Why is the Greek adjective in the neuter plural? Recollect, there is to be a Second Person; and the favorite exposition of the text is, that now he is to be described. He is "in the form of God." Unfortunate at the very first setting out! For think of it, "The same in substance," and yet "in the form"\* of the Almighty! But let us go on. "Thought it not robbery to be equal with God" (v. 6). Now, of all other places in the Bible, a simple singular masculine might at once be expected. "Thought it not robbery to be an equal Person with God." Instead of that, it is neuter: and instead of the singular, it is plural. And I press a distinct answer to the difficulty that in the articulate form of speech there is no rest but in our theory. "Let this mind be in you, which was also in Christ Jesus." According to our theory, this is the great Theanthropos. "Who being in the form of God." What could be more expressive? Having the authority of God; having the name of God, so that he can stand accepted for his people; having the Spirit of God, and that in so marvellous a

---

\* We believe Jesus Christ to be God, even more than our brethren: but if we believed he was a separate God, or, from eternity, a separate person in God, we would expect Paul, in so elaborate a sentence, to say something about that. We would not expect him to begin about his being "in the form of God"; just as we would not expect, in the same case, Gabriel to be telling Mary that the Holy Ghost should overshadow her, and that THEREFORE that holy thing, that should be begotten, should be called the Son of God.

way, that God is in him as One Person,—it is full of significance, as he stood out upon the street " in the form" of the Almighty. And yet, there were some reserves. He was truly God. But his humanity was not truly God. And, therefore, there were certain definitions to be made. There were certain respects in which he was not Almighty. He was Almighty in emptying himself, in making himself of no reputation, in taking upon him the form of a servant, and in being found in fashion as a man; but he was not Almighty in his manhood; and there distinctions had to be made. Hence the beauty of the language, "that there should be equal respects with God" (*to einai isa*). This is no speech of an *Hypostasis*: it is no fixing of a Second Person. It is the portrait of a man: of a man claiming to be divine; of a man, actually God in the incarnation of the whole of Deity; but a man not ceasing to be man; and therefore, when stating his equality with God, exquisite in his speech, and carefully reserving respects in which he has still humanity.

But we must not make these sections too long.

### § 12. *The Angel of Jehovah.*

We think that the angel of Jehovah was a common angel, sent on the errands of the Most High. We believe so for one very strong reason, that the Apostle Paul, speaking of the incarnation of Christ, speaks in this wise, " He does not sure enough take on angels, but he does take on the seed of Abraham" (Heb. ii: 16). That scatters difficulty at a breath. He *seemed* to be actually an angel. That was his appearance. He seemed to be actually a man. But he makes a vast discrimination. He did not sure enough take on an angel; or, to make it more true to the history, any of them (plural), for he appeared in many,—but he did take on the seed of Abraham. And we are to understand that he employed angels, and that they personated him often; but that he became incarnate in the Son; and that he had, therefore, that sure-enough union, which a peculiar Greek word (*depou*) denies in the other case.

If any one asks, Is that your only passage? I say, No. Look at the last chapter of Revelation. The angel, there, rejects the worship of the Apostle (v. 9), and, yet, the next moment personates the Redeemer. "See thou do it not," he says in the ninth verse, and in the twelfth, "Behold I come quickly." This is the manner of angels. They did so at Sodom (Gen. xviii: 2, 13). They did so with Hagar (Gen. xvi: 7, 13), and Lot (Gen. xix: 1, 21); and one did so under the oak at Ophrah (Jud. vi: 11, 16, 20). Our persuasion is, that the "man" who was singled out as Jehovah, was a common angel. And if any one asks, How dare he personate God, I answer, How dare the prophets? (Œhler, Theol. O. T., § 60); or, as a most satisfying instance, how dare Moses? for most undoubtedly he says, "I will give you the rain of your land in his due season, the first rain and the latter rain" (Deut. xi: 14); and most undoubtedly he declares, "I will send grass in thy fields for thy cattle, that thou mayest eat and be full" (v 15).

The fact is, it makes the slenderest sort of difference whether it was an angel or not. If it was an

## God the Son.

angel, God appeared in him, and spoke by him, and wrought miracles by his mouth; and, moreover, gave him a human form, and wrought that miracle in the very act of sending him. If it was not an angel, still it was a human form; and it seems to make not the smallest difference. If it were the Son of God, it would not be his body; nobody pretends that. And if it were a body, God, personally in it, and representing himself by it, would be so like stretching out his arm (Deut. v: 15), as to preclude every possibility of Trinitarian demonstration.

So the matter stands, therefore. We believe that they were angels: but it is unimportant. We believe that they were angels, because the Apostle speaks so, and a distinction is drawn between the ministry of angels and the ministry of Christ (Acts vii: 53; Gal. iii: 19). We believe that they were angels, because Moses deprecated such a convoy, and pled so hard for the presence of God (Ex. xxxiii: 2, 12–15); which surely would be nothing higher than the presence of Christ. We believe that they were angels, out of deference to the straight-forwardness of speech. But grant that they were anything you please. They cannot be built into a hypostatic argumentation; for the rhetoric must remain indifferent. To send an angel, or to send an apparition, or to send a dream, or to send the Second Person in the Trinity, would be all covered under the very same miracle, and there could be no possible distinction that could breed a reasoning.

Now, one thing more.

§ 13. *The Son as Father, Son and Holy Ghost.*

Christ is distinctly called the Father (Is. ix : 6, Jo. xiv : 9). He is distinctly called the Son (Rom. i : 3). He is distinctly called the Holy Ghost (Jo. xiv : 18 ; 2 Cor. iii : 17). We close the chapter with that appeal to the inspired rhetoric. He is not called so, often ; for that would spoil the figures ; just as the " heart" is not called " mind" always or often, but only sometimes, because it is convenient to keep them separate. So the words for the Almighty are not endlessly confused; but sufficiently mixed to keep them from mystic handling.

CHAPTER IV.

GOD THE FATHER.

§ 1. *Meaning of the Name.*

PAUL says, " For this cause I bow my knees unto the Father of the Lord Jesus Christ, of whom all fatherhood in heaven and upon earth is named" (Eph. iii : 14, 15). This immediately sets a Fatherhood up which ought to have a bold and original signification. What is it ? Either a fatherhood of man, or a fatherhood of God. I mean by that, the Bible is an extended revelation, and it ought very quickly to appear whether the Fatherhood that gives pattern to all the fatherhoods of the world, is a fatherhood of the Second Person of the Trinity, or a fatherhood of men ; in other words, whether God was a Father from eternity, or a Father in time ; the

## God the Father.

Son, in the one case, being an Eternal Person, and the Son, in the other, being the Nazarene ; the agreement in either case being that angels (Job xxxviii : 7), and men (Acts xvii : 28), are sons of the same Fatherhood, on earth and in the heavens.

Now, how could we settle such a thing? All agree that it is not debated in the Bible. Indeed, this is but one of very singular agreements. The Trinitarian agrees that his doctrine is nowhere formulated. He goes further. He says, its language is not in the Bible. He often complains of it. Calvin wished the word Trinity had never been invented. Not only is the word Trinity made up, but the word Person. *Hupostasis* is even laughably mistranslated. Not only does it never occur in the Bible to teach a Trinity; but it could not. It means a substance. The only case in which it ever occurs of the Almighty, it is mistranslated, appearing as " person"—" the express image of his person" (Heb. i: 3)—when it means " his substance ;" so that the very terminology of the scheme awakens a suspicion. There is no term, Trinity. There is no dream of connecting it with anything that can be translated Person ; there is no terminology of it as a faith ; there is no controversy about it as of the creed ; and there is no mode of settling it, except in that " Horæ Paulinæ" way, that hovers about the casualties of the expression.

Nevertheless, shut down to this, we offer this argument.

Consult a Concordance.

In the instance of a comet, do we consider the

tail as evolving the head, or the head as evolving the tail?

Turn up the word Father in a Concordance. Observe it. Where does it centre? and where does its great idea rally? It is never used of God but eight times in the Old Testament? It is never used except as of his fatherhood of man save once, and then it is prophetic of the Anointed Man, Our Saviour, the blessed Redeemer (Ps. lxxxix: 26). It is never used of an anterior Fatherhood a single time. And yet when we come to the New, the page fairly glitters with the glorious appellation.

It is never used of God's fatherhood other than as connected with a creature.

And if any body says, That is assuming everything, I speak more carefully. I do not deny that if Christ was begotten from eternity it may be *consistent* with New Testament texts. But we are speaking now of *evidence*. It will not do endlessly to empty from one mere consistency to another. We are looking for the bush where the Trinity turns upon its pursuers and rends them. I say that the Fatherhood of God is never said to be eternal. By a strange occurrence in the prophet, " The Everlasting Father" is Jesus Christ himself (Is. ix : 6). Sonship or filiation, as of eternity, would have been distinctly mentioned. It is impossible that a grand reality would have been slighted. And now, coupling-on the main argument, it is this :—That the big letters in a Concordance, scattered like the rarest stars in the Old Testament, and, when they do occur, centring, in a far off way, in the manger in Bethlehem ; and then spangling the whole heavens in the New Testament revelation,—is as near a proof as it admits, that the Fatherhood of God was not of a Logos other than as of an earth-born Son, the same in substance equal in power and glory.

§ 2. *No Name or Work Sacred to One Person.*

And the same line of remark may be made in respect to the functions of the Trinity. Controversialists are fond of saying, There is no formula, it is true; there is no controversy waged in the Bible. But, then, the facts are there. There is no gravity written in the heavens; but, then, those far off stars bear the facts of it written on their foreheads. There is no herald of the forest,—This is an oak, and, This is an ash: nor is there any schedule of the sense, proclaiming the eye or the ear: but those functionaries stand out, just as the stars shine down. And so, it may be said, Hypostases are not labelled; nor are they discussed in a doctrinal way; but there they are. And the functions of creation, redemption and sanctification mark their boundary, and, like the facts in physics, we are to collate and make their theory appear.

But, alas for the most candid seeker! there is the very difficulty. The stars wear their livery in heaven, and never change it. And so of the tree. The oak is never an ash. And, in the region of sense, the eye never listens, and the ear never looks, and the heart never breathes. But, in this most important of all doctrines as many men declare, how are we treated? There is no theory. That we must give up at once: though Paul pronounces some very strict theories as to morals (Rom. xiii: 8-10; 1 Cor. v: 9-11), and as to the covenants of life (Rom. v: 12-21). Moreover, there is no controversy, and there is no elenchtic discussion, to give the theory shape. The facts occur in the Bible world, like stars upon the heavens. But, now, mark the difficulty. There is no persistency in them. He who is called Creator to-day, is called Sanctifier to-morrow. There is not the abiding law, even of a well pursued emblem. The Father is called the Son, and the Son is called the Father. Both are repeatedly declared to be the Holy Ghost. And, when it comes to function, the Father is called the Redeemer, and the Holy Ghost acts as King (Acts xvi: 6, 7), and Jesus Christ is the electing Head (Jo. xiii: 18; xv: 19), and the divine Father becomes the Sanctifier of the saints (Jo. vii: 17) and, with Christ, the Quickener and the Purifier (Jo. v: 21); with nothing functional left, as the mark-manual of the Holy Ghost.

For example, Isaiah, in his glorious prophecy, says, "I Jehovah am thy Saviour, and thy Redeemer, the Mighty One of Jacob" (Is. xlix: 26; repeated lx: 16). "Thus saith Jehovah, thy Redeemer," is one of his favorite appeals (Is. xlviii: 17; liv: 8). He is spoken of as Jehovah, the Redeemer, at the very time when there is introduced, also, into the prophecy the anticipated Sacrifice (Is. xlix: 7).

In Paul we read, "The very God of peace sanctify you wholly" (1 Thess. v: 23): in Jude, "To them that are sanctified by God the Father" (Jude 1); in Paul again, "That he (Christ) might sanctify

*God the Father.*

and cleanse it" (Eph. v: 26): and in the Hebrews, "Both he that sanctifieth, and they who are sanctified, are all of One" (Heb. ii: 11).

Then, as to Election, "Ye have not chosen me, but I have chosen you" (Jo. xv: 16). And, if choice of officers could be considered distinctive of the Father, then we have this sentence, "The Holy Ghost said, Separate me Barnabas and Saul to the work to which I have called them" (Acts xiii: 2); again, "take heed to the flock over the which the Holy Ghost hath made you overseers" (Acts xx: 28): and now, once more, throwing into new confusion even such a distinctive office as the atonement, —" Feed the church of God, which he hath purchased with his own blood" (ib.).

But let us look at some of these things more distinctly.

§ 3. *The Father as Son.*

Paul says, " God was manifest in the flesh, justified in the Spirit, seen of angels, preached unto the Gentiles, believed on in the world, received up into glory" (1 Tim. iii: 16).

These texts are contraband. A theory of the Trinity is, that each of the Hypostases, in turn, is separately God.

We are driven, therefore, to texts that will say, in terms, that the Son is the Father. Now, as there could be a rhetorical prediction that the book would not so falsify its tropes as to have such a sentence, we wish to be understood as understanding the true nature of the hardship under which we live in the debate.

Still, many passages come near this very thing. Isaiah says, the child is the " Everlasting Father." Christ says, " I and my Father are one." He says, " He that hath seen me, hath seen the Father." He speaks of the Comforter coming; and then he says, " I will not leave you comfortless, *I* will come to you" (Jo. xiv : 18). And then, in another covert but unmistakable way, he cuts off from himself the possibility of having a separate Divine Hypostasis, by never mentioning it : in a long theological discussion he never realizes that. He speaks of himself, and then he speaks of his Father. He speaks of himself as weak, whenever separated from his Father (Jo. v : 19, 30). He never speaks of an Eternal Son. On the contrary, he says, " I live by the Father" (Jo. vi : 57). He says, " Of that day knoweth no man, but the Father"(Matt. xiii : 32). He says, "Father, into thy hands I commend my spirit" (Matt. xxiii : 46). He is said, " by the Eternal Spirit [to have] offered himself without spot to God" (Heb. ix : 14); not by the Eternal Logos. He never lisps of a separate Person to stand by him, and to BE he in all manner of administration. He ties himself to the Father. He says, " The Son can do nothing but what he seeth the Father do" (Jo. v : 19). We hear of " the God of our Lord Jesus Christ, the Father of glory"\* (Eph. i : 17); of " eternal life which was with the Father" (1 Jo. i : 2) ; and evermore of just such things as we should wish to have, if what Ignatius

\* Why not for once end that sentence—" The Eternal Son"?

## God the Father.

says were true, that " God himself was manifested in human form for the renewal of eternal life" (Ig. p. 167 ; Clarks' Ed.) ; that " He is the mouth, altogether free, by which the Father truly spoke ;" " that he is in the Father ;" and that this " is all the more revealed," the more we watch the pages of revelation (Ig. p. 211).

The difficulties are futile. De Pressensé says, " It is simply impossible to conceive that the Father, in all the glory of his Godhead, can have been enshrined in Jesus, leaving as it were the throne of heaven empty" (*Her. and Chris. Doct.* p. 141). We feel helped by such a cavil. That is, God cannot be enshrined in a lily, without leaving the throne of heaven empty!

Let us pass on.

### § 4. *The Father as Spirit.*

Now, as before ; we cannot expect to have much writing that shall say, " The Father is the Spirit;" for the Father is God, and the Spirit is the Breath of God, with more or less subjectivity of rhetoric. We cannot feign to ourselves the Almighty's " Arm," unless the figure is true to us, and keeps up, on occasions of its use, a good degree of tropical consistency.

But, bereft of theory, and of any illustrative polemic, and now, as it appears, of much departure from the emblem,—see what we do encounter. Jesus Christ says, " If I go not away, the Comforter will not come unto you ; but, if I depart, I will send him unto you" (Jo. xvi : 7); and then he says, " Howbeit, when he, the Spirit of truth, is come, he will guide you into all truth: for he shall not speak of himself; but whatsoever he shall hear, that shall he speak; and he will show you things to come. He shall glorify me: for he shall take* of mine, and shall show it unto you" (vs. 13, 14): and then, without any intervening text, " All things that the Father hath are mine; therefore said I, that HE shall take of mine, and shall show it unto you" (v. 15). I say, It would be impossible, if there were a great underlying Trinity, that our Saviour, so grammatical in all his speeches, should drop this stitch in his discourse; and I am the more confirmed of it, because he then had done it previously.

Let us look into another chapter.

He says, "I will pray the Father, and he shall give you another Comforter, that he may abide with you forever; even the Spirit of truth; whom the world cannot receive, because it seeth him not, neither knoweth him: but ye know him; for he dwelleth with you, and shall be in you" (Jo. xiv: 16, 17): and then, without the least reverence for the Trinity, he adds, "*I* will not leave you comfortless: *I* will come to you" (v. 18); and then, a little after, "WE will come" to you (v. 23), referring to the Father.

Now, put all these things together. Remember, we have been told, " The Lord is that Spirit"(2 Cor. iii: 17). Remember we have been told, " Spirit is God" (Jo. iv: 24). Remember that it has been said,

\* " Receive" E. V.) ; but the Greek is the same as in the fifteenth verse.

## God the Father.

Christ liveth in us (Gal. ii: 20); and again, The Spirit liveth in us (1 Cor. xiii: 16); and again, God is in us of a truth (1 Cor. xiv: 25). Remember that Gabriel says, "The Holy Ghost shall come upon thee, and the power of the Highest shall overshadow thee" (Lu. i: 35), and does not stop to declare a difference. Remember that the Psalmist speaks of "the word of God" and of "the Spirit of God," and gives them the same work in the same sentence (Ps. xxxiii: 6); that Christ speaks of "the Spirit of God," in one report of his speech (Matt. xii: 28), and of "the finger of God" in another (Lu. xi: 20); that Paul speaks of the Spirit of God and of power (1 Cor. ii: 4): put all these things together; and I will insist, that, considering the decencies of the trope, there is more, rather than less, invasion of it, than its strict trope-character would idiomatically portend.

### § 5. *The Father as Jehovah.*

At this very late period in our discussion, we bring forward an idea, which might seem to have deserved to be the centralizing one in our whole investigation. It refers to the meaning of *Jehovah*. This word has excited immense attention. Among the books that have been written on this sole subject, none have been so successful, as to narrow, in the least degree, the domain of doubt. Some things have been agreed; but they have been for a long time agreed: and some things are in doubt; but they are the things that have always been in doubt; I mean within the historic period, or that compass of time that hides us from the mind of those that actually received the Pentateuch.

Now, what are the things agreed? The things agreed are, first, that Jehovah was the proper name of God; second, that the Jews were afraid to pronounce it; third, that they used instead, *Adonai*, which our translators, with a singular compliance with the superstition, have rendered "Lord"; fourth, that nothing is to be learned from the vowels in the name, because they are the vowels of *Adonai*; and, fifth, that if we could trace the consonants, that would be the most hopeful track for expounding the signification.

Now, singularly enough, the consonants are not so difficult.

Let me premise: Devas, and other Indian derivations (De Wette, I. p. 183), or, to sum it all up in a single word, all tracings of the term to languages (*Schiller's Heb. Myst.*), or to mythologic forms (*see Bib. Repos.*, No. 13), outside of the Hebrew people, have been confessedly (*Von Cölln über die Theokra* :) illusory and vain. We are thrown back upon the Hebrew: and here, strange to say, there lies nearest to our sight, and not without categorical suggestion from the Scriptures themselves, a strict and most striking signification.

Let me expound it.

Moses said, when he was commanded to go into Egypt, " Behold, when I come unto the children of Israel, and shall say unto them, The God of your fathers hath sent me unto you; and they shall say to me, What is his name? what shall I say to them?

## God the Father. 123

And God said unto Moses, I AM THAT I AM" (Ex. iii: 14).

I was reading this carelessly some months ago, and suddenly there flashed up before me the future form of it. I was perfectly amazed. I seized upon the commentaries, and they recognized the fact ; but languidly; and with a learned exposition how the future was more a tense for EXISTENCE than the Hebrew past. But instantly I seized the Concordance, and I could scarce find one future of the verb *to be*, that did not mean the future ; and I found no cause at all for such a grammatic prepossession. I soon lit up the sentence with its own legitimately relumined lights: and, now, read the result :—"What is his name ? And God said unto Moses, I SHALL BE THAT I SHALL BE: say unto the children of Israel, I SHALL BE hath sent me unto you."

Now it is but three chapters off, when there comes another discussion. " I appeared unto Abraham, unto Isaac, and unto Jacob, by the name of God Almighty; but by the name Jehovah was I not known to them" (Ex. vi: 3).

We glance at the name ; and the unmistakable similarity arrests us instantly. " I SHALL BE" (Ex. iii: 14) is the first person singular future, and Jehovah is the third person singular future, of the same word, in the same exact shape, in the same unmistakable use, and, beyond all question to me now, with the same meaning.

It may be asked, Why has this been hid ? It has not been altogether hid I find upon investigation (*see Bib. Repos.*, No. 13) ; but the reasons why it has not been intelligently accepted, seem, first, that it has not fallen into appreciative hands. The great glory of Heaven, in view of the SHALL BE when the Manhood should be taken in, had not met with appropriate favor. Let me mention further: Jehovah is an old name, older, *perhaps*, than that saying to Moses; and the verb is in an old form. The common Hebrew for the verb *to be*, is *hayah*. The older Hebrew is *havah*. The Hebrew in the speech to Moses, is the later and more common form. The Hebrew in the other would be the earlier. This is as we might expect; but then its more unaccustomed look, and the confusing of everything by the foreign vowels, have laid a veil upon the meaning. Jehovah says, " *Ehyeh esher Ehyeh.*" Jehovah's name, brought down to what was originally inspired, is " *Jehveh.*" The differences are but two: one is the later form of the verb, and the first person singular: the other is the earlier form of the verb, and the third person singular. Would that all riddles could be pressed as close! One means, I SHALL BE WHAT I SHALL BE. And the other means, HE SHALL BE, as the great name of God. And to us, in our present mind, of course, it falls as a glorious confirmation. It may be asked, Why did you not state it in the very preface? I answer, Lest it should give an air of visionariness to all the book. I would rather build upon the very commonest ideas. But now in the superstructure, having refused to allow it to be in the base of the building, it smiles upon us with peculiar beauty. God was always perfect; and, in his power, he was entire; and, in his unity, he was complete. There were no gods beside him; and, in our belief, there was no triplicity in his person. But there was one thing wanting to his work; and that was, union with humanity. Though he might be known, in rolling the stars, as God Almighty; yet when he came to the Iron Furnace, and to the region and to the period of grace, he needed more. He must prophesy there of himself, " I SHALL BE." He must be known by others as HE SHALL BE. "This is my name, and this is my remembrance," he says. And he could not build a foot of earth, or save a lost soul, but on the faith of JEHOVAH; on the bottom of that ordained Theanthropy, that was to be the base of the whole creation.

## § 6. *The Father and His Glory.*

Lit up by this view of JEHVEH, and reading some passages where the word is found, as for example, " I am HE SHALL BE; that is my name; and my glory will I not give to another" (Is. xlii: 8); or again," I, even I, am HE SHALL BE; and beside me there is no Saviour" (xliii: 11); or, "I am HE SHALL BE, your Holy One, the Creator of Israel, your King" (v. 15): hunting up some of the more salient uses of this entitlement, and then remembering, This is the Whole Jehovah, and yet Jehovah confessing that it must needs be that he come in the flesh : taking this case, —" Before me there was no God shaped, neither shall there be after me" (v. 10) ; and understanding that to mean, not ismply that there was no God, but no administrative Father, except the SHALL BE who was to be made complete in Jesus Christ : and that, therefore, the triumph is to be understood when it was known that Jesus Christ was God (Rom. ix: 5), or, as it is expressed in the Philippians, when "every tongue should confess that the Lord is Jesus Christ" (Phil. ii : 11)—putting all these things together,—we learn to appreciate the word GLORY, which did exist from eternity, and was the essential fact with the Lord Jesus. Had he been a Hypostasis, he would have talked more of that; but the GLORY that he had with [*chez*, Fr.] the Father—that it is that fills his eye. Jesus, as man, was nothing. That he says ever (Jo. v: 19, 30; viii: 28). Jesus, as God, was everything. And, therefore, the best part of Jesus was his GLORY, viz., that which gave him a Spirit, and a righteousness, and a power, and a Kingship, and an eternity, which were the essential prerequisites of his whole sacrifice for the lost.

Listen, therefore, how that word occurs.

" Glorify me, O Father, with thine own self" (The word *para* is more like *in* than it is like " *with*." The French *chez* is almost its exact counterpart.) "with the glory that I had with (*chez*) thee before the world was" (Jo. xvii: 5) ; " that is, that I had as HE SHALL BE before the birth of my humanity. Being " raised up from the dead by the glory of the Father" (Rom. vi: 4). " Who being the brightness of his glory, and the express image of his substance" (Heb. i: 3). " Who gave him glory" (1 Pet. i: 21). " The light of the knowledge of the glory of God in the face of Jesus Christ" (2 Cor. iv: 6).

*God the Father.* 127

## § 7. *The Baptismal Formula.*

The acknowledgment having been in recent times arrived at, that the sentence in First John, "There are three that bear record in heaven, the Father, the Word, and the Holy Ghost" (1 Jo. v : 7), is an interpolation, the passage next in order in popular impressiveness is that in Matthew, "Baptizing them in the name of the Father, and of the Son, and of the Holy Ghost."

Indeed, this is so wide a formula, and has been printed on our ear, so, since infancy, that perhaps every body turns to it the soonest, when their faith in the existence of a Trinity is the least endangered.

1. Let me say, first, that this was not in such sense a formula, that the church was bound by it, or, in other words, as that we ever hear of it, afterwards, as of the practice of the Apostles. Were it a rigid formula, the argument would, of course, be greater. But, instead of that, we hear of two acts of baptism, and, in each of them, the person who was baptized, was baptized in the name of the Lord Jesus (Acts ii : 38 ; xix : 5).

2. But, secondly, it may be asked, Why a plurality of names at all? Why not say, Baptize in the name of God? To which I respond, Why not say, Believe in Christ? Christ does say, He that believeth on the Son (Jo. vi : 40), and Paul does speak of "him which believeth in Jesus" (Rom. iii : 26) : why need Peter leap into a wider formula? and why does he say so carefully, "Believe in the Lord Jesus

Christ, and thou shalt be saved, and thy house?" (Acts xvi : 31).

In fact, why does it say "name"? Why does it not say *names*? If Father, Son and Holy Ghost are hypostatically different, they may be the same in substance, and yet difference of Persons would eminently discredit the singular, "name." Our blessed Lord was God and man. As "Lord," he was the Greek for Jehovah; as "Jesus" he was Jehovah a Saviour; as Christ, he was an Anointed Man. In either of the three appellatives, there was a distinct idea; but who says that believing in the Lord Jesus Christ is anything but believing in the one Emmanuel?

3. But, it will be said; and this is by far the strongest consideration,—The Son *is* different; and, therefore, the same may be argued in respect to the Spirit. No man imagines Jesus to be different from Christ; but men do imagine the Father to be different from the Son. The Son is weak (Heb. v : 2). The Son prays (Lu. xxii : 44). The Son is man (Mar. vi : 3). The Son dies (Matt. xxvii : 50); and does what the Father could not do. Whatever may be said of the Spirit, no one denies that the Father is different from the Son : and why then, in the Baptismal Formula, do we not have a like discrepance imagined for the Spirit.

Now we have shown that the Son, as God, is one in substance with the Father. We are talking of theories now, not realities. The implication is, that we are contradicting our own theory. But let it be remembered that, on the side of God, the Father and the Son *are*, with us, but One Person. If it says,

Baptizing them in the name of the Father, the Son and the Holy Ghost, it means in the One Glorious Name (*sing.*), enthroned as the Father, enshrined as the Son, and engrafted as the Holy Ghost.

We see no difficulty. There is but one God, and Jesus Christ is the Son of God: and if any one says, Yes, but Jesus Christ, as Son, has passed into very different relations from the Father; and the argument be pressed, that the discrepance between the Father and the Son seems to imply a like mysterious discrepance between the Father and the Holy Ghost, I take issue even with that, as a fact implied in the mere enumerations of a formula.

For example, take this text,—" Your whole spirit and soul and body" (1 Thess. v: 23). Does the fact that there is a certain discrepance between the soul and body, prove, on the faith of this enumeration, that there is a like discrepance between the soul and the spirit? Or, take this text, " God, and the Lord Jesus Christ, and the elect angels" (1 Tim. v: 21). Does the fact that angels differ from God, show that there is a like discrepance between Christ and God? In fact, is there any proof in the matter? When Allen cried out, "God and the Continental Congress"; or, when the history tells us, " They feared the Lord and Samuel" (1 Sam. xii: 18); or when Isaiah says, "The Lord of Hosts is his name and thy Redeemer, the Holy One of Israel; the God of the whole earth shall he be called" (Is. liv: 5); or when Paul says, " I commend you to God, and to the word of his grace" (Acts xx: 32); or when the Chronicles say, They " worshipped God and the

King" (1 Chr. xxix : 20); or when Isaiah says, " Thus saith Jehovah, the Redeemer of Israel, and his Holy One" (Is. xlix: 7); or when Moses says, " They believed the Lord and his servant Moses" (Ex. xiv: 31); or when Paul says, " By whom we have received grace and apostleship" (Rom. 1 : 5); or when Peter and Paul both speak of " the Spirit and power" (Acts x : 38 ; 1 Cor. ii : 4),—I beg any one to decide, whether, in a great and sober polemic, the discrepance of these terms, or the likeness of these terms, is either to be defined or limited by the mere force of their conjugal location.

But if not, what becomes of the Baptismal Trinity ?

### § 8. *The Apostolic Benediction.*

And if the Baptismal Formula is no argument, I think no one will blame me for passing by the Apostolic Benediction, as offering the same appeal, only with far feebler influence. If the form of baptism reminds each of us, at a solemn moment, of the saving relations of the Deity, the benediction actually specifies those relations. It is a sort of running comment upon the work of God. And " the grace of the Lord Jesus Christ, and the love of God, and the communion of the Holy Ghost," is a *résumé* of all that God does for man : and though, as we have all along confessed, consistent with a Trinity if there be a Trinity, yet, like all the other passages, not a proof of it. What we are looking for is positive proof. The whole course of our argument is, that the proof is illusory : that there is wonderful fencing from attack in the plea that the Trinity are the same in substance ; but that when we

God the Father.   131

summon that evanescent thing a Hypostasis, the showing is not solid. There is the mere emptying of one consistency into another; without that actual proof, that would be demanded in far lower interests.

§ 9. *The Scene at Jordan.*

Witness, for example, the great insisting upon the Scene at Jordan. Turrettin goes so far as to quote, " *Abi, Ariane, ad Jordanem, et videbis Trinitatem* (Tur. Qu. xxv. § 7). Now, exhaust the proof. Jesus Christ says, " No man hath ascended up to heaven, but he that came down from heaven, even the Son of Man which is in heaven" (Jo. iii: 13). According to that, Christ has two Persons. Let us understand precisely the argument. Because the Baptized Person was down in Jordan, and the Accepting Voice was up in heaven, and the Descending Dove was hovering in the air, therefore there are three Persons in the Godhead. That is, because " truth shall spring out of the ground," it is a totally different thing, and springs from a totally different source, from the " righteousness" which looks " down from heaven" (Ps. lxxxv: 11). Because there is a " Son of Man, which is in heaven" (Jo. iii : 13), therefore he is a totally different Person from the Son of man closeted with the Ruler. Because he casts forth lightning and scatters them, therefore he is a heavenly person, and not the earthly person that shoots out arrows and destroys them (Ps. cxliv: 6). What is such argument really worth? The voice, " This is my beloved Son," was not the voice of the Almighty, but a pulsation of the air by which he miraculously revealed himself. The Descending Dove was not God, but the apparition of a bird, representing his Holy Spirit. The flesh in Jordan was not Jehovah, but the Carpenter's Son, in whom he had been pleased to become incarnate. The dramatic dislocations of the Most High are no more evincive of a Trinity, than that the Father lives in the skies, and that the Holy Ghost comes downward from the Father, and pours himself upon the head of the Lord our Advocate.

CHAPTER V.

THE TRINITY NOTHING TO THE GOSPEL.

§ 1. *What are the Gospel Ideas?*

THE shock that our creed will create is, lest it destroy the gospel ideas. This fear is not unreasonable. The denial of the Trinity in God has been like the palsy, a deadly symptom. I mean that, like the palsy, it has been so the symptom of a deadly state, that men pronounce upon it at the start, and it becomes associated, in the diagnosis of the Church, with all the deadly symptoms with which it has had incidental unity.

But this is unfair.

Moreover, the path to it has been different from ours. It has begun in laxities far down beneath it, and which travelled up to it by gradual approach. It began in Arminianism. It is a notorious fact that Geneva learned what it has learned by the track of humanitarianism and Pelagian heresy. Hence the vice of Geneva, and of all her sister cities, is that she denies the Redeemer. It is so in London. It is so in our own land. The glorious gospel of Christ perished by inanition. Now I say, There is a vast difference, in a creed that has sprung from a denial of the gospel; which has ripened in a reverence for man; which has proceeded to a dethronement of Christ; and which has come entirely to deny the Deity of our Redeemer: and one that enforces that Deity: which begins by piling every thing upon it: which makes Christ the plenary Jehovah; and which gets rid of the Trinity *a parte ante* by showing that it degrades Christ, and not *a parte post* by showing that Christ *must* be degraded, because no salvation of men and no miraculous birth is needed for the welfare of the people.

I insist that these two *geneses* of belief are totally different; and that, as the physician discovers sometimes a palsy which is as innocent as a birth; which may be incident to mere childish state; and which may be neither serious or deep,—so an anti-Trinitarian creed may be found deifying Christ, and ennobling all the doctrines of salvation.

What are these doctrines?

A denial of the Trinity, if it uphold (1) Incarnation, (2) Redemption, (3) Mediation, (4) Intercession, (5) Regeneration, (6) Justification, (7) Adoption, (8) Sanctification, (9) the Final Judgment, and (10) the Glorification of the redeemed, cannot be far astray: and if it hold them with peculiar emphasis, and make much of them, and present them in orthodox forms, surely it should be investigated twice, before it should be denounced as a damning heresy.

## § 2. *The Incarnation.*

The Trinitarian believes that the Second Person of the Trinity is incarnate in Christ. We believe that the Whole Person of our Maker is so incarnate. The Trinitarian believes that the Second Person of the Trinity must be incarnate in Christ, to give him a worth and a name adequate to our redemption. We believe that the Whole Deity is so incarnate for the same purpose, and that the Whole Deity gives the power and the worth that makes Christ a sufficient Victor for the soul's salvation.

## § 3. *Redemption*

The Trinitarian believes that Christ, being the Son of God by being united with the Eternally Begotten, lived and died as a substitute for us, both as to merit and to punishment, and that, by force of this vicariousness, he substituted himself in our place, and, so, is ready to welcome us in his own blessed claim at the Final Judgment. We believe precisely the same thing; only, our Christ is united with God; and the Eternally Begotten, like the Eternal Sacrifice of the Mass, or like the Miraculous Wafer, seems, like the Right of Kings, or like the Divine in Baptism, to have been lightly introduced, from unresolved and uninvestigated emblematical expressions.

## § 4. *Mediation.*

To the objection, This leaves no room for Mediation: if Christ is God, and if that is carried so far as to obliterate a Trinity; and if that go to the extreme of making the One Jehovah angry with the lost, and, at the same time, die on the cross to save them,— where is the room for Mediation? and, in fact, where is the Redemption? If the same God die to please himself, where is the angry Judge? and where is the pitiful and aroused and propitiating God our Saviour?

Now, this is, in fact, two questions.

1. In the first place, Where is the Redemption?

Now, the Trinitarian himself believes that God is merciful. He believes that he instituted grace. He believes that the whole universe rang with it before time began. He believes that the Father willeth not the death of the sinner, but that all should turn and live. He believes, or else he ought to, that he taketh no pleasure in the death of him that dieth, but that all should turn and live; and, therefore, that God is no more angry than Christ (Rev. vi: 16), and no more pleased than Christ; for Christ himself is to be our Angry Judge (Jo. v: 22), and God himself was our Redeemer (Acts xx: 28), from the beginning.

He believes, therefore, that what is to be satisfied is justice, and that what is to be exercised is mercy; and he has, doubtless, often emphasized the emblem of a just judge weeping over the culprit, and, nevertheless, dooming him, in a just way, to a bitter execution.

Now, put all these things together; and put in another thing—that the Son is of one substance with the Father,—and surely there can be small complaint. The Trinitarian says, The Son reconciles us to the Father; and we say, The Son reconciles us to Jehovah: and both say, Both the Father and the Son are God, and are of one mind, and have both been concerned, as the One Glorious Jehovah, in reconciling all things to himself.

2. But it will be said, Here is no Mediation. Why not? A is a mediator between C and D. Is that the mediation of Christ? Nobody pretends it. The first Adam was under a covenant; the second Adam was under a covenant. Were they alike? The Apostle declares they were different (Rom. v: 12-21). There was an imputation in either case. Was it the same? Paul carefully argues, No (vs. 15, 16). Then, listen to the lesson. All the emblems of the Bible are to be carefully regarded in their exceptions. If God is said to "repent," we are to look at it. If he is said to be "furious," we are to lay it side by side with passages that speak of him as "grieved," or as "cruel." We are to read the Bible with the usual appreciative guards. When, therefore, it says, "Now a mediator is not a mediator of one, but God is one" (Gal. iii: 20), we are to look at it as what it really is; not a pretext for a thousand glosses (see Meyer, *in loc.*), nay, for whole solid books (Bonitz, Reil, Koppe, *etc.*), but as a simple intimation that Mediatorship is an emblem in the gospel, but not a very perfect emblem, in that the Man-God is not separate from any other God, and in that the God-Man is not altogether separate from certain other men; for, as the Apostle himself argues it, "Ye are all one in Christ Jesus" (v. 28).

The difficulty of the Mediation lies here. Jesus Christ is to reconcile us to the Almighty. He is, however, himself the Almighty. He is, notwithstanding that, also man. Now, as man, he has a separate consciousness; for we learn that he did not "know" certain things that were known by his Divinity. Moreover, he had a separate will; for he says himself, "Not my will, but thine, be done" (Lu. xxii: 42). And, therefore, in this separate consciousness and will, he was "very man," as our Confession expresses it.

What trouble, therefore, in the rhetoric, if Christ, as very man, should be looked on as Mediator between Divinity and Humanity? Recollect, Person is not an inspired word. If anybody were to say, Is the Deity or Humanity of Christ a separate Person, I would decline to answer. I would say, The word is not decisive: I will tell the facts. And when I came to tell the facts, it would be thus: Christ, as having but one authority, and one forensic name, and one administrative power, is the One Almighty; but Christ, as the carpenter's son, can be looked on away from the Almighty; and, on this brother's side, I can look at him as between me and the All Wise.

§ 5. *Intercession.*

And so of Intercession.

In fact, if we look at Intercession, we will see what is the divine Mediation.

In the first place, "Intercession" is not a word of the Bible. The word in the Bible means entreaty; it means direct supplication. The idea of "*inter*" or "*between*" is not expressed in the original

(Heb. vii : 25). Intercession, therefore, as an argument from the language employed, is met already.

But, then, the very idea of prayer! The Trinitarian says, There are three Persons in the Godhead ; and, therefore, the praying of Christ to his Father is perfectly natural ; and is but the entreaty of one Person to another. But discard the Trinity, and what do we behold? The Son, writhing in Gethsemane, is interceding—with himself! The argument seems to be conclusive. Either Christ is two persons ; or else, if Jehovah is without triplicity, we have the preposterous scene of Jehovah wrestling with Jehovah ; that is, the One Grand Divinity wrestling with itself: an idea confounding to faith, and destructive to popular impression.

But now, briefly :—Who says that Christ is not two persons? We have distinctly refused any such language. Let me explain more perfectly. The word Person is not in the Bible.* As applied to God it must be an emblem ; and before I use it, I must know distinctly what it is to mean. For a man to seize it, and use it as a formidable weapon, is idle, unless he first explain what he means by it, and then it will have no force in itself, but only as a *résumé* of the facts and the principles which we must look for first in Scripture.

Accordingly, putting together a whole circle of Scripture truths, and calling it by their name, Christ is one person ; and putting together another circle, he is two persons. Where is the benefit of doing either? We simply decline any such determination

\* I mean, of course, as of the Almighty.

of the use. And as we are free of the word, no such word being used in revelation, we go to the principles at the very first, and refuse to pump our reasoning through this or that perfectly arbitrary expression.

Christ, as God, is one. Christ, as man, is one. Christ as God-Man is two; that is to say, as our Confession expresses it, he is "very God and very man." Nevertheless Christ, as God-Man, is one. And if it were left to us to volunteer a meaning, we would say, Our meaning for Person, if any one insists on employing it, shall be in consistence with this last idea. We would say, Let Christ be a Person; and let us call him one; and let his unity be of this nature,—that, though he is unquestionably two, yet the Godhead and the Manhood have great respects of unity; first, that they are one in Court, the whole world pleading but the One Name, forensically; second, that they are one in Rule, the whole world bowing to the same sceptre; and, third, that they are one in a mysterious incarnation, the Eternal God actually entering and making himself one in Christ Jesus.

It would be these strong unities that would make me refuse to give up the word Person to any other.

But if a man insisted, and said he would use it as he pleased; that Person was not an inspired appellative, and he would say that Christ had two Persons; and if he were then to go on to explain, that Christ was entire and distinct Man, and also Eternal God; and if he were further to explain, that one person was weak and wretched, and the other glorious; that one person was buffeted and tempted, and the other the God in Heaven; if he were to say, One person shrank, and the other comforted and spoke peace,—I could not say that I like his vocabulary, but I would certainly understand it.

Nay, I could use it.

And if the Trinitarian were to press, too much, the word in the other sense, then I could enforce it; and I could say, Neither word is Scriptural; and, therefore, there are facts expounded by the one, which are not at variance with those understood by the other.

For example, prayer!

Christ was weak and wretched. Did that forbid his divine nature helping his human nature? He was ignorant. Where did he go for light? He was tempted. Who helped him? What is meant by that Eternal Spirit by which he offered himself, without spot, to God? (Heb. ix: 14). And if he could trust to that Spirit, why not pray? In other words, we believe that Christ had an entire humanity: that that humanity was equipped for every act known to man; that that humanity was distinct from the divinity; not with a hypostatic difference, leaving it the same in substance equal in power and glory, but making it different in substance, and utterly without glory (Is. xli: 24); and that this inglorious humanity could pray (Heb. v: 7) to the divinity; there being but one Jehovah; and the Father, the Son and the Holy Ghost being but One Person, subject to that complicity of state which resulted from incarnation in the blessed Jesus.

Prayer, therefore, like hunger and fasting; and like many another act; like his pain upon the cross, and like his slumber in the depths of the grave,—was an attribute of the man; and even the Trinity must so link itself with these very ideas (we admitting, of course, that the man must be supported and enforced by the God), that it can find little room for the Eternally Begotten, if the Man Christ Jesus prays directly to his Heavenly Father

§ 6. *Regeneration.*

The Trinitarian believes in a work by the Spirit, and feels confused and discomfited if we obliterate the distinction between Him and the Father. He feels as if we had denied the separateness of the operations of redemption. Yet what does the Trinitarian believe? He believes that we are born of the Spirit. So do we. He believes that that Spirit is God. So do we. All believe that we are " born of God" (Jo. v: 13). He is discomfited if ransom is confounded with the new birth. So are we discomfited. We pass on from point to point; and at last arrive at a single respect of difference. He believes that the new birth is by God, because he believes that the Spirit is one with God, " the same in substance, equal in power and glory." Can we be very far astray? He believes that the Trinity all share in each other's work. We believe that they all do the work. And our sin, if we have any, is that we deny a mysterious difference. We say that the Father new-creates (Jo. vi: 44, 65); and a beautiful fact of our system is, that it agrees with Scripture. The Scripture pays no attention to a Trinity; and just as if the Viceroy and the Pasha and the Khedive were all the same, it speaks indifferently of either. " It is the Spirit that quickeneth" (Jo. vi : 63); and then, as though to forbid our settling upon some new-creating Hypostasis, it says, " As the Father raiseth up the dead, and quickeneth them, even so the Son quickeneth whom he will" (Jo. v : 21); and then, as though the word, God, were the prose announcement for the whole, he says, " Which were born, not of blood, nor of the will of the flesh, nor of the will of man, but of God" (Jo. i: 13).

§ 7. *Justification.*

Justification will have more asserted about it.

The Trinitarian will declare that the angry God and the pacifying Christ *must* be two Persons. And, yet, never did a theory so break down when we come to challenge it. We ask the Trinitarian, Was God angry? He will say, Yes. We ask him, Was Christ angry? He will stop to meditate. Presently we will see that a motion is taking place in his mind. He is moving all the difference of thought and sentiment that exists between the Father and the Son away from the Incarnate Deity, and on to the man Christ Jesus. We let a long pause ensue, and then ask him, and we find that a great change has occurred. There is no such difference in the anger and in the love as he at first imagined. He finds that the Father conceived redemption (Jo. iii : 16). He finds that the Son is angry, like the Father (Matt. xxv ; 41). He finds that their attitudes are shared. And when he comes to run the ploughshare of difference between the Father and the Son, he finds himself forced off on some idea of Justice. Both are trying to satisfy Justice. The Father is no more angry than the Son, both viewed as God. And if it be said, The Father was angry *at* the Son, digestion of detail soon fixes the proper relation. The Father pours out upon a Man the vials of wrath; and when we come to the constitution of that Man, the Father gives him strength (Lu. ii : 40). He is clothed with forensic dignity (Jer. xxiii : 6). Two supplements are made. He is begotten into a divine strength (Rom. i : 4) ; and decked with God's authority (Matt. xxviii : 18): and, when he comes to explain all this himself, he says it is his Father. "I live by the Father" (Jo. vi : 57). At any rate, God is no more angry at sin, than Christ is, as the Great Almighty (Rev. vi : 16).

The Father is said to reconcile all things to himself by Jesus Christ (2 Cor. v : 14). Where would be the propriety of this, if there were a great gospel motive for keeping separate the anger of one original Hypostasis, and the assiduity of another? Christ himself is said to reconcile all things to himself (Col. i : 21, 22); and, as though to give a parting overthrow to all idea of personalities, as between God and God, there is a text from Paul which places Jehovah precisely as we describe him—One God, apart from any distraction till he becomes Emmanuel—and then, One God tabernacling in the flesh—One God, Father Son or Spirit as we may choose our rhetoric— One God, complete in the divine decree from all eternity—but One God completed in Emmanuel, fitted by assuming flesh for the salvation of the world; building upon that en-fleshed Jehovah all creation; and not talking as though God were the Angered, and Christ were the Merciful; but laying all smooth in this crowning text, "Feed the church of God, which he hath purchased with his own blood" (Acts, xx: 28); as though "God so loved the world that he gave his only begotten Son" (Jo. iii: 16): and as though the "begotten Son" were not first an Eternally Begotten, and then a Begotten in Nazareth; but most distinctly this last alone; so that this Divine Begetter is a Father by entering, himself; by coming in, in his Whole Divinity; by pouring down, with every endowment; by making one, in the most solemn way; and by being able to say, therefore, that he reconciles all things TO HIM-SELF (2 Cor. v: 18); and that he is himself the Most High, "our Redeemer," and "the Lord, our Righteousness" (Is. xlvii: 4; Jer. xxiii: 6).

### § 8. *Adoption.*

And so of Adoption. The Trinitarian is confused if we do not allow a separate Father, and a separate Spirit as a Spirit of Adoption, and a separate Son to be associated with us, that he may be the First Born among many brethren.

But singularly enough, Christ is the person that tramples upon all this. He is careful enough, where his humanity needs to be distinguished. He is very express, lest his manhood be forgotten, and lest he be too much confused with God, in his weakness (Lu. xviii: 19) and death as a sacrifice (Jo. xvii: 1);

but, where his divinity is concerned, he becomes confused at once. If Christ was discrepant from the Father, and that discrepance was not human, but began in the original Divinity, he is hard upon his people. He brings us to the brink of almost necessary error. We might have a better teacher. He does not treat us as we are, poor erring children, and keep well in hand the lines of an original triplicity; but he confounds, knowingly. He takes the most preserved peculiarities of the Father, and claims them utterly. "Ye have not chosen me, but I have chosen you, and ordained you:"

### § 9. *Judgment.*

—Nor does he stop short of the Universal Judgment. He seats himself at a bound upon the Father's throne. He speaks exactly as though he were the whole. He says, "The Father judgeth no man, but hath committed all judgment unto the Son" (Jo. v: 22): which cannot mean that the Father will not judge at all (Rom. iii: 6; 1 Pet. i: 17); but must be one of those Eastern phrases,—"They had not had sin" (Jo. xv: 22), or, "I came not to judge the world" (Jo. xii: 47): and must mean that the manhood shall be on the throne, and the plenary Jehovah shall be in judgment in him.

### § 10. *Sanctification.*

We speak, just as the Trinity does, of being sanctified by the Holy Ghost. And let it be observed, there is not one of the liturgical expressions that we do not use, if it is at all a counterpart to what is said in Scripture. We pray for the Spirit. We recognize the appointed Comforter; and think of him as coming down; and of the Holy Ghost as being poured upon us, and as dwelling in us as a perpetual temple. Moreover we believe, as others do, that he is the One God, the same in substance equal in power and glory. We only deny a triplicity. And, therefore, the Holy Ghost, who, in the Trinity, is of one substance with the Father, with us is the same Person. There can be our sole mistake. And that seems to be sanctioned by the Bible, which speaks of the lost sinner as sanctified by the Father (Jude 1), and the Son (Heb. ii: 11), and the Holy Ghost (Rom. xv: 16).

§ 11. *Glorification.*

No act can be kept distinguished. If there could be any, would it not be our being glorified? And, yet, this is constantly confused. Would it not be said, The Father shall glorify us? and should there not be fixed solid ground that must remain unaltered? But, while everything is imputed to the glory of the Father (Rom. vi: 4; xv: 7), Christ, just as if he were the Father (Jo. xiv: 10), seizes upon this last token of a distinctive Fatherhood.

Let us quote.

"Now unto him that is able to keep you from falling, and to present you faultless before the presence of his glory with exceeding joy, to the only wise God our Saviour, be glory and majesty, dominion and power, both now and ever. Amen." (Jude 24, 25). "Who shall change our vile body, that it may be fashioned like unto his glorious body, according to the working whereby he is able even to subdue all things unto himself" (Phil. iii : 21). " That he might present [the church] to himself a glorious church, not having spot or wrinkle or any such thing; but that it should be holy and without blemish" (Eph. v: 27). " Looking for that blessed hope, and the glorious appearance of our great God and Saviour, Jesus Christ" (Titus ii : 13).

# III.

# CONCLUSION.

### CHAPTER I.

#### THE SCANDAL OF THIS BOOK.

THE geography and authorship of this book, and its relation to schools and creeds, are of course not vital to its truth, and not interesting to the general reader. But in the whole of what is called evangelical Christendom, as far as it is read at all, it will awaken a disagreable surprise; and for three reasons.

1. In the first place, it will be thought seriously untrue. This however is the whole question in the book itself.

2. In the second place, it will be thought disagreeably presumptuous. The Trinity, to a most extraordinary degree, lies entrenched in the region of piety. Intellect has often come out against it. Locke and Newton and Milton, whatever their pious claims, are chiefly remarkable in the region of the mind. A man may embolden himself in heresy by saying, Hume is with me, or Boyle is with me, or Shaftesbury thinks as I do; but it is a ghastly comfort; because there are the assurances of Scripture that this worldly intellect is specially to be put to shame

## The Scandal of this Book. 149

Locke certainly denied the Trinity. So did Newton. So did Milton. Moreover they were not infidels; and, what is far more interesting, they were professed worshippers of Christ. But, perhaps, Gamaliel was a good man. We stand in awe, rather, of intellect, when it comes to knocking away the pins of what have been thought great truths of the gospel.

Isaac Watts denied the Trinity. Here we have piety and rare gifts besides. And though there can be no question of the fact, and, after all the efforts of his biographers, it cannot be made out that it was the faltering of his stricken faculties, or the aberration of a crazy mind; though there are sane letters telling why he could not alter his hymns, and how the property in them had passed, and was entirely out of his control, and had been so for thirty years; though there can be no earthly doubt that he who wrote

"Alas! and did my Saviour bleed?"

lived, in the entire ripening of his powers, to deny and disown the separate personality in God, yet, alas! he denied and disowned the Deity of his Redeemer. The shelter is but a forlorn one. Locke and Newton and Milton did the same.

On the whole, it is a pleasant thing, when we find our creed not in the Bible, to say, Newton thought so, and Locke and Milton; and they thought so in their maturest and most pious period: and it is an assuring thing to discover Watts thought so; and in all the aroma of earnest faith, wrote so to the world, just as he was ascending to his heavenly Father: yet, alas! this is but a poor sort of prop. In the first place, These are but a few. In the second place, These are not specimen men, but men of advanced thought; and, in the main, of very enthusiastic ideas. In the third place, They became Arian, or something worse. And though we say, How many more would join them if they were shown, as we have tried to do, how Christ can be preserved, and yet there be a denial of the Trinity,—still, all this remains to be proved. There is a scandalous look of presumption in just such a book as this. Our own feelings, but a few years ago, would have turned from it with disgust. The only excuse for it must be, a very profound conviction. And though it is right to say, Locke and Newton and Milton parry it a little, and Watts spreads over it the mantle of excuse; and though each of these could have dissected away the Trinity and kept Christ, if they had observed the exegesis followed in the preceding plan; yet all this goes for very little. Unless the Trinity, like the Real Presence, has come, in the counsels of eternity, to its period of decline, woe worth the present enterprise, and woe worth the reckoning of any man, who kindles the bale-fires of death in face of the noon-day light of a blessed revelation.

3. In the third place, What doctrine will come next? This is, perhaps, of all others, the most reasonable misgiving of the church. The sin of Presbyterianism has been to deny Emmanuel. Here its plague has begun. It has not been in an overhonored sacrament: the fall of Genevism has begun in an underhonored Lord and Divine Sacrifice.

So the church is fully warned.

And I cannot but emphatically agree, that a finger raised against the Trinity ought to be watched like a match in the magazine of a Monitor. There should be no trifling here. But, beyond all question, there is to be this admission—that error is to be no shelter for the truth. Our Lord said, " Let both grow to the harvest." But he uttered that of men, not of doctrines. The man that teaches that weeds must shelter the crop, debauches his religion. The church, in our day, is not a weakling, such that she cannot bear the most fruitful investigations: and if she were, she would have no right to withhold them. The simple point is, Is there a Trinity? If there is, no weapon formed against it will prosper. If there be not, it is a shameful disrespect to the Master to be sheltering him, as the glorious God, behind a baseless dogma of a Pagan Platonism.

CHAPTER II.

THE BENEFIT OF THIS BOOK

1. ALL truth is of necessary value. If the Trinity is not a fact, it clogs and clouds the actual doctrines of the gospel.

2. The Trinity is hard to teach. We are holding out our hand to distant and stupid Pagans. Men's lives are going into the scheme ; and patient women are withering under unwholesome skies. The dogma of the Trinity costs missionary life ; for, all the time spent in propounding it, if it is false, or defending it, if it be not defensible, is like what Paul speaks

of as beating the air. It is keeping back the lost from mercy, and loading the principia of grace with what Paul calls " unsanctioned fables" (1 Tim. iv : 7).

3. Third, it almost prohibits certain entrances among the perishing.

Oh, if Mohammed had not found the Trinity in Damascus! if that pale-faced youth had not encountered, in his aroused conscientious frame, the *Hypostasis* of the Bishops! if the Old Man of the Sea had not jumped on Sinbad on his first setting out upon the deep,—who can tell what young Mohammed might not have been formed to be?

At any rate, everybody will admit, that, if the Trinity be a mistaken heresy, it will give us new life, to unseat it : and that Southward among the African Lakes, and Eastward among other Mussulmans ; that among the Unitarians of our own land, and among Jews all over the world,—the doctrine of One Great God, and he incarnate in the One Man Our Saviour, would give us a new power to work, and give us altogether a noble form in which to cast the enterprise of the gospel.

THE END.

www.ingramcontent.com/pod-product-compliance
Lightning Source LLC
Chambersburg PA
CBHW022104290426
44112CB00008B/548